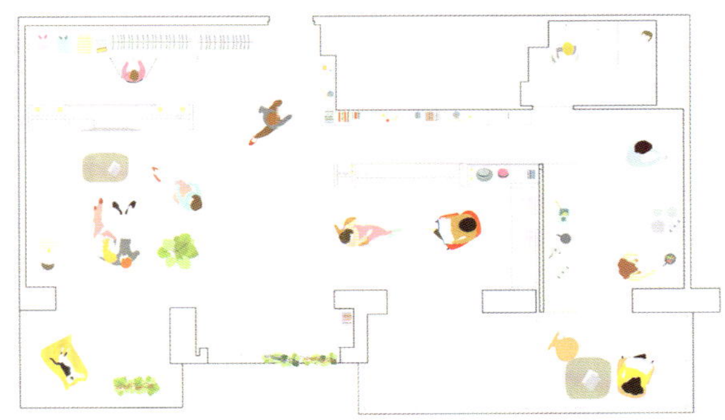

booq
publishing

© 2016 **booq** publishing, S.L.
c/ València, 93, pral. 1ª
08029 Barcelona, Spain

ISBN 978-84-945662-4-0 [EN]
ISBN 978-84-945662-0-2 [DE]

ILUSBOOKS
ILLUSION ILLUSTRATED

Derechos de publicación y distribución
en lengua española en propiedad de:

© 2016 **ILUS BOOKS** Illusion Illustrated
c/ Cobos de Segovia, 19, 5º 1ª
28005 Madrid
España

ISBN 978-84-16574-26-1 [ES]

© 2016 **Éditions du Layeur**
Dépôt légal : septembre 2016
Imprimé chez Litostamp en septembre 2016

ISBN 978-2-915126-29-7 [FR]

Editorial coordination:
Claudia Martínez Alonso

Art direction:
Mireia Casanovas Soley

Edition and layout:
David Andreu Bach

Translation:
Thinking Abroad

Printed in Spain

The current concept of minimum housing dates from the early 20th century, when Modern Movement architects, inspired by the International Congress of Modern Architecture in 1929, began experimenting with the idea of *Existenzminimum* (minimum subsistence level), which had arisen as a response to the housing crisis that followed the First World War.

An exhaustive analysis of both technical and program needs stimulated the search for imaginative solutions which, energized by recently developed construction systems, ensured maximum comfort in smaller spaces that were more accessible financially to residents.

Most of the projects presented in this book go a step beyond *Existenzminimum*, since they generally involve pre-existing spaces, and are even smaller in size. Many are experimental prototypes, which is common in a field such as that of housing, which so readily lends itself to formal and functional research.

There are two essential premises that mark the route of these projects. The first and more important involves having the complete agreement of the client; although this type of housing does not waive basic standards of comfort and liveability, in many instances it denotes a lifestyle that turns its back on ordinary paradigms and puts the basic necessities into perspective. The second is a matter of discerning and distilling the client's program priorities, as these are especially significant in paring down the restrained design of the spaces.

Besides being ingenious and capable, planners must make creative use of construction techniques, often artisanal, to create flexible-use living environments that optimize the use of space. Some recurring elements in this type planning are enclosures that integrate and conceal furnishings, new lofts that take advantage of underutilized interior height, furniture that can be moved to differentiate areas, and independent volumes that focus functional areas.

The construction of minimal living spaces is present in many other areas of design, such as the intereriors of boats or house trailers; however, the design of these is somewhat different from the architectural sensibility reflected in the projects presented here, handed down from masters such as Le Corbusier in works such as his holiday cabin in Cap Martin.

Das derzeitige Konzept der Wohnung für das Existenzminimum stammt aus der Zeit Anfang des 20. Jahrhunderts, als die Architekten der Bewegung „Neues Bauen", denen der Internationale Kongress für Architektur 1929 einen Impuls gab, anfingen, mit der Idee des Existenzminimuns zu experimentieren, die als Antwort auf das drängende Problem des Wohnungsbaus, das der Erste Weltkrieg hinterlassen hatte, entstanden war.

Eine vollständige Analyse der Bedürfnisse in puncto Technik und Zielsetzung regte die Suche nach einfallsreichen Lösungen an, die — unterstützt durch die neuen, in den Jahren davor entwickelten Bausysteme — maximalen Komfort in Räumen geringerer Dimensionen sicherstellen und tragbare Kosten für die Benutzer mit sich bringen sollten.

Die meisten der in diesem Buch vorgestellten Projekte gehen noch einen Schritt weiter als das *Existenzminimum*, da sie die Anwendung ihrer Maximen durchweg in bereits bestehenden und noch kleineren Räumen darstellen. Viele dieser Projekte stellen experimentelle Prototypen dar, was in einem Bereich wie dem Wohnungswesen, welcher so stark der formalen und funktionalen Untersuchung unterliegt, üblich ist.

Zwei wesentliche Prämissen kennzeichnen den Leiftaden für diese Projekte. Die erste und wichtigste Prämisse besagt, den Kunden ganz und gar als Verbündeten zu betrachten; diese Form der Architektur verzichtet nicht auf grundlegende Standards in Sachen Komfort und Bewohnbarkeit, symbolisiert jedoch bei vielen Gelegenheiten einen Lebensstil, der einen großen Bogen um gewohnheitsmäßige Muster macht und Bedürfnisse relativiert. Die zweite Prämisse versucht, die Prioritäten bei den Zielsetzungen des Kunden, die in diesen Fällen die angepasste Gestaltung der Räume besonders deutlich bestimmen, zu erkennen und zu vereinfachen.

Zum Einfallsreichtum und Geschick der Planer kommt der kreative Einsatz von Bautechniken hinzu, die häufig mit dem Handwerk verknüpft sind, um ein bewohnbares Umfeld zu schaffen, das durch Flexibilität in der Nutzung und Raumausnutzung geprägt ist. Ummantelungen, welche Möbel einbinden und verbergen, neue Halbgeschosse, die von der freien Bauöhe im Inneren profitieren, Möbel, die sich verschieben lassen und Bereiche voneinander abheben können, oder unabhängige Volumen, die Funktionsbereiche bündeln, sind einige der wiederkehrenden Elemente bei Verfahren dieser Art.

Der Bau von Wohnraum auf begrenzter Flächeist in vielen weiteren Gestalt ungsbereichengegenwärtig, wie z. B. in der Kabine eines Bootes oder eines Wohnwagens. Doch diese Planung entfernt sich von der architektonischen Sensibilität, die sich in den hier gezeigten Projekten wiederspiegelt, und welche bereits Meister wie Le Corbusier in Werken wie z. B. seinem Ferienhäuschen am Cap Martin gezeigt haben.

Le concept actuel d'habitation minimale remonte au début du XXe s., lorsque les architectes du Mouvement moderne, poussés par le Congrès International d'Architecture de 1929, ont commencé à expérimenter avec l'idée de l'*Existenzminimun* (minimum existentiel), survenu comme une réponse au problème pressant de l'habitat que la Première Guerre Mondiale avait laissé derrière elle.

Une analyse exhaustive des besoins techniques et programmatiques a incité à rechercher des solutions imaginatives qui, soutenues par les nouveaux systèmes de construction développés au cours des années précédentes, assurent le confort maximal dans des espaces aux dimensions plus restreintes avec un coût assumable pour les utilisateurs.

La plupart des projets présentés dans ce livre vont au-delà de l'*Existenzminimum*, car ils représentent l'application de ses préceptes dans des espaces qui, de manière générale, existent déjà et sont plus réduits. Nombre d'entre eux sont des prototypes expérimentaux classiques dans un domaine tel que celui de l'habitat, si enclin à la recherche formelle et fonctionnelle.

Deux prémisses essentielles marquent la feuille de route de ces projets. La première et la plus importante requiert de compter sur l'entière complicité du client. Cette typologie d'habitation ne renonce pas aux standards de base de confort et d'habitabilité, mais symbolise très souvent un style de vie qui évite les modèles classiques et relativise les besoins. La deuxième tente de discerner et de simplifier les priorités programmatiques du client qui, dans ces cas, conditionnent, de manière particulièrement significative, la conception ajustée des espaces.

À l'ingéniosité et l'habileté des concepteurs s'ajoute une utilisation créatrice des techniques de construction souvent liées à l'artisanat afin de créer des espaces habitables caractérisés par la flexibilité des utilisations et la maximisation de l'espace. Des cloisons qui intègrent et dissimulent le mobilier, de nouvelles mezzanines qui tirent profit de la hauteur sous plafond, des meubles déplaçables et limiteurs d'espace ou des volumes indépendants qui concentrent des espaces fonctionnels, tels sont certains des éléments récurrents dans ce type d'interventions.

La construction d'espaces habitables réduits est présente dans de nombreux autres domaines de la conception tels que les habitacles d'un bateau ou l'intérieur d'une caravane. Leur conception s'éloigne néanmoins de la sensibilité architectonique reflétée dans les projets présentés ici et que des maîtres tels que Le Corbusier ont transmis dans des œuvres telles que sa cabane de vacances au Cap Martin.

El concepto actual de vivienda mínima se remonta a principios del siglo XX, cuando los arquitectos del Movimiento Moderno, impulsados por el Congreso Internacional de Arquitectura de 1929, comenzaron a experimentar con la idea del *Existenzminimun* (mínimo existencial), surgida como respuesta al acuciante problema de la vivienda que la Primera Guerra Mundial había dejado tras de sí.

Un análisis exhaustivo de las necesidades técnicas y programáticas incentivó la búsqueda de soluciones imaginativas que, respaldadas por los nuevos sistemas constructivos desarrollados en los años precedentes, asegurasen el máximo confort en unos espacios de dimensiones más ajustadas y supusiesen un coste asumible para los usuarios.

La mayoría de los proyectos presentados en este libro van un paso más allá del *Existenzminimum*, ya que representan la aplicación de sus preceptos en espacios por regla general ya existentes y de tamaño aún más reducido. Muchos de ellos constituyen prototipos experimentales, habituales en un campo como el de la vivienda, tan proclive a la investigación formal y funcional.

Dos premisas esenciales marcan la hoja de ruta de estos proyectos. La primera y más importante implica contar con la total complicidad del cliente; esta tipología doméstica no renuncia a unos estándares básicos de confort y habitabilidad, pero en muchas ocasiones simboliza un estilo de vida que rehúye los patrones habituales y relativiza las necesidades. La segunda intenta discernir y simplificar las prioridades programáticas del cliente, que en estos casos condicionan de manera especialmente significativa el ajustado diseño de los espacios.

Al ingenio y a la habilidad de los proyectistas se une un uso creativo de las técnicas constructivas, frecuentemente vinculadas a la artesanía, para crear unos entornos habitables caracterizados por la flexibilidad de usos y el aprovechamiento del espacio. Cerramientos que integran y ocultan el mobiliario, nuevos altillos que se benefician de la altura libre interior, muebles con capacidad para desplazarse y diferenciar ámbitos, o volúmenes independientes que concentran áreas funcionales, son algunos de los elementos recurrentes en este tipo de actuaciones.

La construcción de espacios habitables mínimos está presente en muchos otros ámbitos del diseño, como pueden ser los casos de los habitáculos de una embarcación o de una caravana; sin embargo, su concepción se aleja de la sensibilidad arquitectónica reflejada en los proyectos aquí presentados y que ya maestros como Le Corbusier transmitieron en obras como su cabaña de vacaciones en Cap Martín.

As she goes about her day, the owner of this home shifts the locations of three wooden containers, suspended from rails in the ceiling. Located in a space with a bathroom on one end and a kitchen on the other, the positions of these containers can be quickly adjusted to the various activities of the day. Adaptable to different uses, the rest of the space is open and connects visually to the functional areas.

Die Verschiebung der drei Holzcontainer, die an Schienen hängen, welche in der Decke angebracht sind, begleitet die Eigentümerin dieser Wohnstätte während des Tages. In einem Bereich der Wohnung befindlich, der an den Enden durch Bad und Küche abgegrenzt wird, passen diese Container ihre Position schnell an die verschiedenen Aktivitäten an, die während des Tages stattfinden. Die übrige Wohnung besteht aus einem durchscheinenden Raum, der sich an die verschiedenen Nutzungen anpassen lässt und optisch mit dem Funktionsbereich verbunden ist.

Le déplacement des trois containers en bois, suspendus à des rails fixés au plafond, accompagne au quotidien la propriétaire de cette maison. Situés dans une partie de la maison délimitée au niveau de leurs extrémités par la salle de bains et la cuisine, ces containers adaptent facilement leur position aux diverses activités réalisées au cours de la journée. Le reste de la maison est composé d'un espace ouvert, adaptable aux différents usages et relié visuellement à l'espace fonctionnel.

El desplazamiento de tres contenedores de madera, suspendidos de unos raíles situados en el techo, acompaña a la propietaria de esta vivienda a lo largo del día. Situados en una zona de la casa delimitada en sus extremos por el baño y por la cocina, estos contenedores adecúan rápidamente su posición a las diferentes actividades que se desarrollan durante la jornada. El resto de la vivienda está constituido por un espacio diáfano, adaptable a diferentes usos y conectado visualmente a la zona funcional.

8

ALL I OWN HOUSE

PKMN architectures

LOCATION Madrid, Spain AREA 45 m² / 484 sq ft PHOTOS © Javier de Paz García

SECURITAS

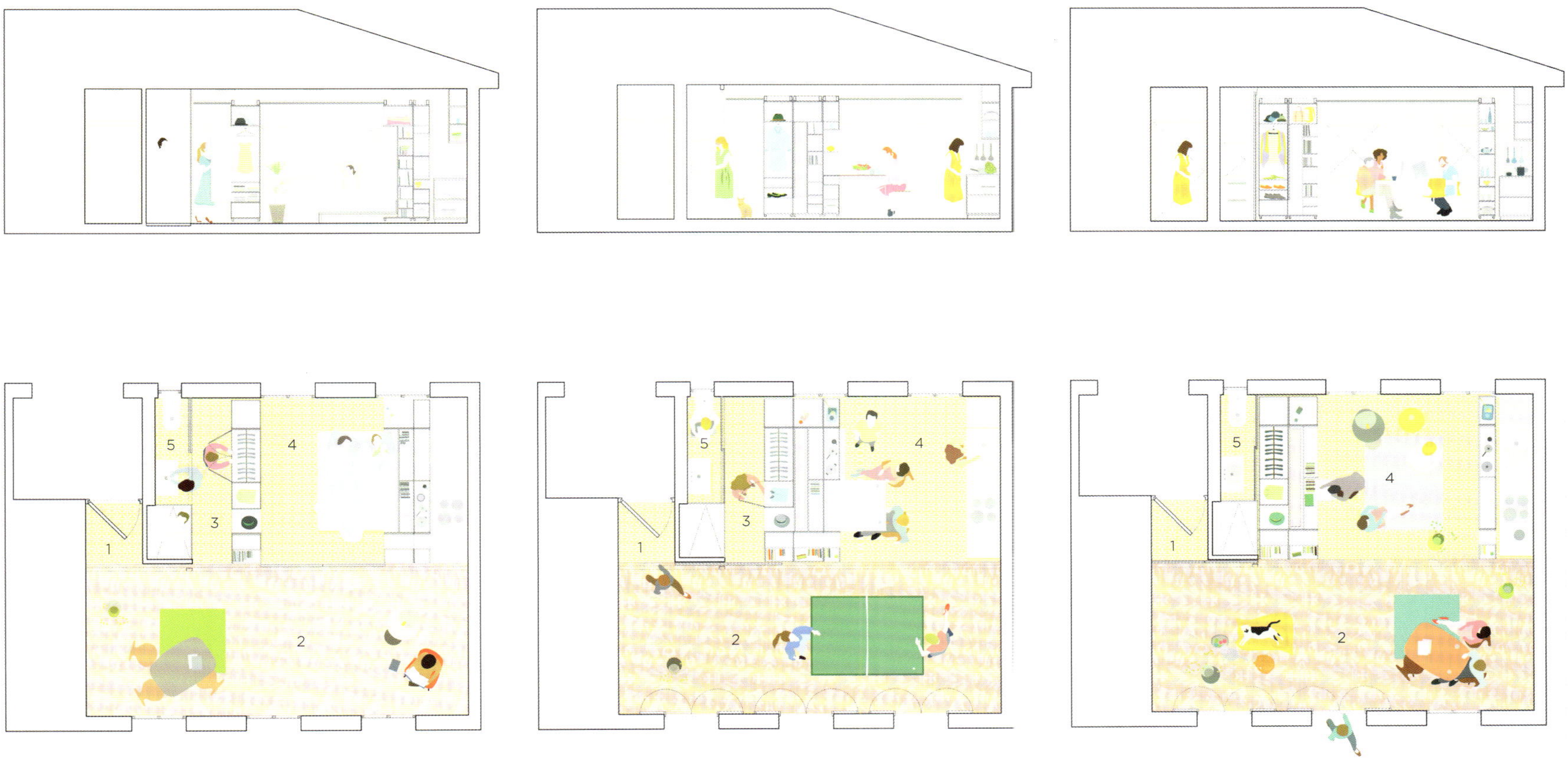

0 1 2m N

Functional diagrams

1. Entrance
2. Living room
   Play room
3. Dressing room
4. Bedroom
   Kitchen/Dining
   Studio
5. Toilet.

The containers are designed to be convertible elements that hold personal belongings, a folding bed, a dining table, and even a round blackboard for work meetings.

Die Container wurden als umwandelbare Elemente entworfen, die persönliche Gegenstände, ein Klappbett, einen Esstisch und sogar eine Schiefertafel unterbringen, die für Arbeitstagungen vorgesehen ist.

Les containers sont présentés comme des éléments transformables qui comprennent des effets personnels, un lit escamotable, une table de salle à manger et un tableau rond pour des réunions de travail.

Los contenedores se plantean como elementos transformables que albergan pertenencias personales, una cama abatible, una mesa de comedor e incluso una pizarra redonda preparada para reuniones de trabajo.

This vacation apartment, located in a penthouse facing a historic fishing port, was redesigned with the goal of fitting two bedrooms, a studio, a living room, a kitchen, and a bathroom into a very small space further constrained by sloping ceilings. The result is a compact floor plan that makes optimum use of the space. The private spaces, conceived as furniture that can be closed after use, flow together into one core area.

Ziel des Umbaus dieser Ferienwohnung, die im Dachgeschoss mit Blick auf einen alten Fischerhafen liegt, war, zwei Schlafzimmer, ein Arbeitszimmer, ein Wohnzimmer, eine Küche und ein Bad auf einer äußerst kleinen Grundfläche mit Dachschrägen anzuordnen. Das Ergebnis ist die Aufteilung äußerst begrenzter Räume, die optimal ausgenutzt wurden. Für den Hauptbereich, in dem die geschlossenen Wohnräume zusammenkommen, wurden Möbel konzipiert, die sich nach der Nutzung schließen lassen.

L'objectif des travaux de cet appartement de vacances, situé au dernier étage, face au vieux port de pêche, était d'avoir deux chambres, un bureau, un séjour, une cuisine et une salle de bains dans une surface très réduite et sous des plafonds mansardés. Le résultat est une répartition des espaces très ajustés et utilisés au maximum, avec un espace principal dans lequel convergent les pièces fermées, conçues de sorte que les meubles, après utilisation, servent de cloison.

El objetivo de la reforma de este apartamento de vacaciones, situado en un ático frente a un viejo puerto pesquero, fue distribuir un programa de dos dormitorios, un estudio, una sala de estar, una cocina y un baño en una superficie muy reducida y de techos abuhardillados. El resultado es una distribución de espacios muy ajustados y aprovechados al máximo, con un ámbito principal en el que confluyen las estancias cerradas, concebidas a modo de muebles que, después de ser utilizados, pueden cerrarse.

14

HARBOUR ATTIC

Gosplan Architects

LOCATION Camogli, Italy AREA 35 m² / 377 sq ft PHOTOS © Anna Positano

In the main space, which faces the sea, a sofa fits into the same unit that holds the kitchenette. A storage unit acts as the back wall of this section, separating it from the bedroom, while being accessible from both sides.

Im Richtung Meer ausgerichteten Hauptraum verbindet die Gestaltung die Küche mit einem Sofa. Ein Containermöbel fungiert als Hintergrund für diesen Bereich und trennt ihn vom Schlafzimmer ab, das von beiden Seiten zugänglich ist.

Dans l'espace principal, orienté vers la mer, l'aménagement allie la cuisine au canapé. Un meuble container sert de toile de fond de ce cadre qui sépare la chambre, accessible des deux côtés.

En el espacio principal, orientado hacia el mar, el diseño funde la cocina con un sofá. Un mueble contenedor actúa como fondo de este ámbito y lo separa del dormitorio, siendo accesible desde ambos lados.

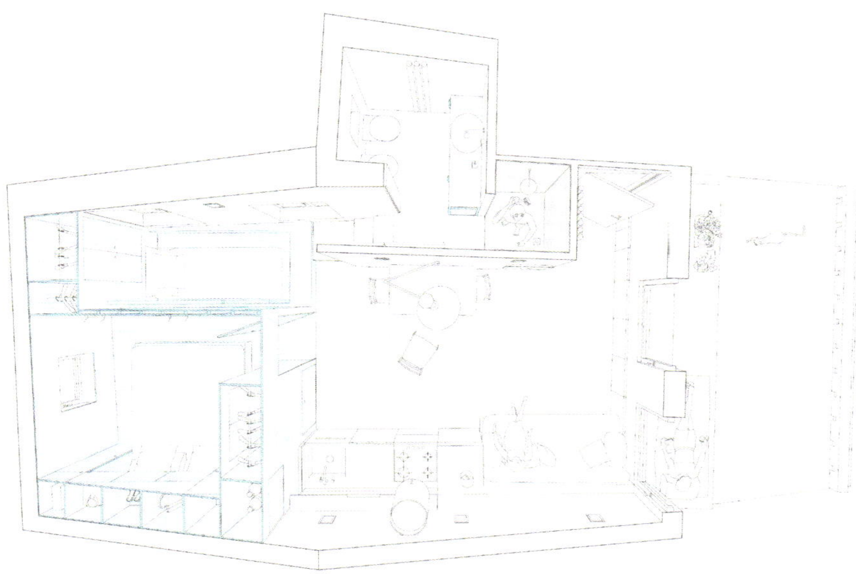

Floor plan

The second sleeping space is a small empty hinged platform, sitting slightly above the level of the house, which opens to reveal a twin-sized bed.

Das zweite Schlafzimmer besteht aus einer leeren Plattform mit Minimalmaßen, in dem eine herunterklappbare Öffnung den Blick auf ein Einzelbett freigibt. Sie ist in einem Boden angebracht ist, der leicht über der Horizontale des Hauses angeordnet ist.

La deuxième chambre est composée d'une plateforme vide aux dimensions minimales dans laquelle se trouve une ouverture rabattable sur un sol légèrement surélevé par rapport au niveau de la maison laisse découvrir un lit simple.

El segundo dormitorio constituye una plataforma vacía de dimensiones mínimas, en el que una abertura abatible situada en un suelo ligeramente elevado sobre el nivel de la casa deja al descubierto una cama individual.

Because available surface area s scarce, the layout is designed to use every corner of the house for storage space, which is built into the rooms.

Der geringe zur Verfügung stehende Platz trägt dazu bei, dass die Verteilung bestrebt ist, alle Ecken des Hauses optimal auszunutzen, um Stauräume zu platzieren, die in den Aufbau der Wohnräume integriert werden.

Le peu de surface disponible fait que l'on cherche à maximiser le moindre recoin de la maison pour disposer d'espaces de rangement intégrés à la composition des pièces.

La escasa superficie disponible hace que la distribución busque aprovechar al máximo todos los rincones de la casa para ubicar las zonas de almacenamiento, que se integran en la composición de las estancias.

This project came about because the homeowners wanted to add a guest room to their house without making significant changes to the layout of the living room. The solution here was to install a motorized moveable wall, four-and-a-half-meters long, that would divide the living space and create two independent rooms whose size could vary according to the requirements of the day: a guest room, a possible office, a game room, or simply a clothes closet.

Diese Maßnahme ergab sich aus der Notwendigkeit seitens der Eigentümer, ihre Wohnstätte mit einem Gästezimmer auszustatten, ohne die Konfiguration des Wohnzimmers übermäßig zu verändern. Die Lösung besteht aus einer beweglichen 4,5 m langen, motorisierten Wand, mit deren Hilfe sich das Wohnzimmer teilen und zwei unabhängige Wohnbereiche schaffen lassen, deren Abmessungen je nach Bedarf jederzeit variieren können: Gästezimmer, bei Bedarf als Büro, Spielzimmer oder einfach Kleiderschrank.

Cette intervention est venue du besoin des propriétaires d'équiper leur maison d'une chambre d'amis, sans pour autant altérer avec excès la configuration du séjour. La solution consiste en un panneau amovible motorisé de quatre mètres et demis de longueur qui permet de diviser l'espace du séjour et créer ainsi deux espaces indépendants dont les dimensions qui peuvent varier selon les besoins à tout moment : chambre d'amis, bureau occasionnel, salle de jeux ou simple dressing.

Esta actuación surge de la necesidad por parte de los propietarios de dotar a su vivienda de una habitación de invitados, sin alterar en exceso la configuración de la sala de estar. La solución consiste en una pared móvil motorizada de cuatro metros y medio de longitud que permite dividir el espacio del estar y crear dos estancias independientes, cuyas dimensiones pueden variar en función de las necesidades de cada momento: habitación de invitados, despacho eventual, cuarto de juegos o simple ropero.

24

STELLA HOUSE

PKMN architectures

LOCATION Madrid, Spain AREA 37 m² / 398 sq ft PHOTOS © Javier de Paz García

Functional diagrams

By moving the wall, it is possible to alternate different layouts. One can create two separate rooms, or, for family gatherings, open up the living room to its largest possible size.

Durch Verschieben der beweglichen Wand lassen sich verschiedene Raumkonfigurationen abwechseln: zwei unabhängige Wohnräume schaffen oder dem Wohnzimmer, Treffpunkt der Familie, den größten Umfang geben.

Le déplacement du panneau amovible permet d'alterner diverses configurations de l'espace : créer deux espaces indépendants ou donner un maximum de grandeur au séjour, lieu de réunion de la famille.

El desplazamiento de la pared móvil permite alternar diferentes configuraciones del espacio: crear dos estancias independientes u otorgar la máxima amplitud a la sala de estar, lugar de encuentro de la familia.

This apartment includes an open, continuous room measuring 50 m², planned to be flexible and dynamic because of a system of room-height revolving furniture that act as separate moveable elements. This special design allows quick changes among three possible layouts; one containing two bedrooms, one with only one bedroom, and one layout with no bedrooms that converts the dwelling into a loft-style setting.

Bei dieser Wohnung wurde ein offener und durchgehender Raum mit 50 m² vorgesehen, entworfen als flexibler und dynamischer Raum dank eines Systems drehbarer Möbel auf der gesamte Höhe, die als bewegliche Trennelemente fungieren. Dank dieser besonderen Gestaltung kann der Nutzer schnell zwischen den drei möglichen Konfigurationen der Raumaufteilung abwechseln: zwei Schlafzimmer, nur einSchlafzimmer bzw. ohne Schlafzimmer, wodurch sich die Wohnstätte in eine Art Loft verwandelt.

Il s'agit d'un appartement dans lequel une pièce ouverte et continue de 50 m² a été prévue, conçu comme un espace modulable et dynamique grâce à un système de meubles mobiles en hauteur qui servent d'éléments séparateurs mobiles. Cette conception particulière permet d'alterner de manière rapide trois éventuelles configurations de répartition : une en deux chambres, une autre en une chambre et un espace sans chambre qui convertit le logement en un espace de type loft.

Se trata de un apartamento en el que se ha previsto una sala abierta y continua de 50 m², planteada como un espacio flexible y dinámico gracias a un sistema de muebles giratorios a toda altura que actúan como elementos separadores móviles. Esta especial concepción permite alternar de forma rápida entre tres posibles configuraciones de la distribución: una de dos dormitorios, otra con un solo dormitorio y una distribución sin dormitorios que convierte la vivienda en un espacio tipo *loft*.

28

MJE HOUSE

PKMN architectures

LOCATION **Salinas, Spain** AREA **70 m² / 753 sq ft** PHOTOS **© Javier de Paz García**

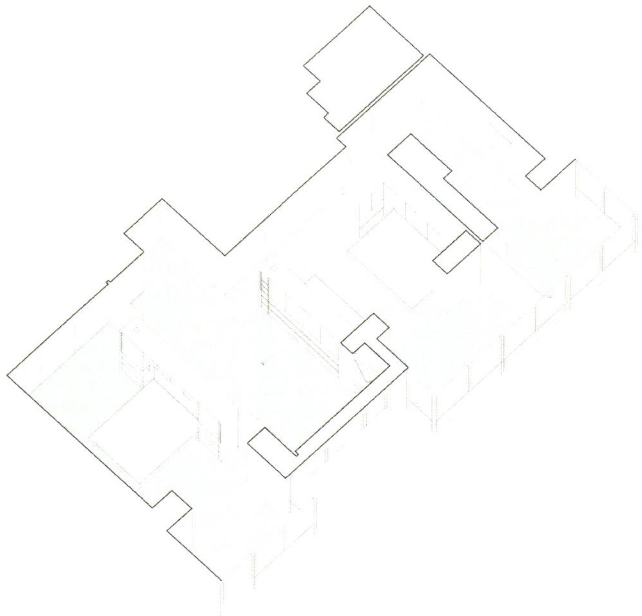

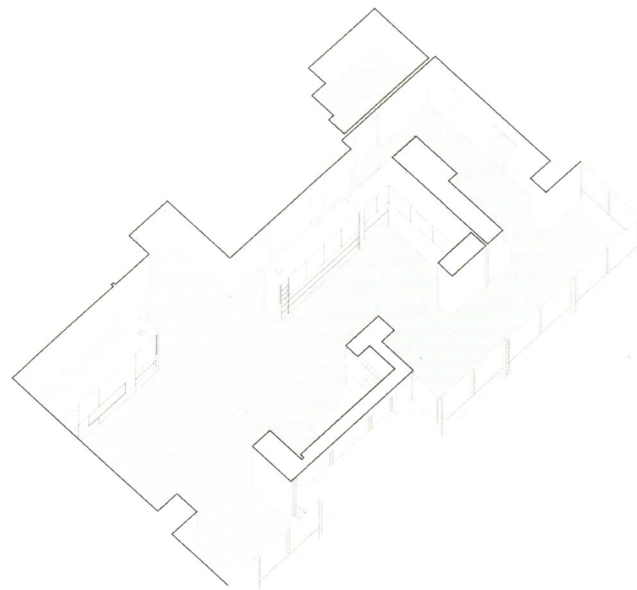

Axonometric views

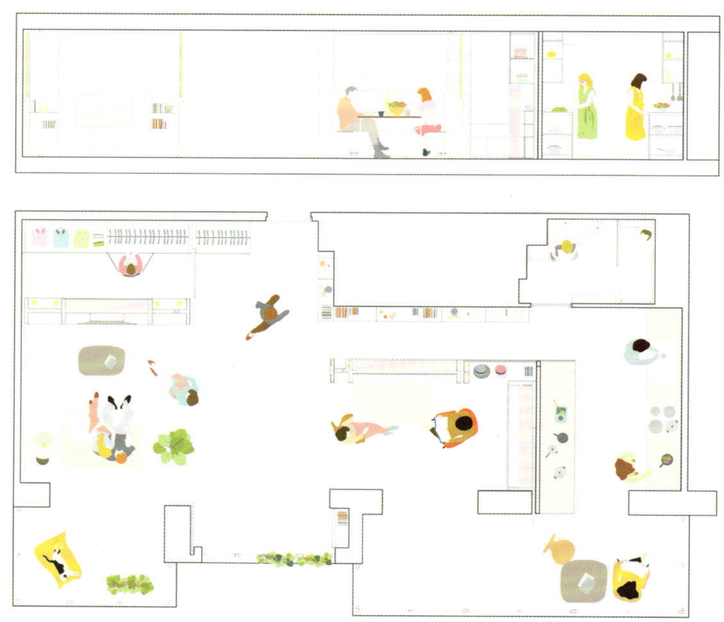

Functional diagrams

The fact that the room dividers are moveable means that it is possib e to try out different placements in the main room and discover new possibilities for structuring the layout.

Dank der Dynamik der beweglichen Trennelemente kann der Nutzer mit den verschiedenen Positionen innerhalb des Hauptwohnbereichs spielen und nach neuen Möglichkeiten suchen, wie er die Aufteilung der Wohnstätte gliedert.

Le dynamisme des éléments séparateurs mobiles permet de jouer sur les diverses positions dans la pièce principale et chercher de nouvelles possibilités d'aménager la répartition de l'appartement.

El dinamismo de los elementos separadores móviles permite jugar con diferentes posiciones dentro del ámbito de la sala principal y buscar nuevas posibilidades de estructurar la distribución de la vivienda.

Here a highly compartmentalized apartment, located in Madrid in a historic *corrala*, a courtyard-centered apartment building, becomes a more ample space with improved light. This was done by putting the living and sleeping areas together on one side of a central cabinet, which is the main element, as it organizes the various ways it is used. The other rooms are opened up and reconfigured to create a fluid space and allow more sunlight into the home.

Das Projekt verwandelt eine Wohnstätte mit einer sehr stark unterteilten Raumaufteilung, die in einem typischem „Corrala"-Wohnblock Madrids liegt, in einen geräumigeren und besser beleuchteten Raum. Hierfür werden Wohn- und Schlafbereich zu einem Bereich zusammengefasst, getrennt durch ein Möbelstück in der Mitte des Raumes, das ein einzigartiges Element darstellt, welches die verschiedenen Arten der Nutzung organisiert. Die übrigen Räume der Wohnung öffnen sich und werden neu konfiguriert, um einen fließenden Raum zu schaffen und die Wohnung für das Sonnenlicht besser zugänglich zu machen.

Le projet transforme une habitation à la répartition très compartimentée, située dans une *corrala* (cour) madrilène typique, en un espace plus vaste et plus lumineux. Pour cela, on intègre dans un même espace le séjour et la chambre, séparés par un meuble situé au centre de la pièce et constitue un élément singulier qui organise les différents usages. Les autres pièces de la maison s'ouvrent et sont configurées de telle sorte à créer un espace fluide et le rendre plus perméable à la lumière du soleil.

El proyecto transforma una vivienda de distribución muy compartimentada, ubicada en una típica corrala madrileña, en un espacio más amplio y mejor iluminado. Para ello, se integran en un mismo ámbito las zonas de estar y dormitorio, separadas por un mueble situado en el centro de la sala y que constituye un elemento singular que organiza los diferentes usos.
El resto de estancias de la casa se abren y se reconfiguran para crear un espacio fluido y hacer la vivienda más permeable a la luz del sol.

32

DWELLING IN LAVAPIÉS

Clap Design!

LOCATION **Madrid, Spain** AREA **50 m² / 538 sq ft** PHOTOS **© Juan Carlos Quindós**

The divider/cabinet makes the sleeping area more private. It can hold a television that revolves as needed, and it also contains shelving and storage spaces.

Das trennende Möbelstück verleiht dem Bereich des Schlafzimmers Privatsphäre. Sein Design ermöglicht die Unterbringung eines Fernsehers, der sich je nach Bedarf drehen lässen. Gleichzeitig bietet es Regale und Stauraum.

Le meuble séparateur confère de l'intimité à l'espace nuit. Sa conception permet également de placer une télévision qui se tourne selon les besoins avec des étagères et des espaces de rangement.

El mueble separador dota de intimidad a la zona de dormitorio. Su diseño permite también albergar la televisión y girarla según las necesidades y, al mismo tiempo, contiene estanterías y espacios de almacenaje.

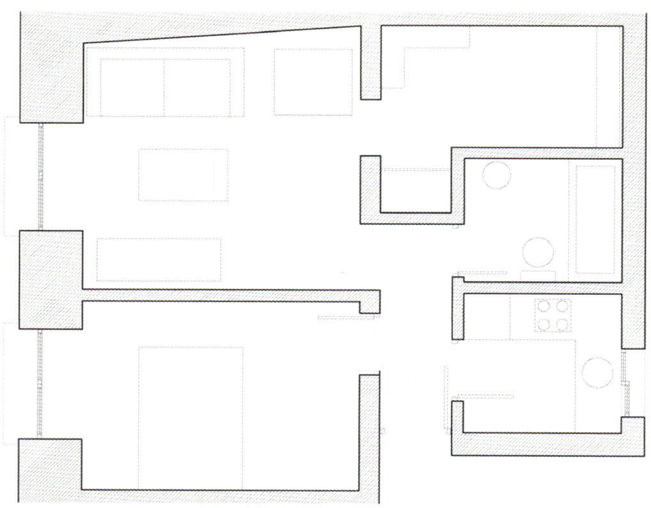

Existing floor plan

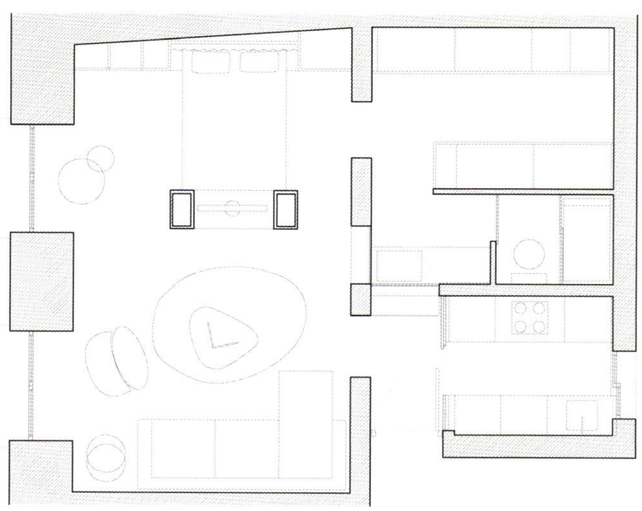

New floor plan

The open plan used in all the rooms, and the relationship it establishes among them, makes for a fluid, continuous environment, with the predominant use of white tones working to increase the sense of spaciousness.

Die offene Gestaltung aller Wohnräume dieser Wohnung und die Beziehung, die zwischen ihnen aufgebaut werden, ergeben einen fließenden und durchgehenden Raum, in dem die überwiegende Verwendung weißer Farbtönen das Gefühl von Geräumigkeit steigert.

La conception ouverte de toutes les pièces de la maison et la relation qui s'établit entre elles créent un espace fluide et continu dans lequel prédominent des tons blancs, ce qui augmente la sensation de grandeur.

La concepción abierta de todas las estancias de la casa y la relación que se establece entre ellas generan un ambiente fluido y continuo, en el que el uso predominante de tonos blancos incrementa la sensación de amplitud.

There are two elements that make this all-in-one space effective. First is the moveable cabinet that can either create a bedroom or make more space for the living area on the opposite side, where there is a sofa. The second is a cupboard built into the wall, perpendicular to the room divider. Its doors slide open to reveal flexible shelving, work nooks, or clothes storage spaces, depending on how the spaces are arranged.

Zwei Elemente organisieren die Nutzung dieser Wohnung mit einem einzigen Bereich. Das erste ist ein bewegliches Möbelstück zur Trennung, das alternativ einen Schlafzimmerbereich schafft oder den Raum zum Wohnbereich erklärt, der auf der entgegengesetzten Seite liegt, wo sich ein Sofa befindet. Das zweite Element ist ein Wandschrank, der in der Wand senkrecht zu dem trennenden Möbelstück eingebunden wird, in dem je nach Nutzung ein Satz Schiebetüren Regale, Arbeitsbereiche oder Stauraum für Kleidung freigibt.

Deux éléments organisent le fonctionnement de cet appartement à espace unique. Le premier est un meuble séparateur mobile qui créé en alternance une chambre ou assigne l'espace au séjour situé à l'opposé, où se trouve un canapé. Le deuxième est une armoire intégrée au mur perpendiculaire au meuble séparateur dans lequel un jeu de portes coulissantes révèle des étagères, des espaces de travail ou des zones de rangement pour les vêtements selon la configuration d'utilisation.

Dos elementos organizan el funcionamiento de este apartamento de un solo ambiente. El primero es un mueble separador móvil que, de forma alternativa, genera una zona de dormitorio o asigna el espacio a la zona de estar situada en el lado opuesto, en la que se ubica un sofá. El segundo es un armario integrado en la pared perpendicular al mueble separador, en el que un juego de puertas correderas revela estanterías, zonas de trabajo o zonas de almacenaje de ropa en función de la configuración de los usos.

38

5:1 APARTMENT

Michael K Chen Architecture (MKCA)

LOCATION **New York, USA** AREA **36 m² / 387 sq ft** PHOTOS **© Alan Tansey**

When the cabinet is moved, a folding bed in the sleeping area can be opened out. The sliding cabinet has a spot for a television, which can be adjusted to face either way.

Durch Verschieben des trennenden Möbelstücks lässt sich ein Bett im Bereich des Schlafzimmers ausklappen. Das bewegliche Möbelstück bietet Platz für den Fernseher, der sich nach beiden Seiten ausrichten lässt.

Le déplacement du meuble séparateur permet de déployer le lit abattable dans la chambre. Le meuble amovible comprend un espace pour la télévision qui peut se tourner des deux côtés.

El desplazamiento del mueble separador permite extender una cama abatible en el ámbito del dormitorio. El mueble móvil incorpora un espacio para la televisión que puede orientarse hacia ambos lados.

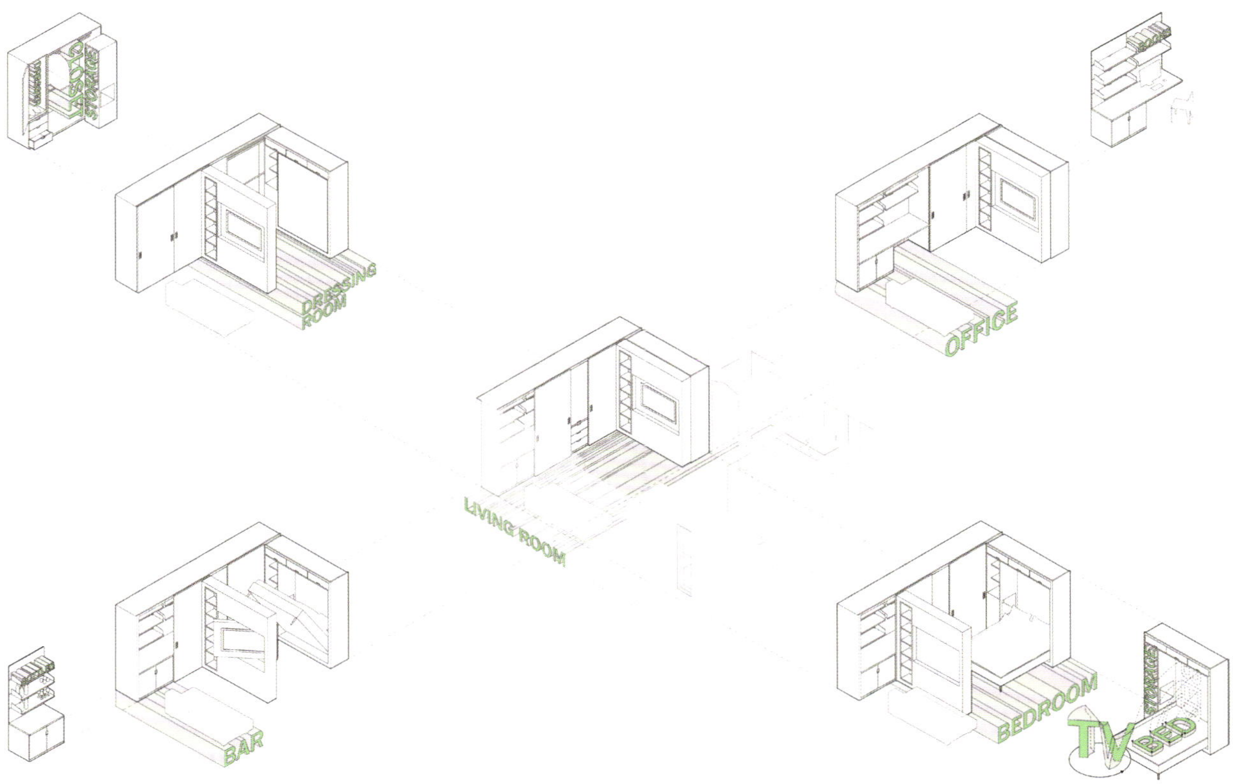

Expanded axonometric

Trevlig
sommar!

The existing kitchen and bathroom have been rebuilt to maximize their surface area, create storage, and update the fixtures. Near the entry to these is a small four-person dining area.

Die vorhandene Küche und das bestehende Bad sind renoviert worden, um deren Fläche zu erweitern, Stauraum zu schaffen und die Einrichtung zu modernisieren. Neben dem Zugang zu beiden befindet sich ein kleiner Essbereich für vier Personen.

La cuisine et la salle de bains existantes ont été refaites afin d'agrandir leur surface, créer des espaces de rangement et moderniser leur équipement. Une petite salle à manger pour quatre personnes a été créée à proximité de l'accès des deux pièces.

La cocina y el baño existentes han sido reformados para ampliar su superficie, crear zonas de almacenaje y actualizar su equipamiento. Una pequeña zona de comedor para cuatro personas se sitúa junto al acceso a ambos.

The plan for this split-level abode with a square floor-plan gave priority to creating internal passageways that would be pleasing to the eyes of its inhabitants. Starting in the spacious living-dining room on the first floor, an isolated stairway ascends over the foyer on the lower level toward a bridge suspended in space. This bridge, joining the master bedroom and the dressing room on the second floor, overlooks the continuous space of the house.

Bei der Planung dieses Hauses mit drei Etagen und quadratischem Grundriss räumten die Gestalter der Entfaltung einiger Kreisläufe im Innenraum, die dem optischen Genus seiner Bewohner dienen, Vorrang ein. Von dem geräumigen Wohn-Esszimmer im Erdgeschoss steigt eine isolierte Treppe über den Flur der unteren Etage in Richtung einer Brücke, die im Leerraum schwebt. Diese Brücke, die das große Schlafzimmer und dem Ankleidezimmer im ersten Stock verbindet, verwandelt sich in einen Aussichtspunkt über den fortlaufenden Raum des Hauses.

Dans le projet de cette maison sur trois niveaux avec une surface carrée, les concepteurs ont donné la priorité aux circulations intérieures pour un meilleur visuel des utilisateurs. Depuis l'espace séjour-salle à manger du rez-de-chaussée, un escalier isolé monte au-dessus du dégagement du niveau inférieur vers une passerelle suspendue dans le vide. Cette passerelle qui permet de communiquer entre la chambre parentale et le dressing du premier étage, se transforme en un mirador au-dessus de l'espace continu de la maison.

En el proyecto de esta vivienda de tres niveles y planta cuadrada, los diseñadores dieron prioridad al desarrollo de unas circulaciones interiores destinadas al goce visual de sus usuarios. Desde el espacioso estar-comedor de la planta baja, una escalera aislada asciende por encima del distribuidor del nivel inferior hacia un puente suspendido en el vacío. Este puente, que comunica el dormitorio principal y el vestidor de la primera planta, se convierte en un mirador sobre el espacio continuo de la casa.

44

BLOCK VILLAGE

HAO Design

LOCATION Kaohsiung City, Taiwan AREA 40 m² / 431 sq ft PHOTOS © Hey!Cheese

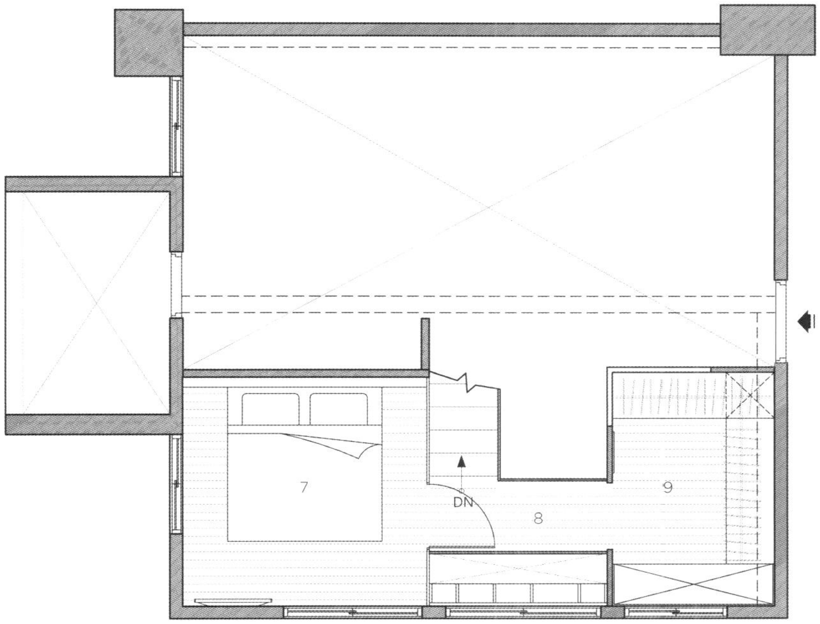

Second floor

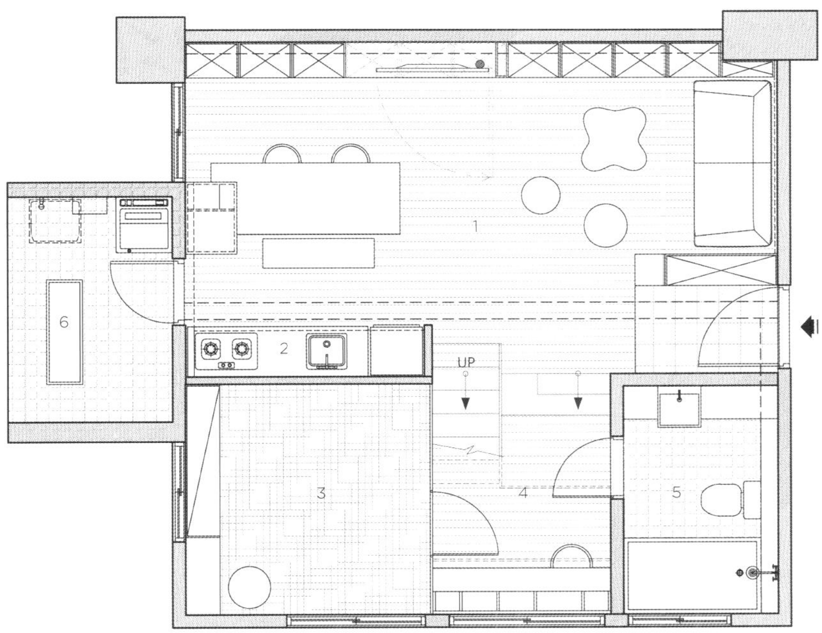

Ground floor

1. Living/Dining
2. Kitchen
3. Bedroom
4. Aisle & stairs
5. Bathroom
6. Patio
7. Bedroom
8. Bridge
9. Dressing room

From the foyer under the stairway, which is used as a study, part of a book shelf rises to the second floor ceiling, emphasizing the double height of the space and acting as a backdrop for the bridge.

Vom Flur, der sich unter der Treppe befindet und als Arbeitszimmer genutzt wird, beginnt ein Bücherregal, das sich bis zur Decke der ersten Etage hinauf erstreckt, wodurch die doppelte Höhe des Raumes betont wird und als Kulisse für die Brücke fungiert.

Du passage situé en dessous de l'escalier, utilisé comme bureau, part une bibliothèque qui va jusqu'au plafond du premier étage, mettant ainsi en valeur la double hauteur de l'espace et servant de toile de fond pour la passerelle.

Del distribuidor situado bajo la escalera, utilizado como estudio, parte una librería que se eleva hasta el techo de la primera planta, enfatizando la doble altura del espacio y actuando de telón de fondo para el puente.

The simple and harmonious interior design combines the simple texture of pine wood with different green tones and a few luminous white walls.

Die harmonische und einfache Innengestaltung kombiniert die Schlichtheit der Textur des Kiefernholzes mit dem Einsatz unterschiedlicher Grüntöne und hellen vertikalen Wandflächen in Weiß.

Le design intérieur, harmonieux et simple, combine simplicité de la texture du pin et utilisation des divers tons de vert et des murs verticaux lumineux de couleur blanche.

El armonioso y sencillo diseño interior combina la simplicidad de la textura de la madera de pino con el uso de diferentes tonos de color verde y con unos luminosos paramentos verticales de color blanco.

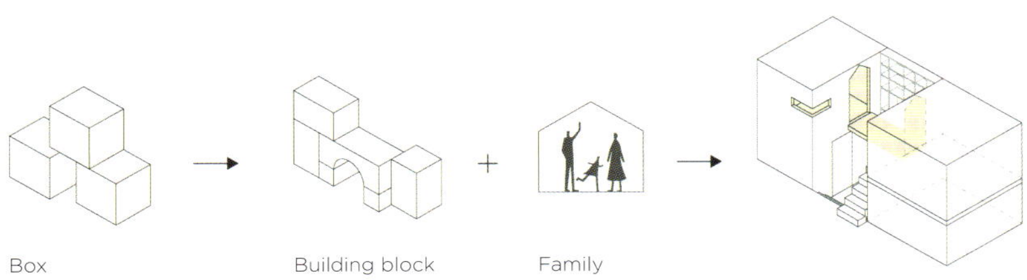

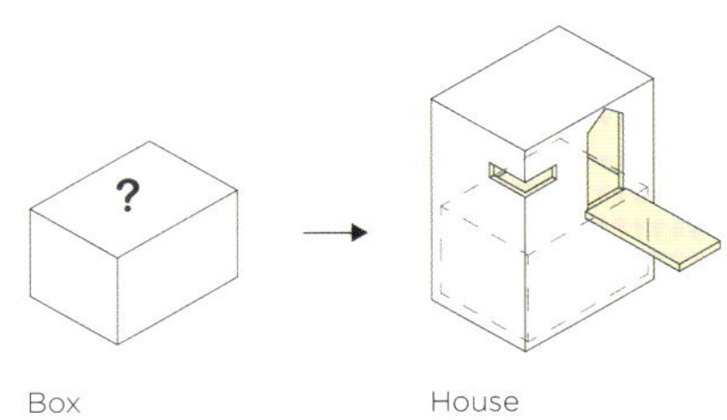

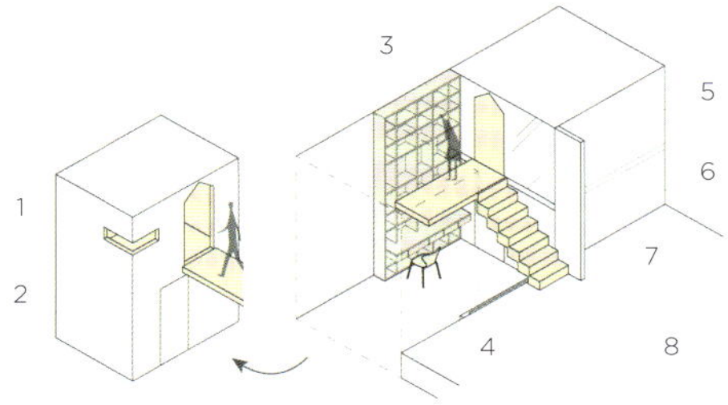

1. Closet
2. Bathroom
3. Study
4. Entrance
5. Bedroom
6. Japanese-style room
7. Kitchen
8. Living/Dining

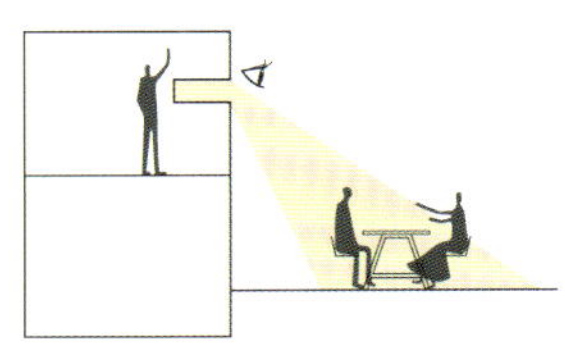

The bedroom and dressing room are connected as part of an optical illusion that defines them as one sole space. A horizontal corner opening in the dressing room provides the best view of the floor below.

Schlaf- und Ankleidezimmer bringen sich durch ein visuelles Spiel in Verbindung, das sie als eine Einheit definiert. Im Ankleidezimmer bietet eine horizontale Kerbe in der Ecke die beste Perspektive auf die untere Etage.

La chambre et le dressing s'entrelacent par un jeu visuel qui les définit comme un seul élément. Dans le dressing, une ouverture horizontale à l'angle offre une meilleure perspective de l'étage inférieur.

El dormitorio y el vestidor se interrelacionan mediante un juego visual que los define como una sola entidad. Dentro del vestidor, una hendidura horizontal en esquina ofrece la mejor perspectiva sobre la planta inferior.

This comprehensive housing plan stems from the increase in one-person homes in the larger cities. This experimental proposal, agreed upon by the owner, brings 54 assembled modules, containing an entire domestic infrastructure, into an open space. These modules, which expand and contract as needed, are laid out so as to organize the various spaces of the home.

Dieser umfassende Eingriff in eine Wohnung hängt mit der Zunahme der Single-Haushalte in Großstädten zusammen. Als Experiment entworfen, stellt der Vorschlag innerhalb eines durchscheinenden Raumes ein Reihe von 54 zusammengebauten Modulen vor, welche die gesamte häusliche Infrastruktur enthalten und deren Charakter mit dem Eigentümer abgestimmt wurde. Die Anordnung dieser Module, die sich je nach Bedarf erweitern und verkleinern lassen, gliedern die verschiedenen Bereiche der Wohnstätte.

Cette intervention complète dans une maison est liée à l'augmentation des maisons indépendantes dans les grandes villes. Conçue à titre d'expérimentation, la proposition introduit dans un espace ouvert une série de 54 modules assemblés qui contiennent toute l'infrastructure de la maison et dont la nature a été réalisée avec l'accord du propriétaire. La disposition de ces modules qui s'agrandissent et se contractent en fonction des besoins organise les divers espaces de la maison.

Esta intervención integral en una vivienda está relacionada con el incremento de hogares unipersonales en las grandes ciudades. Planteada a modo de experimento, la propuesta introduce dentro de un espacio diáfano una serie de 54 módulos ensamblados que contienen toda la infraestructura doméstica y cuya naturaleza fue consensuada con el propietario. La disposición de estos módulos, que se expanden y se contraen en función de las necesidades, organiza los diferentes ámbitos de la vivienda.

54

POP-UP HOUSE

TallerDE2

LOCATION **Madrid, Spain** AREA **58,5 m² / 630 sq ft** PHOTOS **© Imagen Subliminal**

All the modules are constructed of plywood. They are designed to either reveal their functional components or act as a neutral, uniform backdrop for the interior.

Alle Module sind aus Pressholzplatten gefertigt. Ihre Gestaltung ermöglicht es, die Funktionsbauteile zu entdecken, die sie enthalten, oder einen neutralen und einheitlichen Hintergrund für den Innenraum der Wohnstätte zu schaffen.

Tous les modules ont été construits en panneaux de bois pressé. Leur conception permet de découvrir les composants fonctionnels qu'ils contiennent ou de créer un fond neutre et uniforme pour l'intérieur de la maison.

Todos los módulos se construyeron con paneles de virutas de madera prensada. Su diseño permite descubrir los componentes funcionales que contienen o generar un fondo neutro y uniforme para el interior de la vivienda.

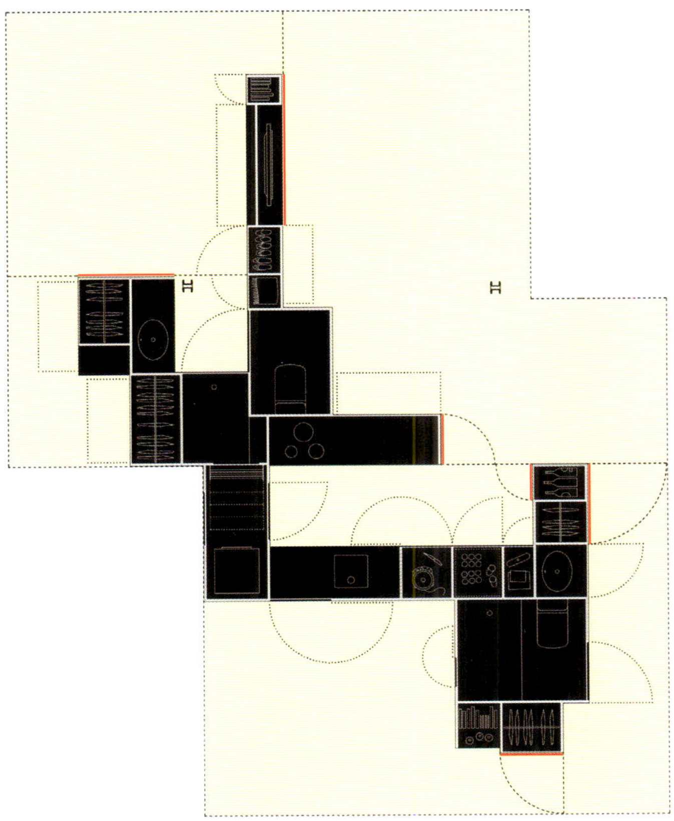

Floor plan

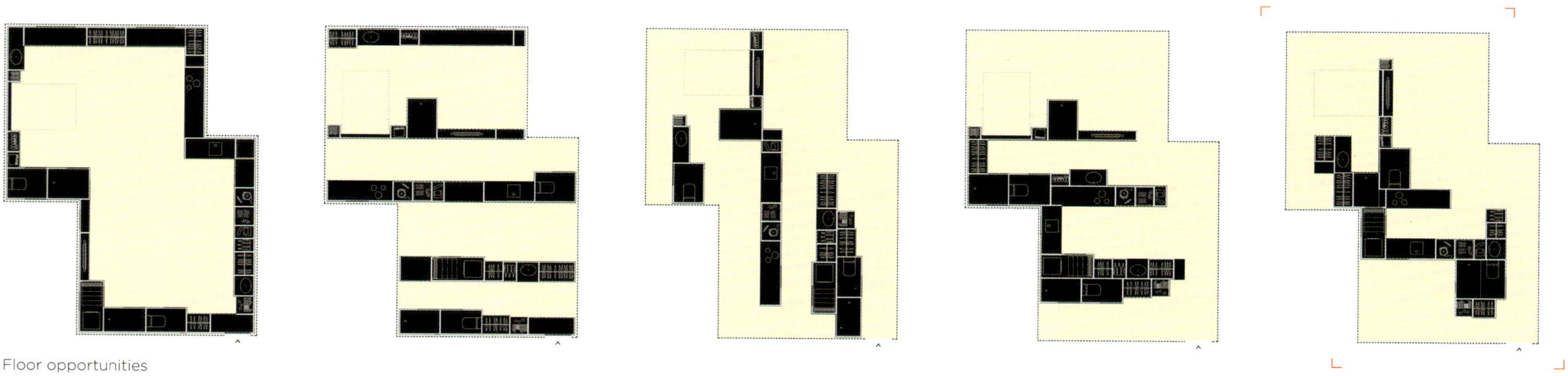

Floor opportunities

The concept of independent functional modules opens up a wide array of possible combinations that can be adapted to any space.

Das Konzept der unabhängigen Funktionsmodule, die bei der Planung dieser Wohnung zu Einsatz kommen, eröffnet ein breites Spektrum an Kombinationsmöglichkeiten, die an jeden beliebigen Raum angepasst werden können.

Le concept des modules fonctionnels indépendants utilisé dans le projet de cette maison offre un large éventail de possibilités de combinaisons qui peuvent être adaptées à n'importe quel espace.

El concepto de módulos funcionales independientes utilizado en el proyecto de esta vivienda abre un extenso abanico de posibilidades combinatorias, que pueden ser adaptadas a cualquier espacio.

Functionality is the concept behind this renovation, given its limitations on the amount of available space. A strip of space near the entryway groups the bathroom and kitchen together. This frees up a multipurpose space with ample storage, including a double-height closet with shelving, and drawers underneath a tatami mat next to the window, which can also be used as a sofa or a bed. A loft located over the technical strip, but also opens to the main room, is used as a sleeping area.

Das Konzept der Funktionalität lenkt die Renovierung dieser Wohnung und akzeptiert die Beschränkung des zur Verfügung stehenden Raumes. Ein Streifen neben dem Zugang verbindet Bad und Küche, wodurch einen Multifunktionsbereich frei wird, in dem Stauräume ins Rampenlicht gerückt werden und zwar in Form eines Wandschrank-Regals mit doppelten Höhe oder eines Behälters unter einem Tatami neben dem Fenster, der auch als Sofa oder Bett genutzt wird. Ein Zwischengeschoss, das über dem technischen Bereich liegt und zum Hauptraum hin offen ist, beherbergt das Schlafzimmer.

Le concept de fonctionnalité domine les travaux de rénovation de cette maison, assumant la limitation de l'espace disponible. Une bande située à proximité de l'accès agglutine la salle de bains et la cuisine libérant ainsi un espace multifonctionnel dans lequel les espaces de rangement jouent le rôle d'armoire-étagère à double hauteur ou de container sous un tatami à proximité de la fenêtre, servant aussi de canapé ou de lit. Une mezzanine située au-dessus de la bande technique et ouverte sur l'espace principal abrite la chambre.

El concepto de funcionalidad dirige la renovación de esta vivienda, asumiendo la restricción del espacio disponible. Una franja situada junto al acceso aglutina el baño y la cocina, liberando un espacio multifuncional en el que las zonas de almacenamiento adquieren protagonismo en forma de armario estantería a doble altura o de contenedor bajo un tatami junto a la ventana, utilizado también como sofá o cama. Un altillo situado sobre la franja técnica y abierto al espacio principal alberga el dormitorio.

60

APARTMENT WITH SLEEPING LOFT

A Little Design

LOCATION **Taipei, Taiwan** AREA **22 m² / 237 sq ft** PHOTOS **© Hey!Cheese**

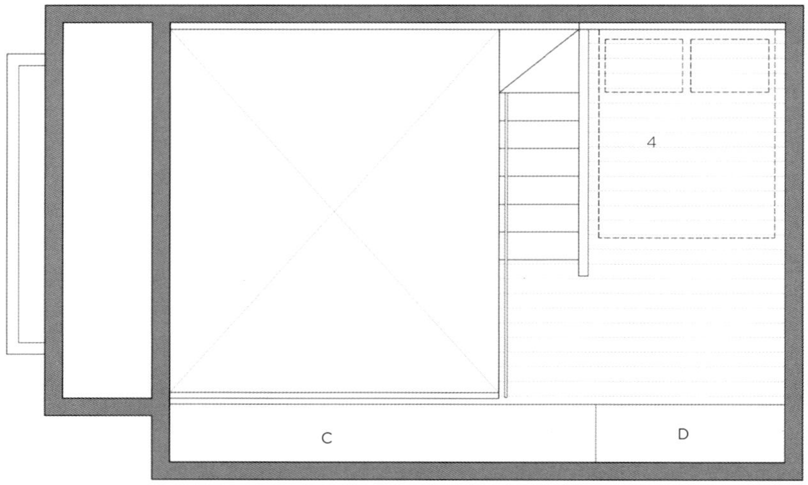

Mezzanine

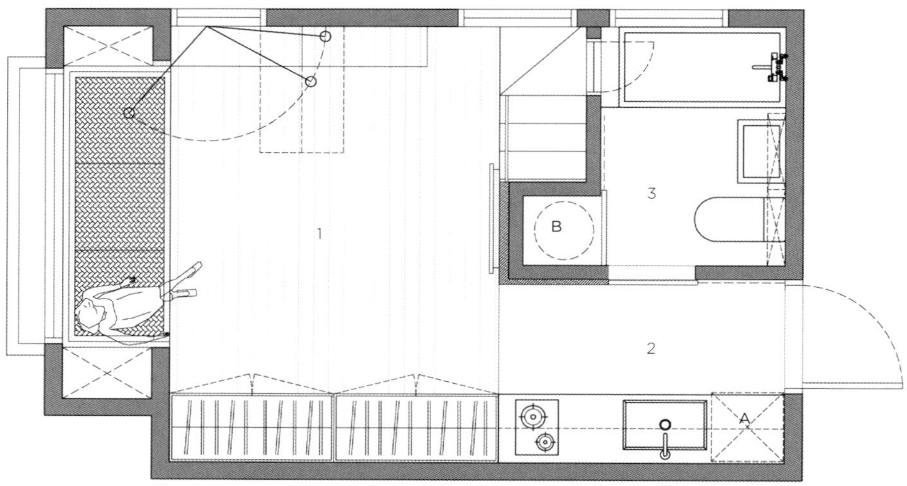

Floor plan

1. Living room
2. Kitchen
3. Bathroom
4. Bedroom

A. Washer
B. Heater
C. Shelf
D. Desk

The project takes advantage of the 3.3 available meters of height to implement a two-level plan. The abundant natural light, and the choice to use a white paint/oak wood color scheme, make the interior more spacious and bright.

Das Projekt nutzt die 3,3 Meter an lichter Höhe, um die Planung auf zwei Ebenen zu entfalten. Das reichlich vorhandene Tageslicht sowie die Weißtöne und die Farbtöne des eingesetzten Eichenholzes machen den Innenraum geräumiger und heller.

Le projet profite des 3,3 mètres de hauteur sous plafond pour réaliser le programme sur deux niveaux. L'abondante lumière naturelle et les tons blancs et en bois de chêne utilisés rendent l'espace intérieur plus spacieux et lumineux.

El proyecto aprovecha los 3,3 metros de altura libre para desarrollar el programa en dos niveles. La abundante luz natural y los tonos blancos y de madera de roble utilizados hacen el espacio interior más amplio y luminoso.

Despite its limited head space, the bedroom area has a small writing desk that matches the shelving in the main space, and that can also be accessed from this level.

Trotz seiner geringen lichten Höhe ist der Schlafzimmerbereich mit einem kleinen Schreibtisch ausgestattet, der an die Regalwand des Hauptraumes anschließt, der auch von dieser Ebene aus zugänglich ist.

Malgré sa hauteur sous plafond réduite, l'espace de la chambre comprend un petit bureau qui donne sur la bibliothèque de l'espace de vie, également accessible depuis ce niveau.

A pesar de su reducida altura libre, el ámbito del dormitorio está equipado con un pequeño escritorio que enlaza con el mueble estantería del espacio principal, que también es accesible desde este nivel.

The layout of this open-plan square space shuns the separation between public and private areas and creates one dynamic space that can be transformed as the users wish. The design used strategies that provide the required mobility, such as building the bathroom door and the folding bed into the furniture, or maximizing the versatility of the sideboard, which becomes a dining table and also acts as a linking element among the different configurations.

In dieser Wohnung mit quadratischem Grundriss und einem einzigen Bereich vermeidet die Raumaufteilung eine Trennung zwischen privatem und gemeinsam genutztem Bereich und schafft so einen dynamischen Raum, der je nach Ansprüchen der Bewohner umgewandelt wird. Seine Gestaltung verwendet Ressourcen, welche die erforderliche Mobilität ermöglichen, wie etwa die Einbindung der Badtür und des Klappbetts bei der Anordnung der Möbel oder die vielseitige Verwendbarkeit des Sideboard, das sich in einen Esstisch verwandelt und als Verbindungsglied zwischen den verschiedenen Konfigurationen fungiert.

Dans cet appartement carré à espace unique, la répartition évite la séparation entre l'espace privatif et l'espace de vie afin de créer un espace dynamique qui se transforme à la demande des utilisateurs. Pour sa conception, on a utilisé des ressources qui offrent la mobilité requise telle que l'intégration de la porte de la salle de bains et du lit escamotable dans la composition du mobilier ou la versatilité du buffet qui se transforme en table de salle à manger et qui joue le rôle d'un élément charnière dans les diverses configurations.

En esta vivienda de planta cuadrada y un único ambiente, la distribución rehúye la separación entre zona privada y zona pública y crea un espacio dinámico que se transforma según las demandas de los usuarios. Su diseño utiliza recursos que aportan la movilidad requerida, como la integración de la puerta del baño y de la cama abatible en la composición del mobiliario, o la versatilidad del aparador que se convierte en mesa de comedor y que actúa como elemento bisagra entre las diferentes configuraciones.

68

APARTMENT LP

BEP Arquitetos

LOCATION **Brasilia, Brazil** AREA **30 m² / 323 sq ft** PHOTOS **© Haruo Mikami**

GRAMMOFONO
PARIS
New York

PARIS

ABCDE
FGHIJK
LMNOP
QRTSU
VXYZ
Mr. right
Mrs. always right

This layout allows for three possible combinations of furniture, so the space can become either a bedroom, dining room, or living room. The kitchen zone is integrated into this main space.

Die Aufteilung spielt mit drei Kombinationen von Einrichtungselementen, um alternativ ein Schlaf-, ein Ess- und ein Wohnzimmer zu schaffen. Der Bereich der Küche wird in diesem Hauptraum integriert.

La répartition joue avec trois combinaisons d'éléments de mobilier afin de créer en alternance une chambre, une salle à mange et un séjour. L'espace cuisine s'intègre dans cet espace principal.

La distribución juega con tres combinaciones de los elementos del mobiliario para crear de forma alternativa un dormitorio, un comedor y una sala de estar. El ámbito de la cocina se integra en este espacio principal.

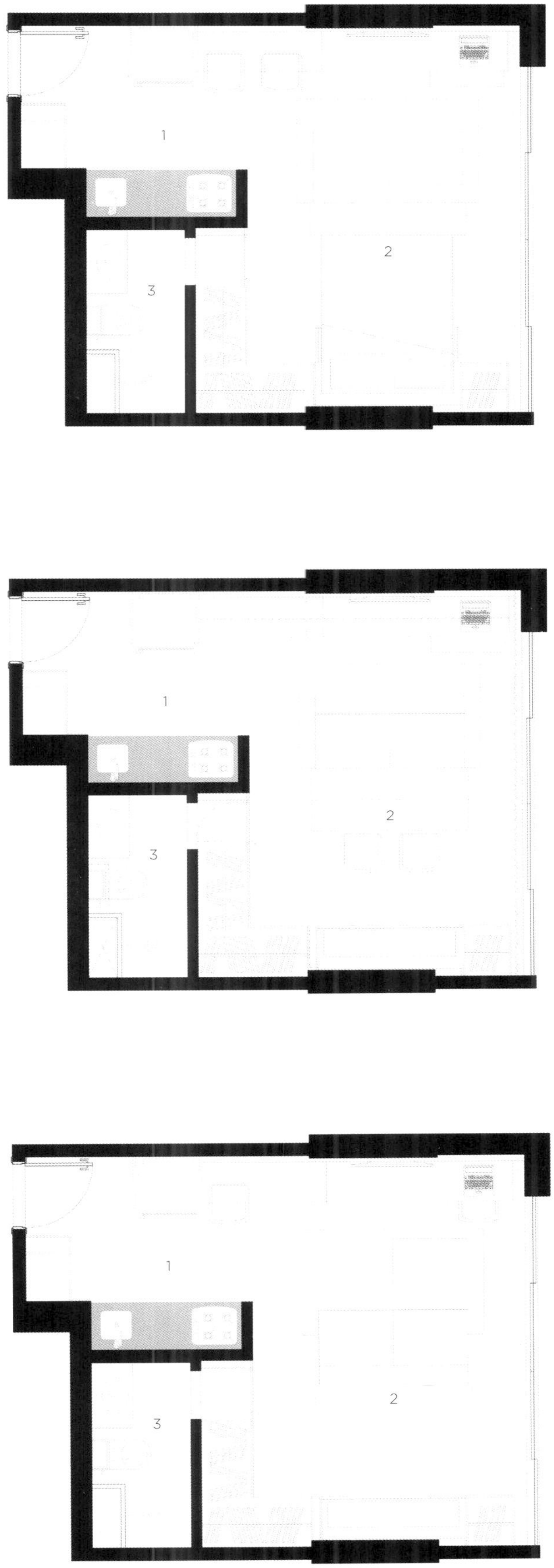

1. Kitchen
2. Living room
   Dining room
   Bedroom
3. Bathroom

Floor plan

In this project, a small office is transformed into a one-person home. The renovation started with a single space of considerable height. Into this was placed a compact piece of furniture, build of medium density fiberboard that contains the bathroom, kitchen, several storage areas, and a sleeping space atop a one-and-a-half-meter-high loft. This strategy brings together all the elements needed for a comfortable home, and frees up space for the generous living area.

Das Projekt setzt die Umwandlung eines kleinen Büros in eine Wohnung für eine Person um. Dabei wird in einem einzigen Raum mit beträchtlicher lichter Höhe ein kompaktes Möbelteil aus mitteldichten Holzfaserplatten eingebaut, das Bad, Köche, verschiedene Ablagebereiche und ein Schlafzimmer, das in einem Zwischengeschoss auf 1,50 Metern lichter Höhe liegt, beherbergt Diese Strategie verbindet alle notwendigen Elemente für eine bequeme Nutzung der Wohnung und setzt Fläche für einen großzügigen Wohnbereich frei.

Le projet envisage la transformation d'un petit bureau en appartement pour une seule personne. Les travaux reposent sur l'implantation dans un seul espace, d'une hauteur sous plafond considérable, d'une pièce meublée compacte, construite en MDF. Elle comprend une salle de bains, une cuisine, divers rangements et une chambre située sur une mezzanine de 1,50 mètre de hauteur. Cette stratégie permet de rassembler tous les éléments nécessaires pour une utilisation pratique de l'appartement tout en libérant de l'espace pour le grand séjour.

El proyecto desarrolla la transformación de una pequeña oficina en vivienda para una sola persona. La intervención se basa en la implantación dentro de un único espacio, de considerable altura libre, de una pieza-mueble compacta, construida con tablero DM, que alberga baño, cocina, diversas zonas de almacenaje y un dormitorio situado en un altillo de un metro y medio de altura interior. Esta estrategia aglutina todos los elementos necesarios para un cómodo uso de la vivienda y libera superficie para la amplia zona de estar.

72

OFFICE CONVERTED INTO DWELLING

Beriot, Bernardini Arquitectos

LOCATION **Madrid, Spain** AREA **28 m² / 301 sq ft** PHOTOS **© Yen Chen**

When the multifunctional piece is viewed from the living area, all the "windows" in the different areas are also visible. This gives depth to the dwelling, and contributes to the perception that it is one seamless space.

Der Anblick des Multifunktionsmöbels vom Wohnbereich aus zeigt gleichzeitig alle „Fenster" der verschiedenen Bereiche, was der Wohnung Tiefe verleiht und dazu beiträgt, ihren gesamten Raum als einen Bereich wahrzunehmen.

La vision du meuble multifonctionnel depuis le séjour présente simultanément toutes les «ouvertures» des divers espaces conférant ainsi de la profondeur à l'appartement et contribuant à la perception de tout son espace comme unique.

La visión del mueble multifuncional desde la sala de estar muestra simultáneamente todas las "ventanas" de los diferentes ámbitos, otorgando profundidad a la vivienda y contribuyendo a percibir como único todo su espacio.

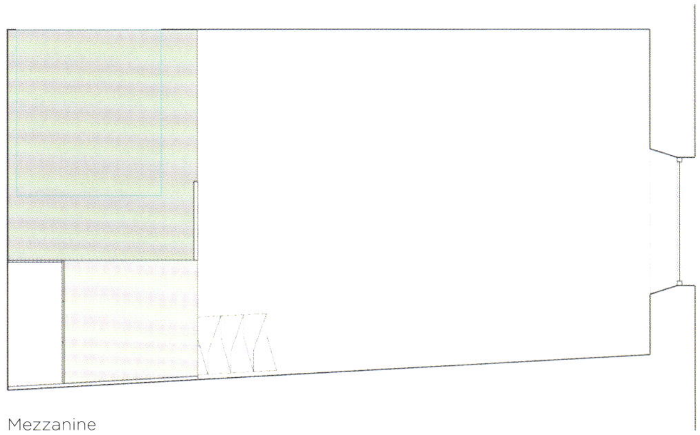

Mezzanine

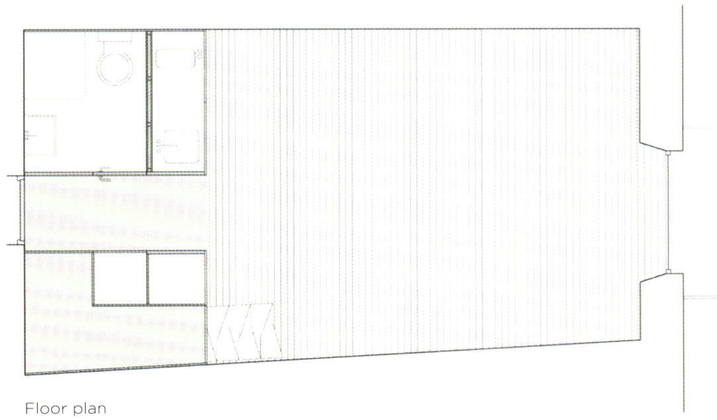

Floor plan

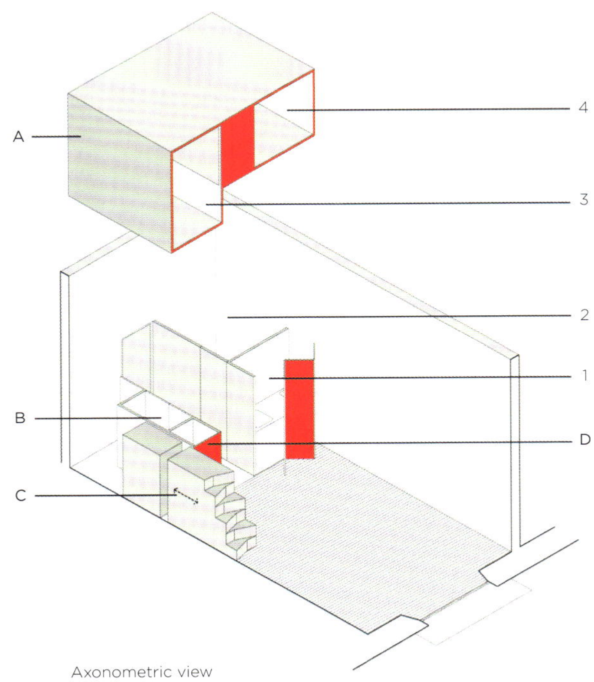

Axonometric view

1. Kitchen
2. Bathroom
3. Dressing room
4. Bedroom 1

A. Bedroom wardrobe
B. Closet
C. Staircase storage
D. Refrigerator

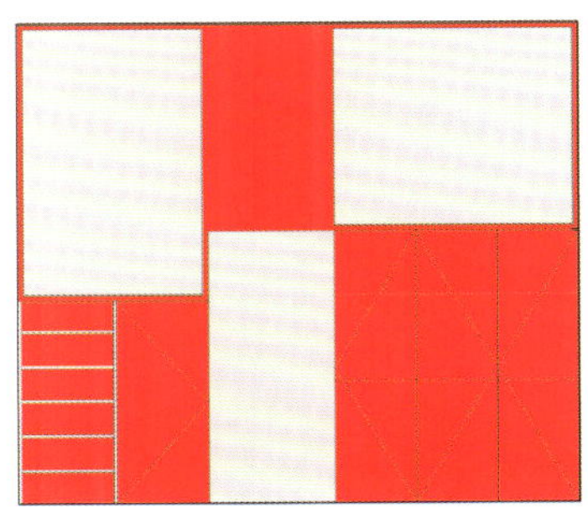

Elevation

The living area is the main element of the interior design of this one-family home on the outskirts of the capital. Here a continuous perimeter of uniform vertical white panels, which conceal the access doors and cover the storage areas and kitchen appliances, provides a practicable way to achieve a sizeable, ample and minimalist central space. Only some niches for shelving, apparently placed at random, indicate the architectural nature of the intervention.

Das Wohnzimmer wird zum Hauptelement der Inneneinrichtung dieses Einfamilienhauses, das in einem Vorort der Hauptstadt liegt. Darin sorgt ein durchgehender Bereich aus weißen, einheitlichen und begehbaren Verkleidungen, welche die Zugänge verbergen und Stauraum sowie die Kücheneinrichtung beherbergen, für einen geräumigen und zentralen Multifunktionsbereich mit minimalistischem Ambiente. Nur einige Nischen für Regale, die anscheinend zufällig platziert wurden, weisen auf den Eingriff eines Architekten hin.

Le séjour devient l'élément principal de la conception intérieure de cette maison individuelle située aux abords de la capitale. Elle comprend un périmètre continu de panneaux verticaux, uniformes et réalistes, cachant les portes d'accès et renfermant des rangements et les éléments de cuisine, ce qui offre un vaste espace central multifonctionnel et de design minimaliste. Seules quelques niches pour des étagères, placées apparemment au hasard, dénotent l'intervention architectonique.

La sala de estar se convierte en el elemento principal del diseño interior de esta vivienda unifamiliar situada en las afueras de la capital. En ella, un perímetro continuo de paneles verticales blancos, uniformes y practicables, que oculta puertas de acceso y que alberga zonas de almacenaje y el equipo de cocina, da lugar a un espacio central multifuncional, amplio y de aire minimalista. Solo unos nichos destinados a estantería, colocados aparentemente al azar, constatan la intervención arquitectónica.

76

FOLDING WALL APARTMENT

Arhitektura d.o.o.

LOCATION **Ljubljana, Slovenia** AREA **180 m² / 1,937 sq ft** PHOTOS **© Jure Goršič**

The succession of modules that makes up two of the living room walls conceals a number of closets, the entry door from the vestibule, and the door to a clothes closet.

Die Reihenfolge der Module, welche zwei Seiten der vertikalen Umbauung des Wohnzimmers bilden, verbirgt eine Reihe von Wandschränken, die Zugangstür vom Hausflur sowie die Zugangstür zu einem Kleiderschrank.

La succession de modules formant deux des côtés du cloisonnage vertical du séjour cache une multitude d'armoires, la porte d'entrée depuis le vestibule et la porte donnant sur un dressing.

La sucesión de módulos que conforman dos de los lados del cerramiento vertical de la sala de estar oculta una batería de armarios, la puerta de acceso desde el vestíbulo y la puerta de acceso a un armario ropero.

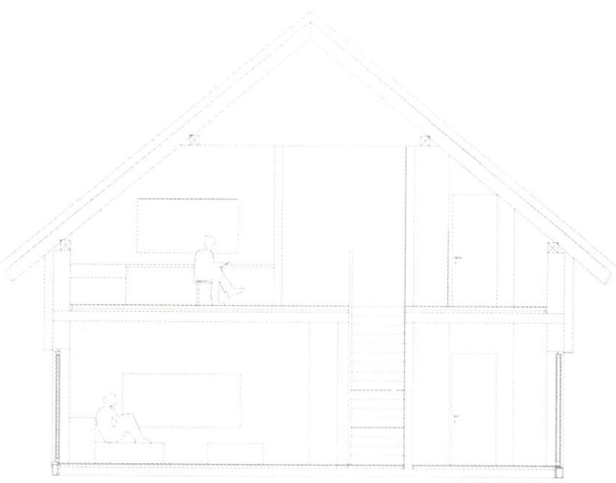

Sections

The interior design contrasts the predominant color, white, with elements made of oak, which is abundant in the surrounding woods. This creates the tension between urban and traditional looks that the clients were seeking for their home.

Die Gestaltung des Innenbereichs kombiniert die überwiegende weiße Farbe mit dem Eichenholz, das in den Wäldern der Umgebung reichlich vorhanden ist, und schafft so eine Spannung zwischen städtischem und traditionellem Ambiente, was die Kunden für ihr Haus suchten.

La conception de l'intérieur combine le blanc prédominant avec le chêne, arbre abondant dans les forêts avoisinantes, ce qui crée une tension entre le style urbain et celui traditionnel que les clients recherchent pour leur résidence.

El diseño del interior combina el color blanco predominante con la madera de roble, abundante en los bosques del entorno, creando la tensión entre lo urbano y lo tradicional que los clientes buscaban para su vivienda.

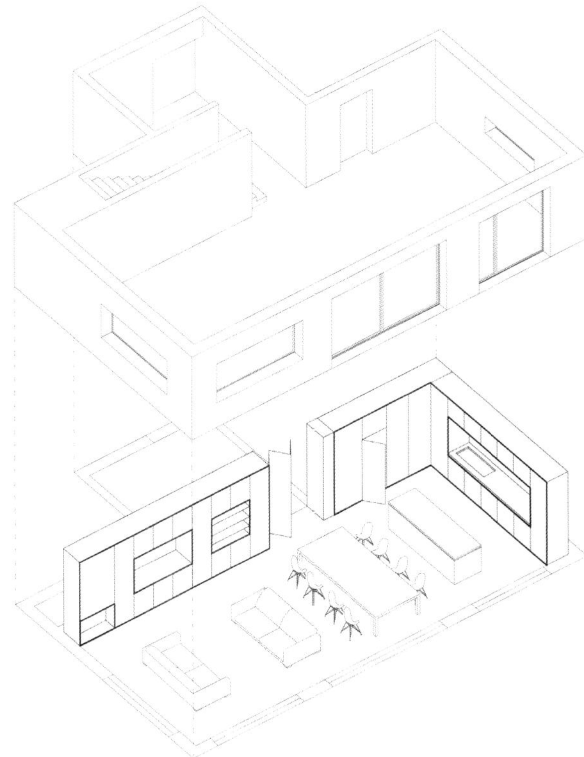

Axonometric view

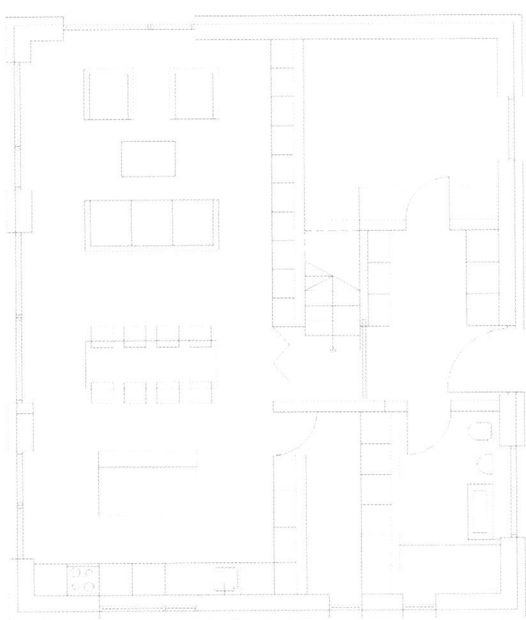

Ground floor plan

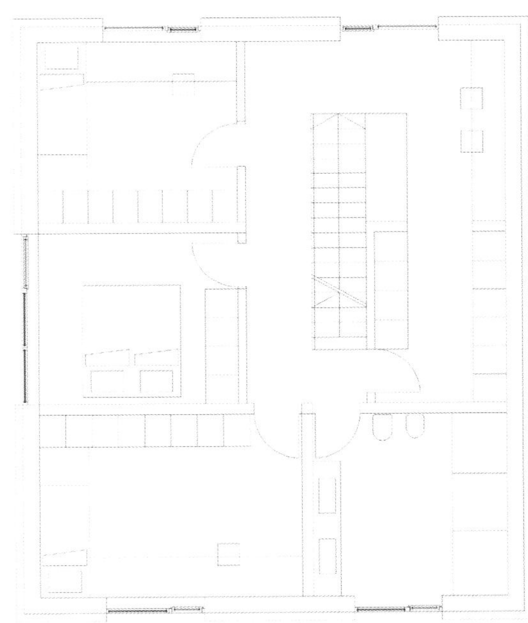

Second floor plan

This house is set on a narrow strip of land between two buildings. Because its dimensions do not meet official guidelines, it is officially known as an artistic installation. It's inner width varies between 72 and 122 centimeters. The building is constructed as a steel cage separate from its two neighboring buildings. Its side walls are clad in sandwich paneling, and the sheets of translucent polycarbonate on the facades guarantee that there will be abundant indirect light within.

Diese Wohnung liegt auf einem schmalen Trennstreifen zwischen zwei Gebäuden. Aufgrund ihrer außerhalb der Norm liegenden Maße wird sie offiziell als künstlerische Installation betrachtet: die freie Breite im Innenraum schwankt zwischen 122 und 72 Zentimetern. Von der Bausubstanz her ist die Wohnung ein von den benachbarten Gebäuden abgetrennter Stahlkäfig, der an den seitlichen Umfassungen mit Sandwichpaneelen und an den Fassaden mit lichtdurchlässigen Polycarbonat-Platten verkleidet ist, welche dafür sorgen, dass im Innenraum reichlich indirektes Licht vorhanden ist.

Cette maison se situe dans une étroite ruelle entre deux bâtiments. Ses dimensions hors-normes font qu'elle est officiellement considérée comme une installation artistique : sa largeur intérieure varie entre 122 et 72 centimètres. De manière constructive, la maison est une cage en acier séparée des bâtiments contigus, dont les cloisons latérales sont revêtues de panneaux sandwich et les façades de planches en polycarbonate transparent, ce qui confère une importante luminosité indirecte à l'intérieur.

Esta casa se sitúa en una angosta franja de separación entre dos edificios. Sus dimensiones fuera de normativa hacen que oficialmente se considere una instalación artística: su anchura libre interior oscila entre 122 y 72 centímetros. Constructivamente, la casa constituye una jaula de acero separada de los edificios vecinos, revestida de paneles sándwich en sus cerramientos laterales y de planchas de policarbonato translúcido en sus fachadas, que garantizan la presencia de abundante luz indirecta en el interior.

84

KERET HOUSE

Jakub Szczęsny

LOCATION **Warsaw, Poland** AREA **14 m² / 151 sq ft** PHOTOS **© Bartek Warzecha**

A steep staircase and a trap door lead into the second floor of the house. Here can be found a "living area", a two-person dining area, a kitchen, and a bathroom whose design is inspired by those on airplanes.

Eine steile Treppe und eine Luke ermöglichen den Zugang zur ersten Ebene der Wohnung, wo sich der „Wohn"-Bereich, ein Esszimmer für zwei Personen, die Küche und eine Badzimmerausstattung befinden, die von der Toilette eines Flugzeuges inspiriert ist.

L'accès au premier étage de la maison s'effectue par un escalier raide et une trappe, où se trouve un « séjour », une salle à manger pour deux personnes, la cuisine et les éléments de la salle de bains inspirée de l'intérieur d'un avion.

Una empinada escalera y una trampilla permiten acceder al primer nivel de la casa, donde se ubican la zona de "estar", un comedor para dos personas, la cocina y un equipo de baño inspirado en el de un avión.

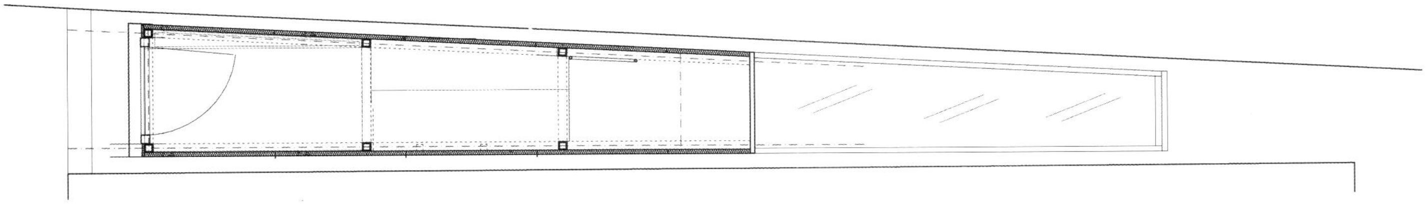

Level 1

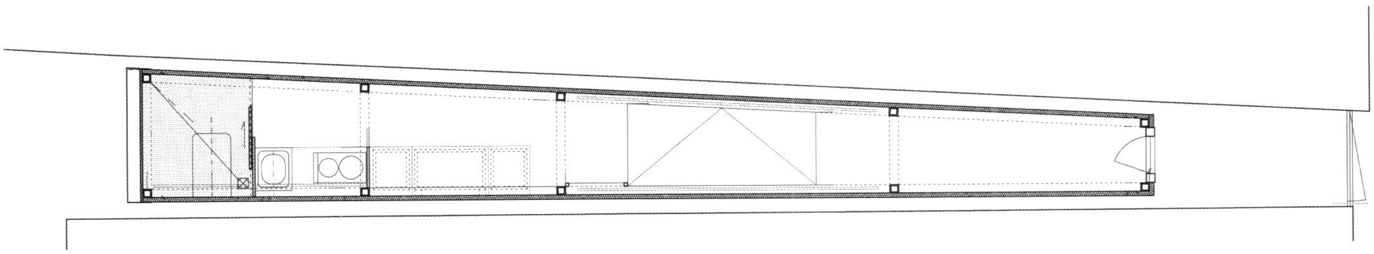

Level 0

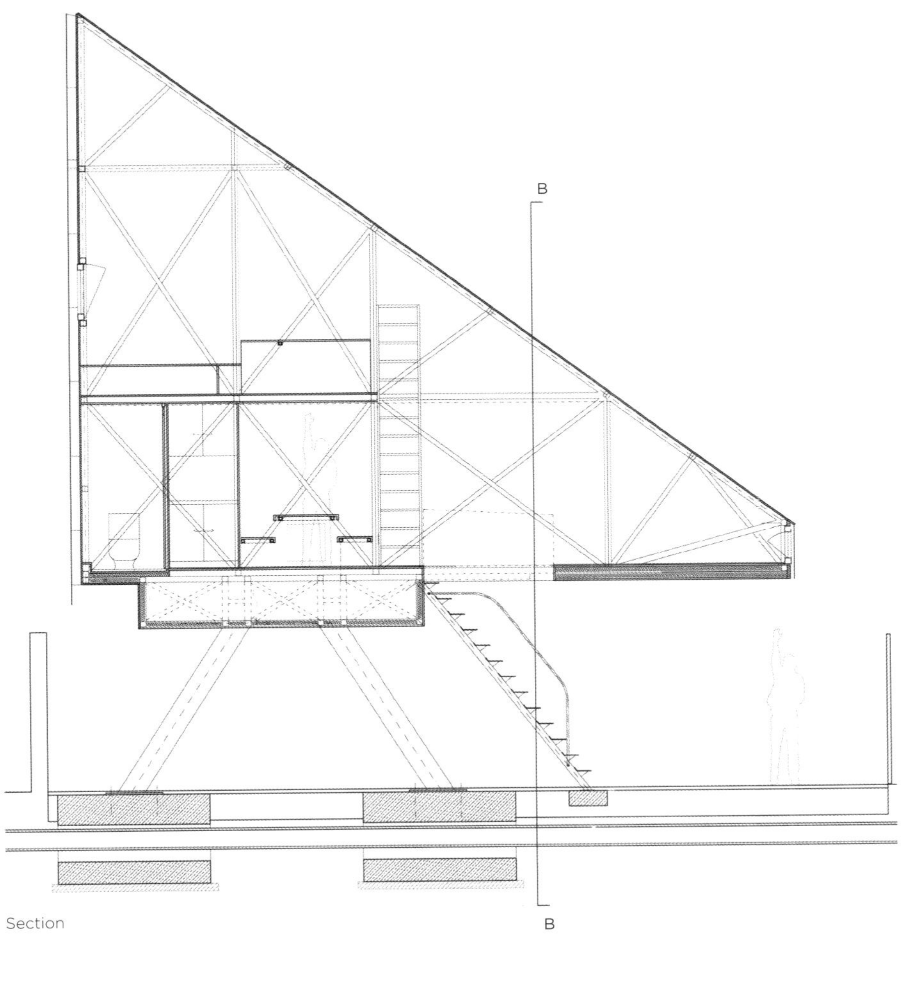

Section

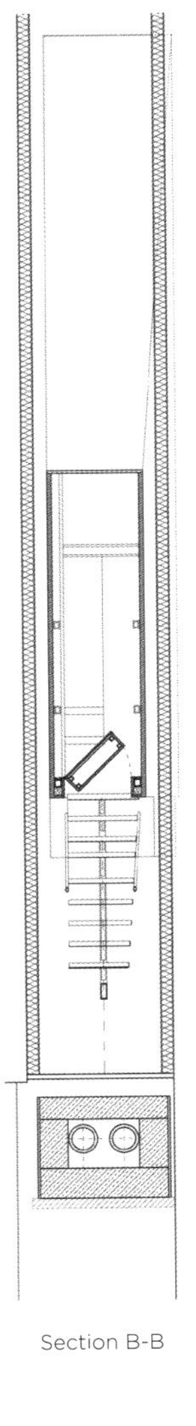

Section B-B

A vertical ladder leads to the upper floor, which has a work table, and a sleeping compartment with a ninety-centimeter mattress. White is used throughout the interior to mitigate the sense of tightness.

Eine vertikale Treppe führt in den oberen Stock, wo sich eine Schlafkoje mit einer 90 cm breiten Matratze und ein Schreibtisch befinden. Der Einsatz von Weiß trägt dazu bei, das Gefühl von Enge im Innenraum abzuschwächen.

Un escalier vertical mène à l'étage supérieur où se trouve un espace pour dormir avec un matelas de 90 centimètres et une table de travail. Le recours à la couleur blanche contribue à mitiger la sensation d'étroitesse de l'intérieur.

Una escalera vertical conduce al piso superior, que contiene un compartimento para dormir con un colchón de noventa centímetros y una mesa de trabajo. El uso de color blanco contribuye a mitigar la sensación de estrechez del interior.

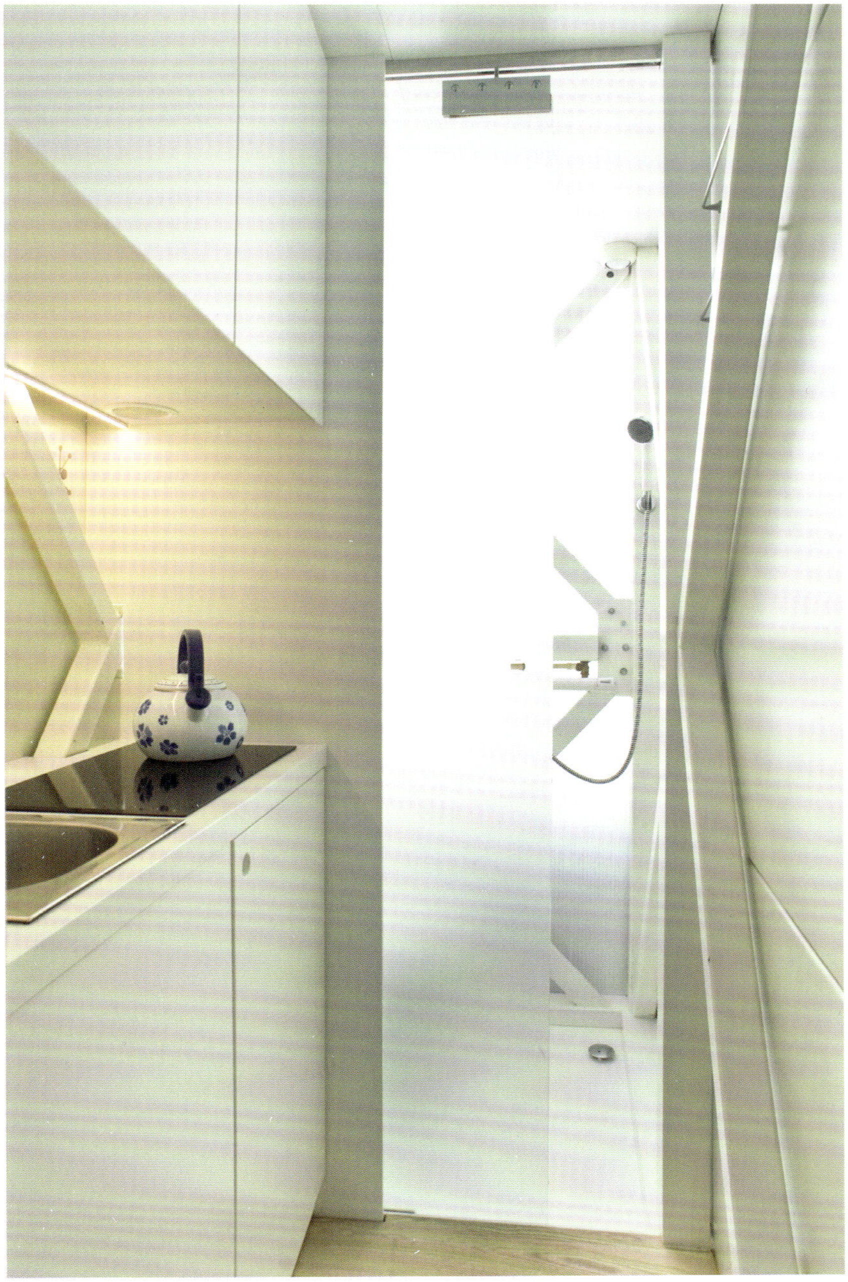

Constructing a mezzanine in the section with greater headroom was a key objective of the transformation of this three-person apartment. The layout structures two differentiated linear environments: the first contains the living room, kitchen, and dining room; the second has one bedroom on the upper level and two bedrooms below. These are separated by the support structure for the loft and open onto a common study/storage area, with which they comprise one whole space.

Der Bau eines Zwischengeschosses, welcher den Bereich ausnutzt, der über eine größere Raumhöhe verfügt, bestimmte die Umwandlung dieser Wohnung für drei Personen. Die Aufteilung gliedert linear zwei verschiedene Bereiche: der erste umfasst, Wohnzimmer, Küche und Esszimmer; der zweite umfasst ein Schlafzimmer auf der oberen Etage und zwei Schlafzimmer auf der unteren Etage, getrennt durch die Trägerstruktur des Dachbodens und hin zum gemeinsam genutzten Studierbereich und Stauraum offen, mit dem sie einen einzigen Raum bilden.

La construction d'une mezzanine qui bénéficie d'une zone dotée d'une plus grande hauteur sous-plafond, a conditionné la transformation de ce logement pour trois personnes. La répartition structure de manière linéaire deux espaces : le premier comprend un séjour, une cuisine et une salle à manger ; le deuxième, une chambre à l'étage supérieur et deux chambres au niveau inférieur, séparées par la structure de support de la mezzanine et ouvertes sur un espace d'étude et de rangement commun, ce qui en fait un espace unique.

La construcción de una planta altillo, que aprovecha una zona dotada de mayor altura libre, condicionó la transformación de esta vivienda para tres personas. La distribución estructura de forma lineal dos ámbitos diferenciados: el primero contiene estar, cocina y comedor; el segundo contiene un dormitorio en el nivel superior y dos dormitorios en el inferior, separados por la estructura de soporte del altillo y abiertos hacia una zona de estudio y almacenaje común, con la que configuran un único espacio.

90

FUJIGAOKA T

Chikara Ohno / Sinato

LOCATION Kanagawa, Japan AREA 68 m² / 732 sq ft PHOTOS © Toshiyuki Yano

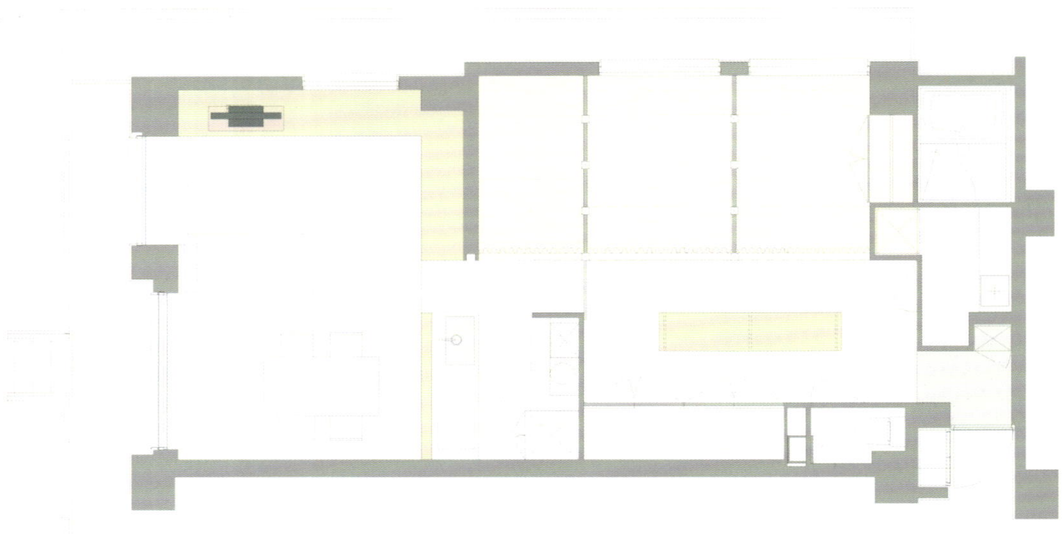

Floor plan

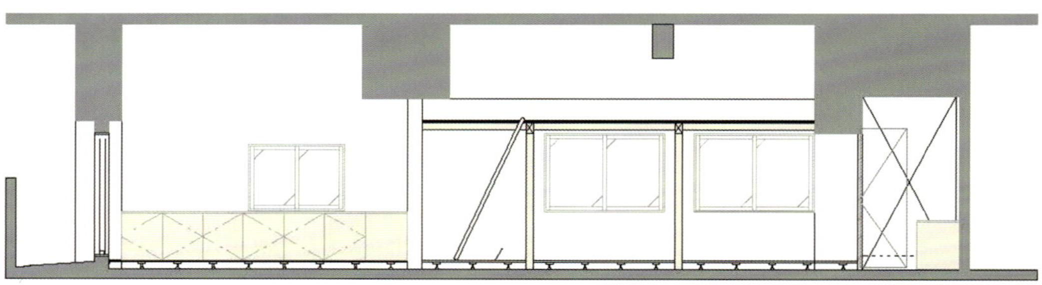

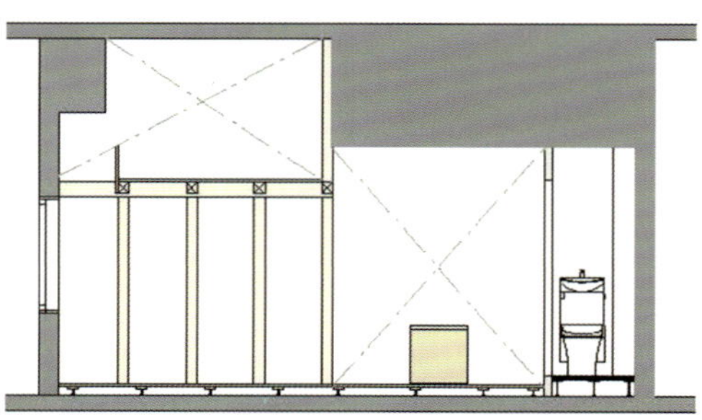

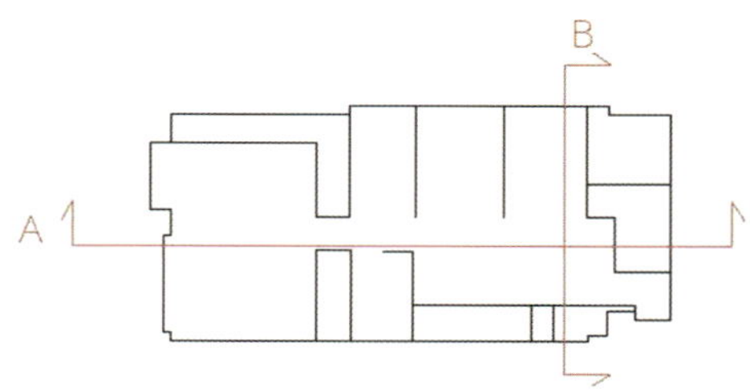

Sections

The minimalist design of all the architectural and decorative elements, together with the open plan of the entire dwelling, increase the feeling of fluidity and continuity of space.

Das minimalistische Design sämtlicher architektonischer und ornamentaler Elemente, gemeinsam mit der offenen Konzeption aller Bereiche der Wohnung,steigert das Gefühl von Fließen und Kontinuität des Raumes.

Le design minimaliste de tous les éléments architectoniques et décoratifs, associé à la conception ouverte de tous les espaces de vie, augmente la sensation de fluidité et de continuité de l'espace.

El diseño minimalista de todos los elementos arquitectónicos y ornamentales, unido a la concepción abierta de todos los ámbitos de la vivienda, incrementa la sensación de fluidez y continuidad del espacio.

A review of the structure's building plans indicated that there were two areas with significant unobstructed height. This allowed the sleeping quarters to be split into two levels, 2 m and 1.5 m high.

Die Durchsicht der Baupläne des Gebäudes ergab das Vorhandensein von Bereichen mit einer lichten Höhe, durch die sich der Schlafzimmerbereich auf zwei Ebenen von 2 bzw. 1,5 Metern Höhe ausbreiten lässt.

La révision des plans structurels de l'édifice a fait état de la présence de zones avec une hauteur sous-plafond permettant de diviser l'espace chambre en deux niveaux, de 2 et 1,5 mètres de hauteur, respectivement.

La revisión de los planos estructurales del edificio constató la existencia de zonas dotadas de una altura libre que permitía desdoblar la zona de dormitorios en dos niveles, de 2 y 1,5 metros de altura respectivamente.

The remodeling of this hundred-year-old village house was managed and executed in several phases, with the final result being a home with two stories and a loft. The ground floor contains a kitchen/dining area that leads into an inner courtyard; there is also the owner's small workshop, which can be accessed from the street. The upper level is one light-filled space with a high vaulted ceiling; there is a living room and study on the lower level, and a bedroom and bath above it.

Der Umbau dieses hundertjährigen Dorfhauses wurde als mehrstufig konzipiert und ausgeführt, wobei ein Haus mit zwei Etagen und einem Zwischengeschoss entstand. Im Erdgeschoss koexistieren der Bereich Küche-Esszimmer, der mit einem Innenhof verbunden ist, und der kleine Arbeitsraum des Eigentümers, der von der Straße aus zugänglich ist. Der obere Bereich des Hauses bildet einen einzigen durchscheinenden Raum mit einer großen lichten Höhe, der auf der unteren Ebene Studier- und Aufenthaltsbereiche und auf der oberen Ebene Schlafzimmer und Bad kombiniert.

Les travaux de cette maison de campagne centenaire ont été gérés et exécutés en plusieurs étapes aboutissant à une demeure sur deux niveaux avec mezzanine. Au rez-de-chaussée cohabitent un espace cuisine-salle à manger donnant sur une cour intérieure et le petit atelier de travail du propriétaire, accessible depuis la rue. L'étage supérieur de la maison comprend un espace unique ouvert avec une hauteur sous plafond qui réunit le séjour et le bureau du niveau inférieur et la chambre et la salle de bains de l'étage supérieur.

La reforma de esta centenaria casa de pueblo fue gestada y ejecutada en varias fases, que dieron como resultado una vivienda de dos plantas y un altillo. En la planta baja conviven una zona de cocina comedor vinculada a un patio interior y el pequeño taller de trabajo del propietario, al que se accede desde la calle. La zona superior de la casa constituye un único espacio diáfano y de gran altura libre, que aúna zonas de estar y estudio en el nivel inferior y de dormitorio y baño en el superior.

96

STUDIO HOUSE WITH MEZZANINE

Fernando Abellanas

LOCATION Paiporta, València AREA 90 m² / 969 sq ft PHOTOS © Javier Ferrer Vidal

The wooden stairway leading to the upper floor starts in the charming kitchen/dining area, which is an open, functional space that is the true heart of this home.

Die Treppe mit Holzstufen, die in die erste Etage hinaufführt, beginnt in einem einladenden Raum, welcher den offenen und funktionalen Küche-Esszimmer-Bereich beherbergt, der so zum wahren Herz des Hauses wird.

Les escaliers en bois menant au premier étage partent du vestibule où se trouve la cuisine-salle à manger, espace ouvert et fonctionnel qui se transforme en véritable cocon.

La escalera de peldaños de madera que conduce a la primera planta arranca del acogedor ámbito que alberga la cocina comedor, espacio abierto y funcional que se convierte en el auténtico corazón de la vivienda.

The roof was raised as part of the renovation, allowing space for the loft, which is one undivided space.

Während des Umbauprozesses des Hauses wurde die Dachhöhe angehoben, was den Bau eines Zwischengeschosses möglich machte, das als ein einziger leerer Bereich ohne Abtrennungen im Inneren konzipiert wurde.

Au cours des travaux de rénovation de la maison, le toit a été surélevé, ce qui a permis de construire une mezzanine, conçue comme un espace unique sans aucune division intérieure.

Durante el proceso de reforma de la casa se dio más altura al nivel de la cubierta, lo cual permitió la construcción de la planta altillo, concebida como un único ámbito carente de divisiones interiores.

The composition of this apartment was determined by an exhaustive analysis of the functional requirements, and the unwavering intention of making the best possible use of the space. What stands out here is the original and welcoming position of the dining area at one end of the kitchen. This frees up space for the living room. In the bedroom, an elevated platform holding the bed structures the room and disguises its narrow width. The bathroom retains its original size, but has been updated with an elegant design.

Eine umfassende Analyse der Anforderungen an die Funktion sowie die feste Absicht, den Raum auszunutzen, bestimmten die Struktur dieser Wohnung. Die originelle und gemütliche Lage des Esszimmers tritt hervor, das an einem Ende der Küche liegt, wodurch Fläche für das Wohnzimmer frei wird. Im Schlafzimmer gliedert eine erhöhte Plattform, auf der das Bett platziert ist, das Zimmer und verbirgt dadurch dessen geringe Breite. Das Bad behält seine ursprünglichen Abmessungen, wird jedoch durch elegantes Design auf den neuesten Stand gebracht.

L'analyse exhaustive des exigences fonctionnelles et une ferme intention d'utiliser l'espace ont déterminé l'aménagement de cet appartement. Il convient de remarquer la situation originale et accueillante de la salle à manger, située dans un coin de la cuisine, ce qui libère de l'espace pour le séjour. Dans la chambre, une plateforme surélevée sur laquelle se trouve le lit qui structure la pièce et masque l'étroite largeur. La salle de bains conserve ses dimensions initiales, mise au goût du jour avec un style élégant.

El análisis exhaustivo de los requisitos funcionales y una firme intención de aprovechar el espacio determinaron la composición de este apartamento. Destaca la original y acogedora posición del comedor, situado en un extremo del recinto de la cocina, que libera superficie para la sala de estar. En el dormitorio, una plataforma elevada sobre la que se sitúa la cama estructura la estancia y enmascara su escasa anchura. El baño mantiene sus dimensiones originales, pero se actualiza con un elegante diseño.

102

APARTMENT FILIPPO

STUDIO ALEXANDER FEHRE

LOCATION **London, Great Britain** AREA **45 m² / 484 sq ft** PHOTOS **© Studio Alexander Fehre**

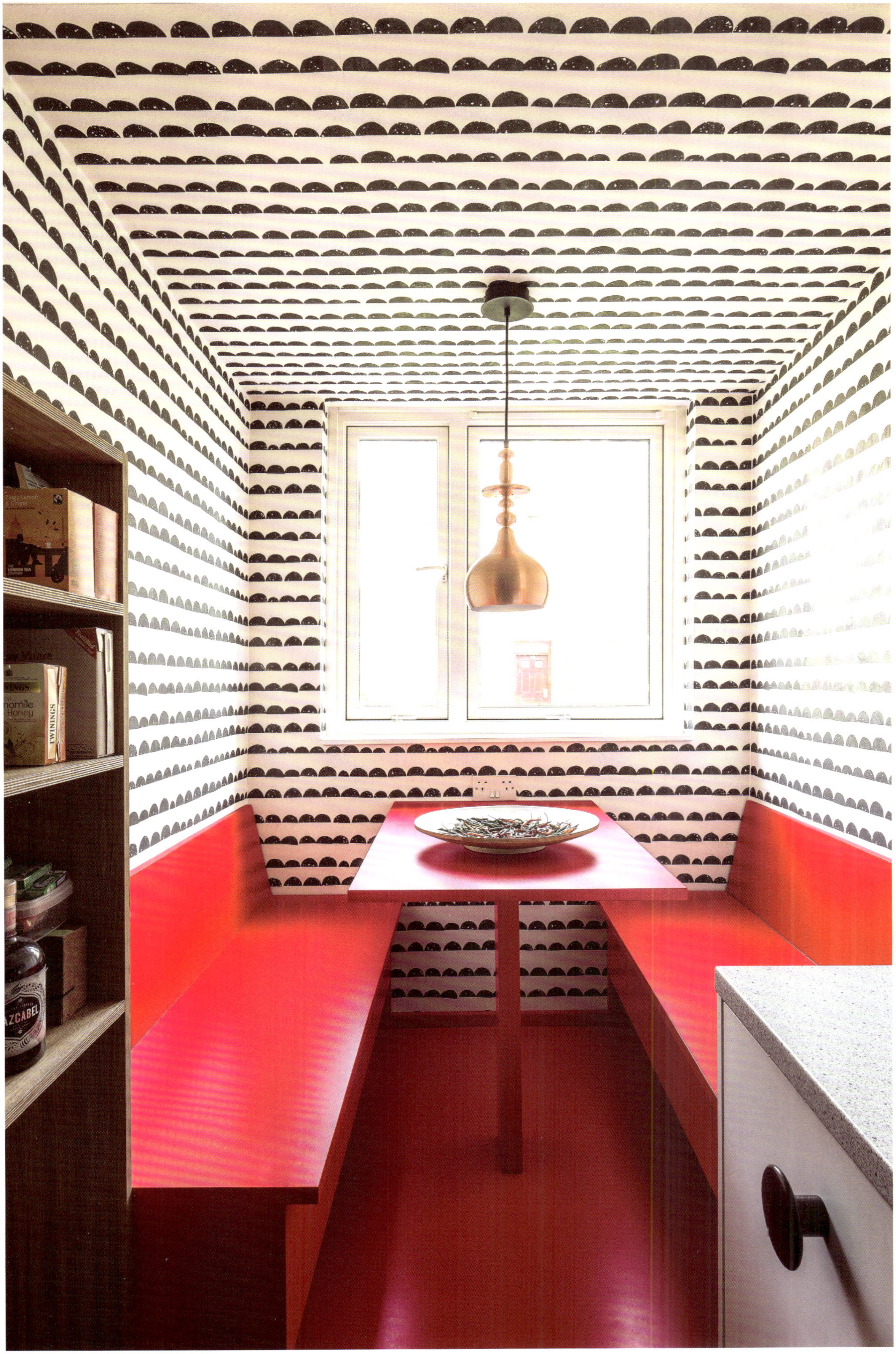

The striking decor of the dining area defines its uniqueness; floor, table, and seats are painted in an ardent Valentino red, and the walls and ceiling are decked out in wallpaper decorated with stripes formed by lines of small semicircles.

Die auffällige Dekoration des Esszimmerbereichs definiert dessen Eigenheit. Boden, Tisch und Stühle sindbestechen durch ein potentes Valentino-Rot, und Wände und Decke sind mit Streifentapeten mit Halbkreisen bedeckt.

La décoration frappante de la salle à manger détermine sa singularité. Le sol, la table et les chaises sont peints dans un rouge vif Valentino contrastant avec les murs et le plafond revêtus d'un papier peint à frange avec des demis-cercles.

La llamativa decoración de la zona de comedor define su singularidad; suelo, mesa y asientos se tiñen de un potente rojo Valentino y paredes y techo se visten con un papel pintado de franjas con semicírculos.

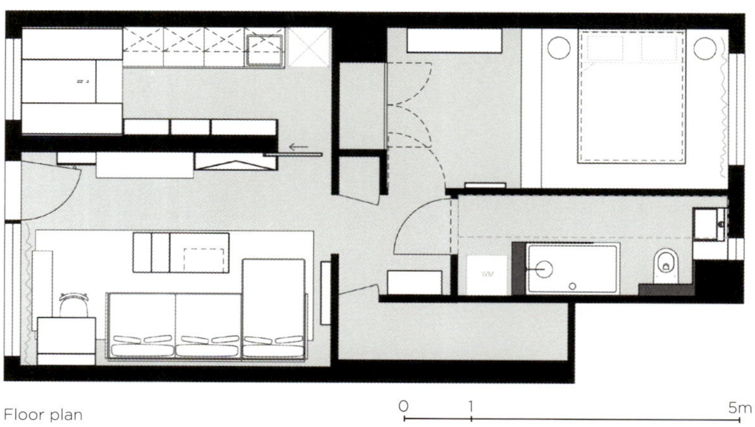

Floor plan

The living and kitchen areas are perceived as one spatial unit; first, because of the continuity of the black flooring, and secondly, because of the kitchen shelving unit that extends into the adjacent room.

Die Bereiche Wohnzimmer und Küche sind dank des durchgehenden Bodenbelags aus schwarzem Holz und des Küchenregals, das sich zum angrenzenden Zimmer hin erstreckt, als räumliche Einheit konzipiert.

Les espaces du séjour et de la cuisine sont organisés comme un seul espace grâce à un revêtement unique en bois noir et au buffet de la cuisine qui va jusqu'au séjour contigu.

Las zonas del estar y de la cocina se conciben como una unidad espacial gracias al pavimento continuo de madera de color negro y al mueble estantería de la cocina, que se extiende hacia la estancia contigua.

The bathroom design takes on the long, narrow shape of the space using a combination of painted wallpaper, mirrors, projectors, a two-story false ceiling, and a generously deep shower.

Die Gestaltung des Badezimmers greift die lange und enge Form des Raumes mittels eines Spiels auf, das Tapete, Spiegel, Scheinwerfern, eine Zwischendecke auf zwei Ebenen und die großzügige Tiefe der Dusche kombiniert.

La conception de la salle de bains offre une forme longue et étroite de l'espace grâce à un jeu qui mélange le papier peint, les miroirs, les leds, le faux plafond à deux hauteurs et la généreuse profondeur de la douche.

El diseño del baño asume la forma larga y estrecha del espacio mediante un juego que combina papel pintado, espejos, proyectores, un falso techo de dos alturas y la generosa profundidad de la ducha.

This house, which was initially planned as a studio, is surrounded by woods, and sits on a plot of land with a steep south-facing slope. With a rectangular floor plan and a sloping roof, it was constructed entirely of wood, based on bioclimatic and sustainable criteria. Its interior is perceived as one sole space, visually subdivided into two separate areas by a metal fireplace. It is designed so that it in the future it can be reconverted into a dwelling, with no need of alterations to its structure.

Diese Wohnstätte, die anfänglich zum Studieren gedacht war, befindet sich in der Nähe eines Waldes auf einem Gelände mit einer starken nach Süden ausgerichteten Neigung. Mit einem rechteckigen Grundriss und Dachschräge, wurde sein Aufbau auf der Grundlage bioklimatischer und nachhaltiger Kriterien ganz aus Holz gefertigt. Sein Innenraum erscheint als ein einziger Bereich, durch einen Metallkamin optisch in zwei getrennte Bereiche unterteilt und konzipiert, um künftig wieder in einen Wohnraum umgewandelt zu werden, ohne in das Tragwerk eingreifen zu müssen.

Cette maison, initialement destinée à un studio, est située en pleine forêt, sur un terrain à forte pente, orientée côté sud. De forme rectangulaire avec une toiture inclinée, cette maison a été entièrement construite en bois et selon les critères bioclimatiques et écologiques. À l'intérieur, elle se présente comme un espace unique, visuellement divisé en deux zones séparées par un poêle en métal et conçu pour devenir une résidence qui à l'avenir ne nécessitera pas de toucher la structure.

Esta casa, destinada inicialmente a estudio, se sitúa dentro del entorno de un bosque, en un terreno con fuerte pendiente orientado a sur. De planta rectangular y cubierta inclinada, su construcción se realizó íntegramente en madera y se basó en criterios bioclimáticos y sostenibles. Su interior se presenta como un único espacio, subdividido visualmente en dos zonas separadas por una chimenea metálica, y concebido para ser reconvertido en vivienda en un futuro sin tener que intervenir en la estructura.

110

WOOD STUDIO HOUSE

Dom Arquitectura

LOCATION **Sant Cugat, Spain** AREA **76 m² / 818 sq ft** PHOTOS **© Jordi Anguera**

VM

Summer, south orientation

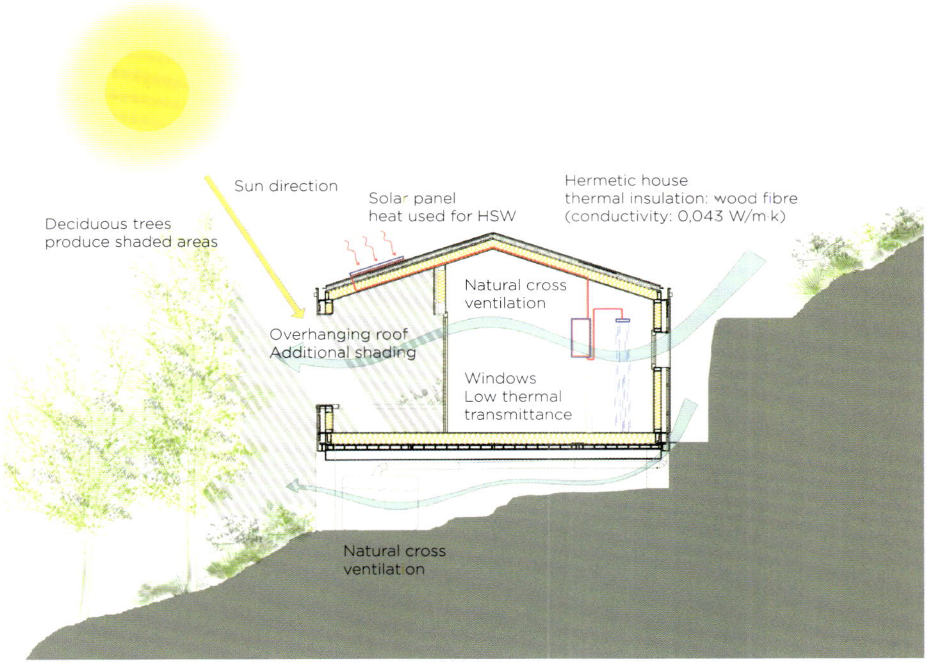

Winter, south orientation

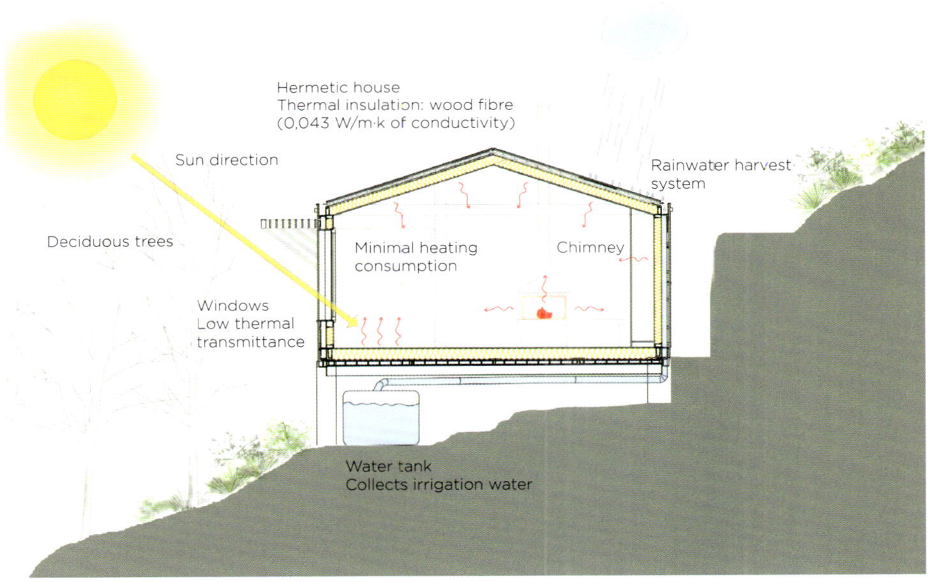

Prefabricated and recyclable construction system. Ecologic timber

The building's energy consumption is reduced by the use of resources such as an overhang, which protects it from direct solar radiation in the summer; and cross ventilation, which helps control the interior temperature.

Der Energieverbrauch des Gebäudes wird durch den Einsatz von Ressourcen wie Auskragungen gesenkt, die es im Sommer vor der direkten Sonneneinstrahlung schützen, oder die Querlüftung, welche bei der Wärmeregulierung der Luft behilflich ist.

La consommation énergetique de la maison est minime compte tenue des ressources utilisées telles que les saillies qui protègent des rayons du soleil directs en été ou la ventilation croisée qui permet le contrôle thermique de l'environnement.

El consumo energético del edificio se reduce con el uso de recursos como los voladizos que protegen de la radiación solar directa en verano o la ventilación cruzada que ayuda al control térmico del ambiente.

The structure itself, the interior paneling, and the exterior cladding were all built of wood. Linoleum was chosen for the interior flooring, as it is made of renewable raw materials.

Sowohl das Tragwerk als auch die Verkleidungen im Innen- und Außenbereich des Hauses wurden aus Holz gebaut. Als Bodenbelag im Innenbereich wurde aufgrund der Zusammensetzung aus erneuerbaren Rohstoffen Linoleum gewählt.

La structure et les revêtements intérieurs et extérieurs de la maison sont en bois. Pour le revêtement intérieur, on a choisi du lino en raison de sa composition en matières premières renouvelables.

Tanto la estructura como los revestimientos interiores y exteriores de la casa se construyeron en madera. Para el pavimento interior se escogió el linóleo por su composición a base de materias primas renovables.

The study area has access to a porch with views of the woods. The angle of the roof shields the space from the summer sun; however, in winter, it admits sunlight freely into the interior.

Der Studierbereich hat einen Zugang zur Veranda, die einen Blick auf den Wald bietet. Die Neigung des Dachs schützt im Sommer von Sonneneinstrahlung, doch im Innenbereich erlaubt sie im Winter den Einfall von Licht.

L'espace d'étude dispose d'un accès à un porche qui offre des vues sur la forêt. Le toit incliné protège des rayons du soleil en été, permettant néanmoins l'entrée de la lumière à l'intérieur en hiver.

La zona de estudio dispone de acceso a un porche que ofrece vistas sobre el bosque. La inclinación de la cubierta protege de la radiación solar en verano pero permite la entrada de luz al interior en invierno.

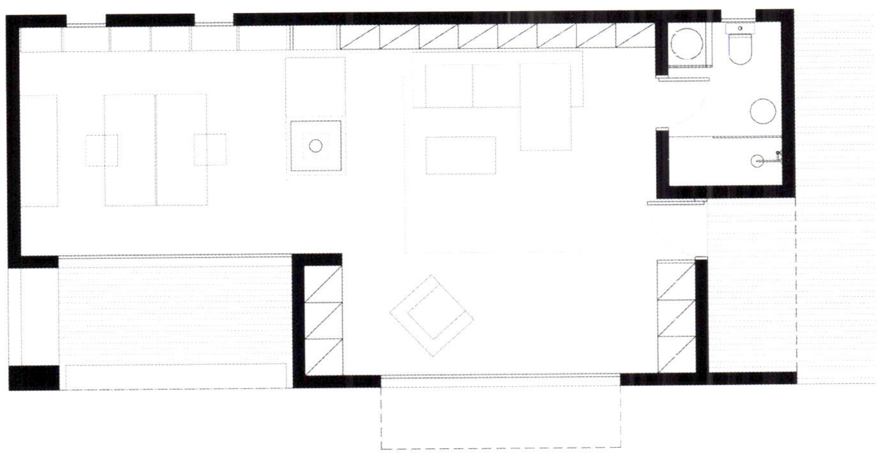

Floor plan

This studio was transformed by inserting two wooden modules into one empty space. The design accents the views of the surrounding mountains. The two-story "cube" that is the bedroom contains one double bed and one twin. The cube for the living space frames the view of the landscape beyond the picture window. The continuous black linoleum floor accents the positioning of the two modules within the empty space.

Die Umwandlung dieses Studios beruht auf der Einfügung von zwei Holzvolumen in einem leeren Bereich, deren Gestaltung dem Genuss der Aussicht zur umgebenden Gebirgslandschaft hin Vorrang gibt. Eine Art „Kasten", der als Schlafzimmer dient, erstreckt sich über zwei Ebenen und umfasst ein Doppelbett und ein Einzelbett. Der „Kasten", der als Wohnzimmer dient, fungiert als Umrahmung der Landschaft, die hinter der großzügigen Fensterfront liegt. Der durchgehende Boden aus schwarzem Linoleum betont die Position der beiden Volumen in der Leere des Raumes.

La transformation de ce studio repose sur l'intégration de deux volumes en bois dans un espace vide dont la conception donne la priorité au plaisir des vues sur le paysage des montagnes avoisinantes. La « case » destinée à la chambre sur deux hauteurs comprend un lit double et un lit simple. La « case » destinée au séjour sert de cadre du paysage situé derrière la grande baie vitrée. Un sol continu en lino noir met en valeur la situation des deux volumes dans le vide de l'espace.

La transformación de este estudio se basa en la inserción de dos volúmenes de madera dentro de un ambiente vacío, cuyo diseño prioriza el disfrute de las vistas hacia el paisaje de montañas circundante. La “caja” destinada a dormitorio se desarrolla en dos alturas y contiene una cama doble y una sencilla. La “caja” destinada a sala de estar actúa como marco del paisaje situado tras el amplio ventanal. Un suelo continuo de linóleo negro resalta la ubicación de los dos volúmenes en el vacío del espacio.

118

STUDIO IN A MOUNTAIN RESORT

Beriot, Bernardini Arquitectos

LOCATION **Puerto de Navacerrada, Spain** AREA **25 m² / 269 sq ft** PHOTOS **© Yen Chen**

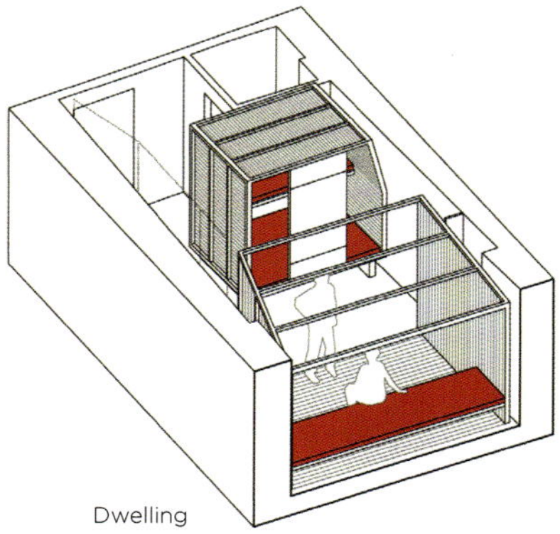

Dwelling

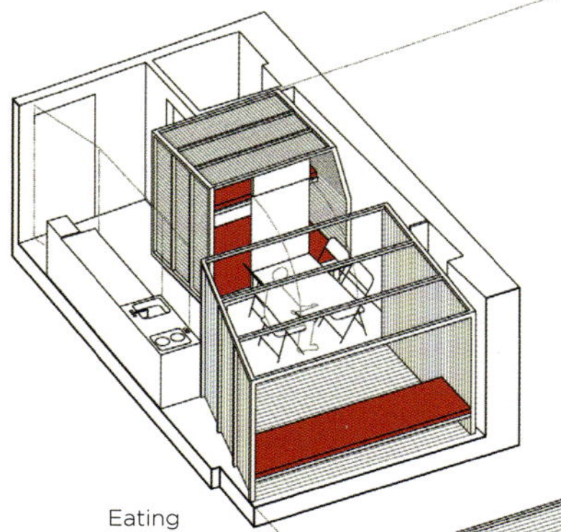

Eating

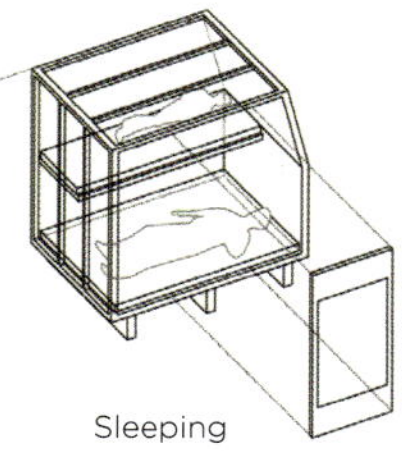

Sleeping

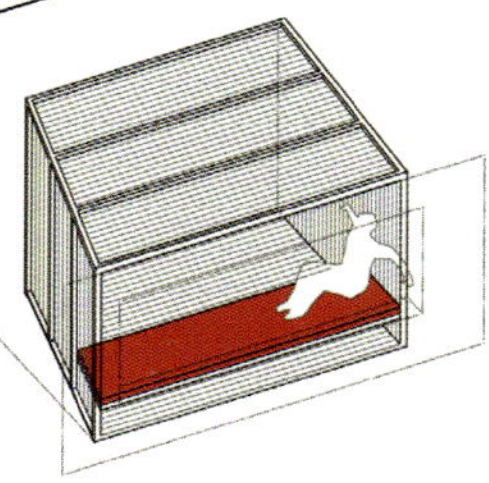

Resting/Lookout

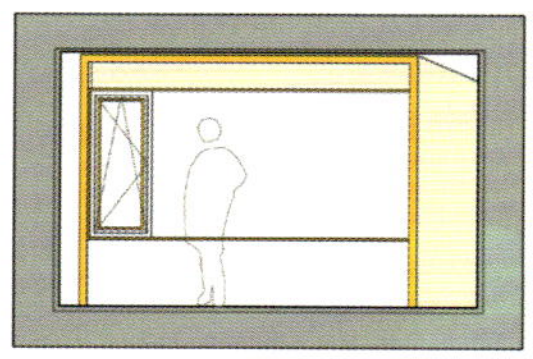

Cross section

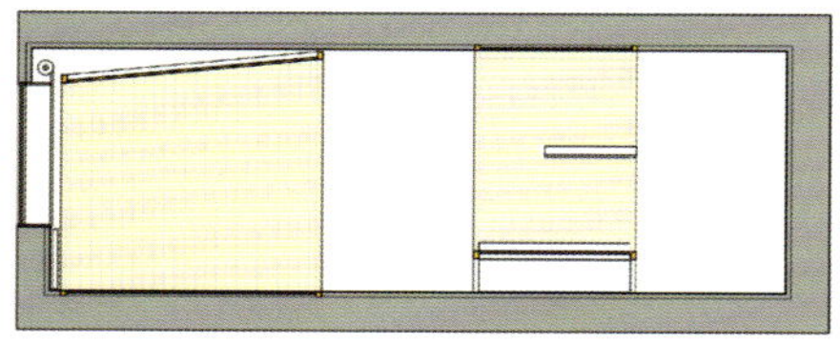

Longitudinal section

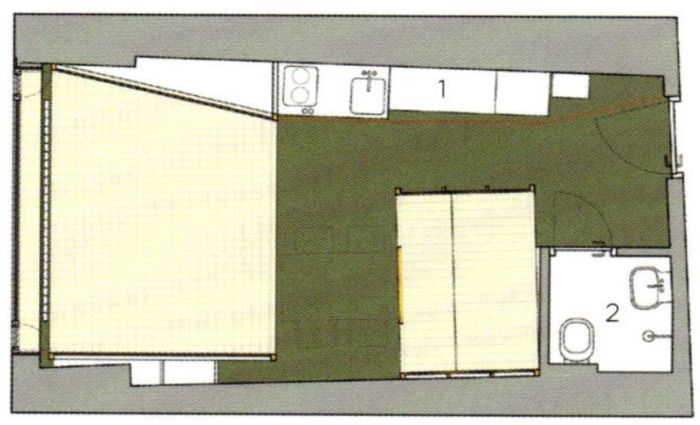

1. Kitchen
2. Bathroom

Floor plan

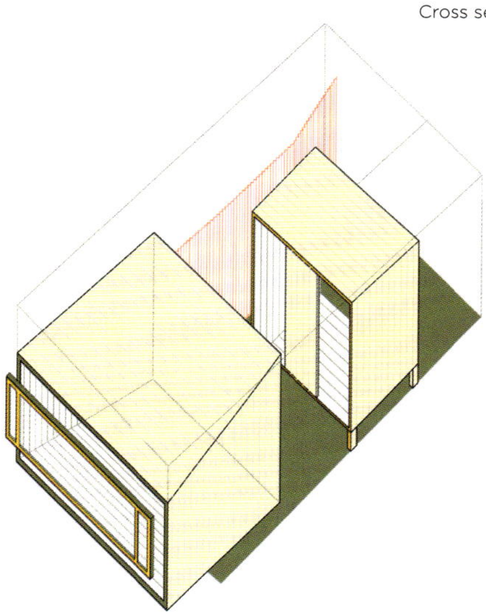

The two cubes are set side-by-side within the rectangular floor space. A small existing bathroom, and a narrow strip hidden behind a curtain, used for cooking and storage, complete the equipment of the studio.

Die beiden Kästen sind auf der rechteckigen Grundfläche aufeinanderfolgend angeordnet. Ein kleines vorhandenes Bad und ein hinter einem Vorhang verborgener Streifen, der als Küche und Stauraum dient, ergänzen die Einrichtung des Studios.

Les deux cases sont situées de façon séquentielle sur une surface rectangulaire. Une petite salle de bains et une section longitudinale qui sert de cuisine et de rangements, cachés derrière un rideau, complètent l'équipement du studio.

Las dos cajas se sitúan de forma secuencial dentro de la planta rectangular. Un pequeño baño existente y una franja destinada a cocina y almacenamiento, oculta tras una cortina, completan el equipamiento del estudio.

The starting point for this project was the relocation of the kitchen and the bedroom. This divided the apartment into two areas: a generous living room, kitchen, and dining room; and a private section holding the storage spaces (the location of which was one of the objectives of the project), as well as the bedroom and the bath. The dividing wall between them works as one continuous piece of furniture. It integrates shelving and closets and, by means of sliding panels, conceals the entryways to the rooms.

Die Neuplatzierung von Küche und Schlafzimmer dient als Ausgangspunkt dieses Eingriffs, der die Fläche dieser Wohnung in zwei Bereiche aufteilt: einen großzügigen Wohnbereich mit Küche und Essbereich und einen privaten Bereich, der Stauräume umfasst, deren Position eine der Zielsetzungen des Projektes, Schlafzimmer und Bad, bildet. Die Trennwand zwischen beiden wird als durchgehendes Möbelstück behandelt, das Bücherregale und Wandschränke beherbergt und den Zugang zu den Zimmern mithilfe von beweglichen Paneelen verbirgt.

La nouvelle situation de la cuisine et de la chambre sert de point de repère à cette intervention qui divise la surface d'un appartement en deux zones : un vaste séjour, une cuisine et une salle à manger et un espace privatif qui propose des rangements dont l'emplacement est un des objectifs du projet, la chambre et la salle de bains. Le mur séparateur entre les deux est un meuble continu avec des étagères et des armoires et qui cache l'accès aux pièces grâce à des panneaux amovibles.

La reubicación de la cocina y del dormitorio sirve de punto de arranque a esta intervención, que divide la superficie de un apartamento en dos zonas: una amplia zona de estar, cocina y comedor y una zona privada que contiene los espacios de almacenamiento, cuya ubicación constituye uno de los objetivos del proyecto, el dormitorio y el baño. La pared divisoria entre ambas se trata como un mueble continuo que integra estanterías y armarios y que oculta el acceso a las estancias mediante paneles móviles.

122

DARLINGHURST APARTMENT

Brad Swartz Architect

LOCATION **Darlinghurst, Australia** AREA **27 m² / 291 sq ft** PHOTOS **© Katherine Lu**

Exploded axonometric

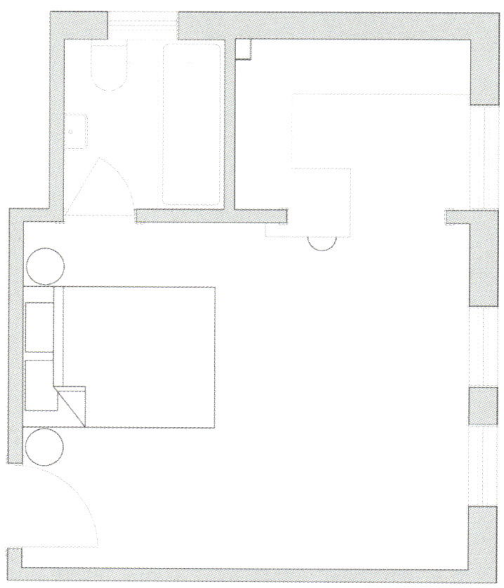

Existing apartment

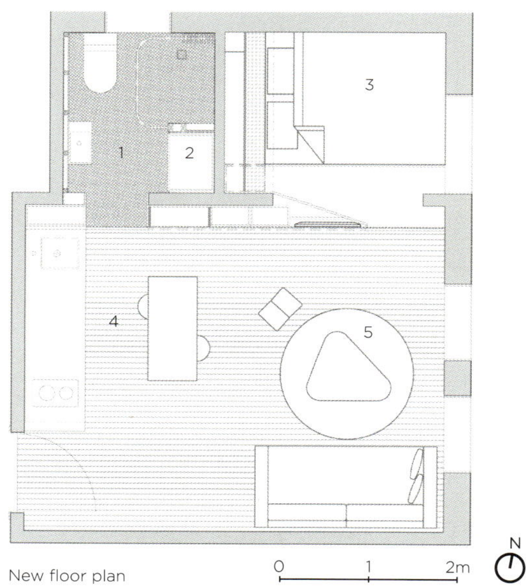

New floor plan

1. Bathroom
2. Laundry
3. Bedroom
4. Kitchen/Dining
5. Living

In the bedroom, the bed area is reduced to the absolute minimum, thus freeing up space for storage purposes. The kitchen is designed to be one single room, with a mirror that helps open up the space.

Im Schlafzimmer wird der Bereich des Betts auf ein unentbehrliches Minimum beschränkt, um dadurch mehr Stauraum zu gewinnen. Die Küche ist als einzelnes Teil gestaltet, in dem der Spiegel dazu beiträgt, den Raum zu erweitern.

Dans la chambre, l'espace-lit se limite au minimum requis pour ainsi obtenir un espace de rangement. La cuisine est conçue comme une pièce singulière, dans laquelle un miroir agrandit l'espace.

En el dormitorio, el ámbito de la cama se reduce al mínimo indispensable para así obtener espacio de almacenamiento. La cocina se diseña a modo de pieza singular, en la que un espejo contribuye a expandir el espacio.

For the project for this dwelling, the architects developed the prototype for a modular cube, designed to be used in small flexible spaces. It contains the kitchen, bathroom, and a double bed, components that can be arranged in several different ways, and then augmented with new elements. In this case, the position of the cube within the rectangular floor plan divides the space into two areas: one living/dining room, and one more private area, which contains a study, off the bedroom.

Für das Projekt dieser Wohnung entwickelten die Architekten den Prototyp eines modularen Würfels, der für kleine und flexible Räume gedacht ist und Küche, Bad und ein Doppelbett umfasst. Diese Komponenten können auf verschiedene Art und Weise angeordnet und mit neuen Elementen ergänzt werden. Im Falle dieser Wohnung gliedert die Position des Würfels innerhalb des rechteckigen Grundrisses den Raum in zwei Bereiche: ein Wohn-Essbereich und ein etwas privaterer Bereich, der mit dem Schlafzimmer verbunden ist, der ein Arbeitszimmerumfasst.

Pour le projet de ce logement, les architectes ont élaboré un prototype de cube modulaire, conçu pour des espaces petits et modulables comprenant la cuisine, la salle de bains et un lit double. Des composants qui peuvent être organisés de manière différente et être complétés par des nouveaux. Pour ce logement, l'emplacement du cube à l'intérieur de la surface rectangulaire structure l'espace en deux zones : un séjour-salle à manger et un espace plus intime associé à la chambre qui comprend un bureau.

Para el proyecto de esta vivienda, los arquitectos desarrollaron un prototipo de cubo modular, concebido para espacios pequeños y flexibles, que contiene la cocina, el baño y una cama doble, componentes que pueden organizarse de diferentes formas y completarse con nuevos elementos. En el caso de esta vivienda, la posición del cubo dentro de la planta rectangular estructura el espacio en dos zonas: una sala de estar comedor y una zona más privada vinculada al dormitorio, que contiene un estudio.

128

CITY CUBE

BYTR architecten

LOCATION Utrecht, The Netherlands AREA 28 m² / 301 sq ft PHOTOS © Richèl Lubbers

The off-center position of the cube within the room means that the living/dining area has more space, partly taken up by the kitchen module that is across from it. A small terrace extends the living room toward the outdoors.

Die dezentrale Position des Würfels im Inneren der Wohnung schenkt dem Wohn-Essbereich, auf den das Modul der Küche ausgerichtet ist, mehr Platz. Eine kleine Terrasse vergrößert dieses Wohnzimmer nach außen hin.

L'emplacement décentral sé du cube dans le logement concède un plus grand espace au séjour-salle à manger qui donne sur le module de la cuisine. Ce séjour se prolonge à l'extérieur par une petite terrasse.

La posición descentrada del cubo dentro de la vivienda concede un mayor espacio al ámbito del estar comedor, hacia el cual se orienta el módulo de la cocina. Una pequeña terraza prolonga esta sala de estar hacia el exterior.

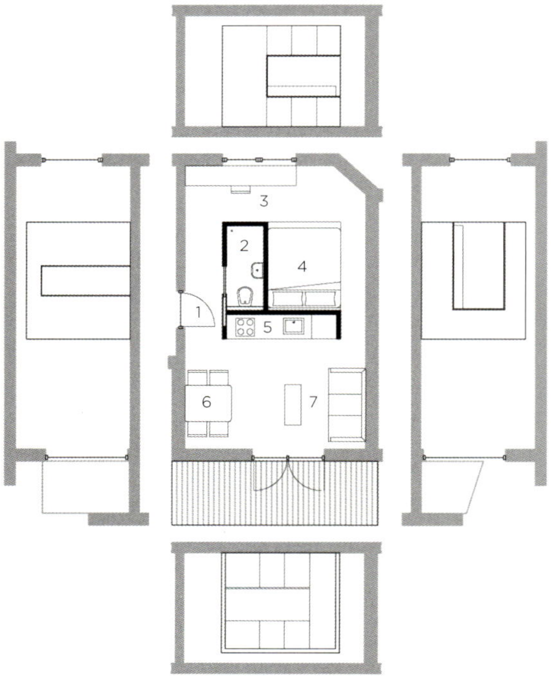

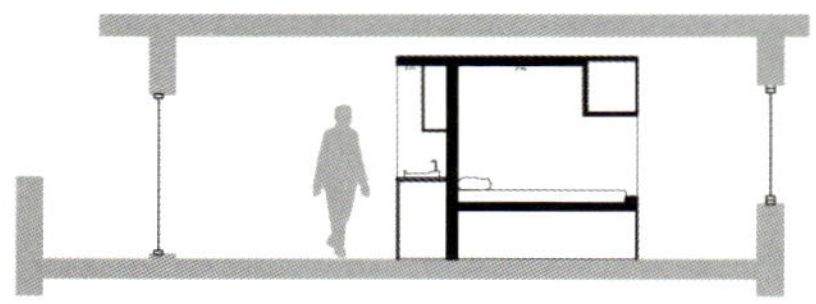

Section

Floor plan/Elevation

1. Entrance
2. Bathroom
3. Study
4. Bedroom
5. Kitchen
6. Dining
7. Living

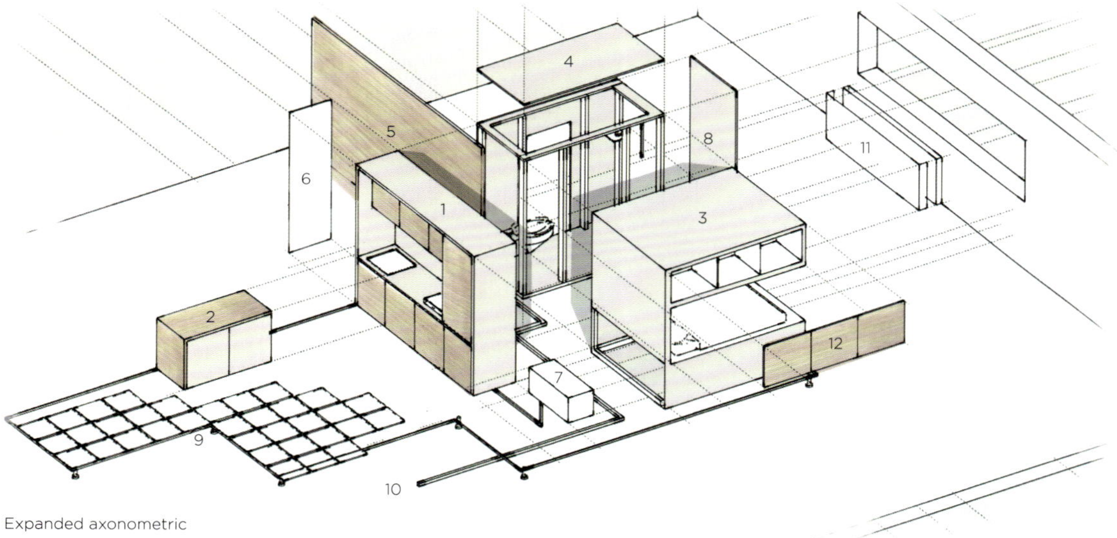

Expanded axonometric

1. Kitchen
2. Kitchen extension
3. Bedroom
4. Bathroom
5. Sliding wall
6. Infrared panel
7. Boiler
8. Biobased boards
9. Raised floor
10. Sanibrayeur

Passageways around the cube connect the living/dining room with the studio space. One of these side hallways contains the entry to the bathroom and the main doorway that leads into the living space.

Um den Würfel herum werden Bahnen geschaffen, die den Wohn-Essbereich mit dem Studierbereich verbinden. In einem dieser seitlichen Flure befinden sich der Zugang zum Bad und die Wohnungseingangstür.

À proximité du cube, ont été créés des couloirs qui relient le séjour-salle à manger à l'espace bureau. L'un ce ses couloirs latéraux donne sur la sal e de bains et la porte d'entrée du logement.

Alrededor del cubo se generan las circulaciones que conectan la sala de estar comedor con la zona del estudio. En uno de estos pasillos laterales se sitúan el acceso al baño y la puerta de entrada a la vivienda.

This project renovates a small apartment in an early twentieth century Berlin *Altbau* (historic neighborhood), to adapt it to the requirements of today's world. Its original high ceilings allow for a two-level layout. Space in the bathroom was tightened up as much as possible so as to gain free space in the other rooms. The light woods and white tones used in the interior design open up the space and fill it with light.

Dieses Projekt beschäftigt sich mit dem Umbau einer kleinen Wohnung, die in einem Berliner*Altbau*aus der Zeit zu Beginn des 20. Jahrhunderts liegt und an die Anforderungen des modernen Lebens angepasst werden soll. Dank der ursprünglichen lichten Höhe lässt sich die Aufteilung auf zwei Ebenen entfalten, bei der die Maße der Wandverkleidungen des Bades maximal angeglichen wurden, um im restlichen Wohnraum freien Raum zu gewinnen. Der überwiegende Einsatz von hellen Hölzern und Weißtönen bei der Inneneinrichtung verleiht dem Raum Weite und Helligkeit.

Ce projet concerne les travaux d'un petit appartement situé dans un *Altbau* berlinois du début du XXe s., pour répondre aux besoins de la vie contemporaine. Sa hauteur sous plafond originale permet d'organiser une répartition sur deux niveaux, dans laquelle les dimensions des cloisons de la salle de bains sont ajustées au maximum afin d'obtenir un espace libre dans le reste des pièces. L'utilisation prédominante de bois clairs et de tons blancs dans le design intérieur confère de la grandeur et de la luminosité à l'espace.

Este proyecto constituye la reforma de un pequeño apartamento situado en un *Altbau* berlinés de principios del siglo XX, para adaptarlo a las necesidades de la vida contemporánea. Su altura libre original permite desarrollar una distribución en dos niveles, en la que las dimensiones de los cerramientos del baño se han ajustado al máximo para obtener espacio libre.en el resto de estancias. El uso predominante de maderas claras y tonos blancos en el diseño interior otorga amplitud y luminosidad al espacio.

136

MICRO-APARTMENT MOABIT

spamroom + johnpaulcoss

LOCATION **Berlin, Germany** AREA **21 m² / 226 sq ft** PHOTOS **© Ringo Paulusch**

An elegant and sturdy staircase made of five-milimeter-thick folded steel plate, attached to one of the structural walls, connects the original main floor with the newly created upper level over the core of the bathroom.

Eine elegante und robuste 5 mm starke Stahltreppe, die sich an eine der Tragmauern anlehnt, verbindet die Ebene der ursprüngliche Etage mit der neuen Ebene, die auf dem Zentrum des Bades geschaffen wurde.

Un escalier, élégant et solide, en acier plié de cinq millimètres d'épaisseur, adossé à un des murs porteurs, enlace le rez-de-chaussée d'origine et le nouvel étage créé sur la base de la salle de bains.

Una elegante y robusta escalera de acero plegado de cinco milímetros de grosor, adosada a uno de los muros estructurales, enlaza el nivel de la planta original con el nuevo nivel creado sobre el núcleo del baño.

Mezzanine

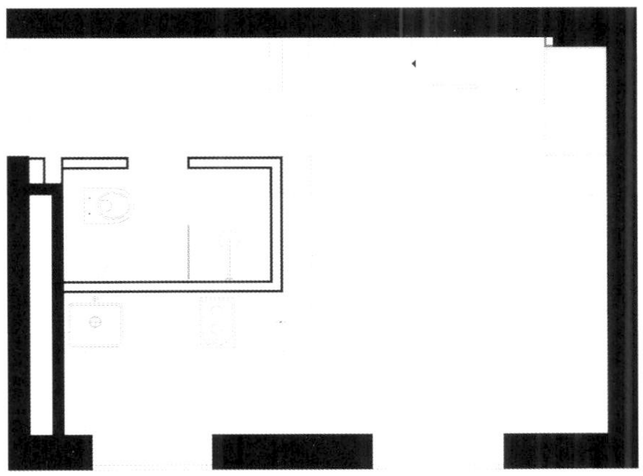

Floor plan

Sections

At the client's request, the design of the apartment includes elements of *Art Nouveau*, such as the blue tiles in the small washbasin, which contrast with the beige tones of the rest of the space.

Auf Kundenwunsch bindet die Gestaltung der Wohnung Elemente des Jugendstils (Art Nouveau) ein, wie beispielsweise die blauen Fliesen im kleinen Bad, die mit den Beigetönen des übrigen Raumes kontrastieren.

À la demande du client, la conception de l'appartement intègre des éléments du *Jugendstil* (Art Nouveau), tels que la faïence bleue du petit lavabo qui contraste avec les tons beiges du reste de l'espace.

A petición del cliente, el diseño del apartamento incorpora elementos del *Jugendstil* (*Art Nouveau*), como los azulejos de color azul del pequeño lavabo, que contrastan con los tonos beis del resto del espacio.

This two-story home is on the top floor of a mid-twentieth century building, with numerous views of the gardens that surround it. The lower floor has a main open space that includes the kitchen, living, and dining rooms; it contains the entryways to the other rooms, built in as part of decorative items and furniture. The upper floor, which contains a living room and small bathroom, can be remodeled into a separate bedroom.

Diese zweistöckige Wohnung befindet in der obersten Etage eines Gebäudes, das Mitte des 20. Jahrhundert erbaut wurde, und bietet verschiedene Ausblicke auf die umliegenden Gärten. Die Raumaufteilung der unteren Etage umfasst einen offenen Hauptraum mit Küche, Wohnzimmer und Esszimmer und gestaltet die Zugänge zu den übrigen Wohnbereichen durch die Einbindung in Dekorationselemente und Möbel. Die obere Etage beherbergt ein Wohnzimmer und ein kleines Bad, die sich in ein unabhängiges Schlafzimmer verwandeln lassen.

Cet appartement sur deux étages est situé au dernier étage d'un bâtiment construit au milieu du XXe siècle. Il offre une multitude de vues sur les jardins qui l'entourent. La répartition de l'étage inférieur présente un espace principal ouvert avec cuisine, séjour et salle à manger et prévoit les accès aux autres pièces en les intégrant comme des éléments de décoration et mobilier. L'étage supérieur comprend un séjour et une petite salle de bains qui peuvent se transformer en une chambre indépendante.

Esta vivienda de dos plantas se sitúa en el último piso de un edificio construido a mediados del siglo XX y disfruta de múltiples vistas sobre los jardines que la rodean. La distribución de la planta inferior contiene un espacio principal abierto que incluye la cocina, el estar y el comedor, y plantea los accesos al resto de las estancias integrándolos en elementos de decoración y mobiliario. La planta superior alberga un estar y un pequeño baño, que pueden reconvertirse en un dormitorio independiente.

142

APARTMENT H01

dontDIY

LOCATION **Sofia, Bulgary** AREA **92 m² / 990 sq ft** PHOTOS **© Asen Emilov**

501
CINEMA NOW

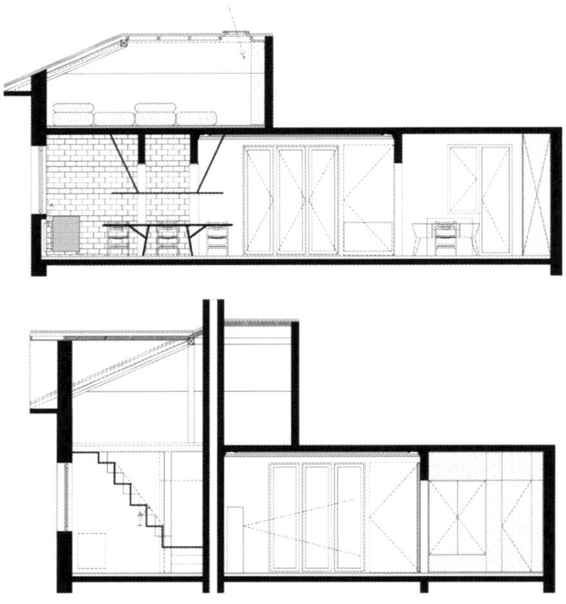

Section 1

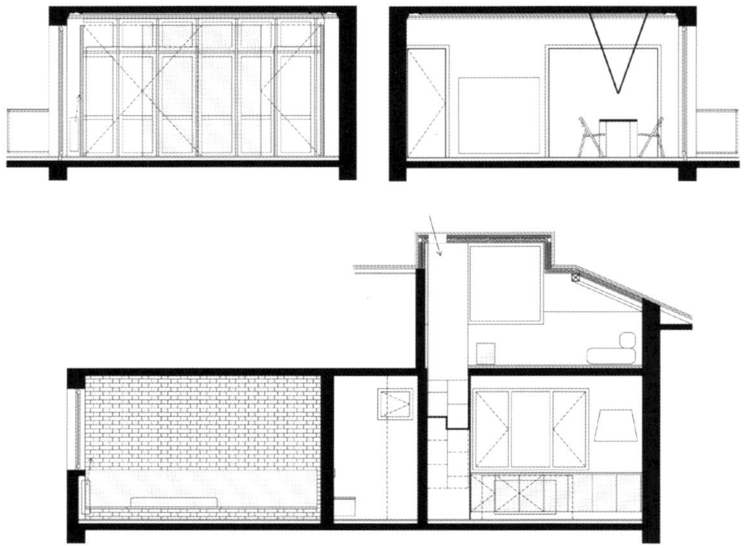

Section 2

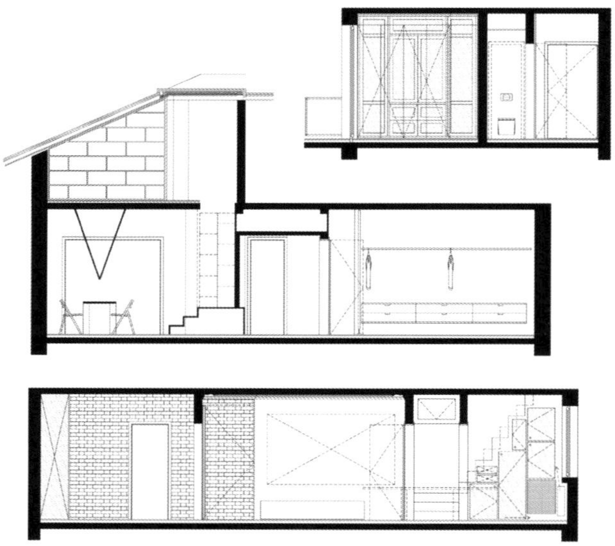

Section 3

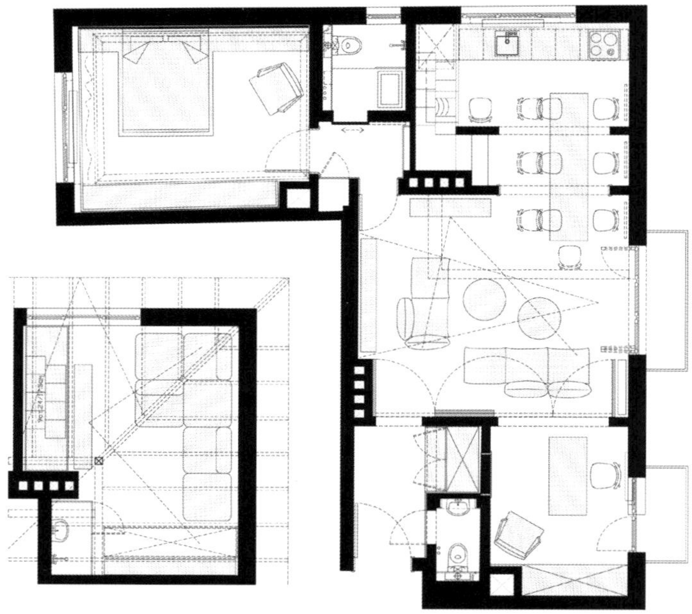

Upper floor plan

Main floor plan

Large sliding foldable panels separate the main space from the vestibule and the study. They create one continuous wooden enclosure that contrasts with the white walls.

Große verschiebbare und klappbare Verkleidungen trennen den Hauptraum von Diele und Arbeitszimmer, und bilden ein durchgehende Umschließung aus Holz, die mit dem Weiß der Wandflächen kontrastiert.

De grands panneaux coulissants et rabattables séparent l'espace de vie du vestibule et du bureau et forme une cloison continue en bois qui contraste avec le blanc des murs.

Unos grandes paneles correderos y abatibles separan el espacio principal del vestíbulo de acceso y del estudio, y conforman un cerramiento continuo de madera que contrasta con el blanco de los paramentos.

The striking green staircase leading from the main room to the loft becomes one more piece of furniture for the home, as it is used to store kitchenware.

Die auffällige Treppe in Grün, welche die Hauptetage mit dem Zwischengeschoss verbindet, wird zu einem weiteren Möbelstück des Hauses und dient als Aufbewahrungsort für Küchengeräte.

L'étonnant escalier vert qui relie l'étage principal et la mezzanine se transforme en une pièce supplémentaire du mobilier de l'appartement et sert d'élément de rangement pour les éléments de la cuisine.

La llamativa escalera de color verde que comunica la planta principal con el altillo se convierte en una pieza más del mobiliario de la casa y sirve de elemento de almacenaje para los útiles de cocina.

The layout for this apartment renovation avoids doors and dividers in favor of having one continuous, transparent space. To define the dwelling's four different living areas, it relies on variations in materials and subtle changes in the heights of ceilings and floors. This visual permeability makes it possible for inhabitants to contemplate, from any point inside, the line of metasequoias that faces the building. The view is framed by a wide picture window that can be completely opened.

Die Aufteilung, die für dem Umbau dieser Wohnung geplant ist, vermeidet Türen und Zwischenwände, um einen fortlaufenden und transparenten Raum zu schaffen, in dem der Einsatz von verschiedenen Materialien und subtilen Veränderungen bei der Höhe von Decken und Böden die vier Bereiche definieren, die sie bilden. Die visuelle Durchlässigkeit des Raumes hat als Betrachtungsziel von jedem Punkt des Innenraums einer Reihe von Urweltmammutbäumen vor dem Gebäude, deren Anblick von einem großzügigen Fenster eingerahmt wird, das sich ganz öffnen lässt.

La répartition proposée au cours des travaux de cet appartement prévoit le retrait des portes et cloisons afin de créer un espace continu et transparent dans lequel l'utilisation des divers matériaux et les modifications utiles des hauteurs sous plafond et des sols déterminent les quatre pièces qui le composent. Sa perméabilité visuelle permet d'admirer depuis l'intérieur d'une haie de séquoias géants située en face du bâtiment dont la vue est marquée par une grande baie vitrée qui peut entièrement s'ouvrir.

La distribución propuesta en la reforma de este apartamento huye de puertas y tabiques para crear un espacio continuo y transparente, donde el uso de diferentes materiales y los sutiles cambios en la altura de techos y suelos definen los cuatro ámbitos que lo integran. Su permeabilidad visual tiene como objetivo la contemplación, desde cualquier punto del interior, de una hilera de metasecuoyas ubicada frente al edificio, cuya visión queda enmarcada por un amplio ventanal que puede abrirse por completo.

150

APARTMENT 37

Atelier Mearc

LOCATION **Shanghai, China** AREA **37 m² / 398 sq ft** PHOTOS **© Lu Haha**

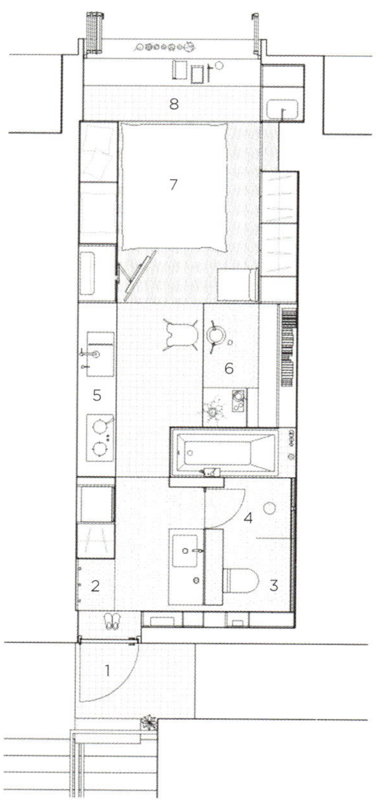

Floor plan

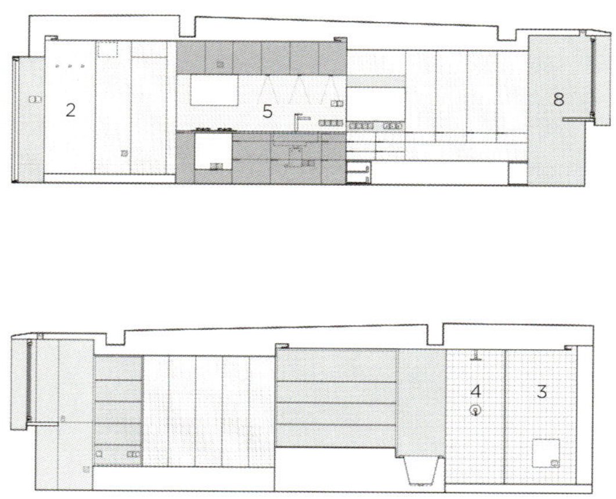

Facade

1. Entrance
2. Entryway
3. Toilet
4. Bathroom
5. Cooking area
6. Dining area
7. Bed
8. Balcony

The apartment's furnishings and appliances are built into the space as architectural elements, whose form and position are less important than the materials of which they are made.

Mobiliar und Einrichtung dieser Wohnung werden in die Gestaltung des Raumes als architektonische Elemente eingebunden, bei denen Form und Standort nicht so wichtig sind wie das Material, das sie kennzeichnet.

Le mobilier et les éléments de l'appartement s'intègrent à la conception de l'espace comme des éléments architectoniques dans lesquels la forme et l'emplacement ne sont pas aussi importants que le matériau qui les caractérise.

El mobiliario y el equipamiento de la casa se integran en el diseño del espacio como elementos arquitectónicos, en los que la forma y la posición no son tan importantes como el material que los caracteriza.

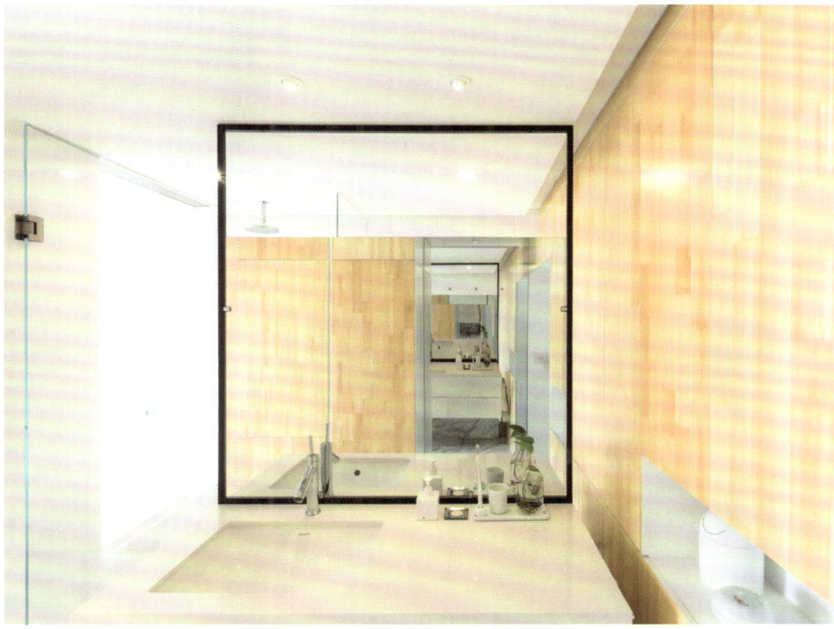

The image of a female nude in an Edward H. Weston photograph inspired the curved outline of the cabinet that runs the length of this home from front to back, and gives both character and continuity to its public space. This cabinet, made of medium density board lined with oukoume wood, holds the two folding beds that are in a hidden second bedroom, the entry to the laundry, the basic kitchen appliances, and some of the furniture for the living room and the seafront terrace.

Das Bild eines weiblichen Akts auf einer Fotographie von Edward H. Weston inspiriert den gebogenen Verlauf eines Möbelstücks, dass diese Wohnung in Längsrichtung durchkreuzt und dadurch die beiden gegenüberliegenden Fassaden verknüpft und dem allgemeinen Bereich Charakter und Kontinuität verleiht. Dieses Möbelstück, das aus mit Okumen-Holz gefütterten MD-Holzplatten gefertigt ist, integriert zwei Klappbetten eines zweiten verborgenen Zimmers, den Zugang zur Waschküche, die Grundausstattung der Küche und einen Teil der Möbel des Wohnzimmers und der auf das Meer ausgerichteten Terrasse.

La représentation d'une femme nue sur une photo d'Edward H. Weston inspire le tracé courbé d'un meuble qui traverse cette maison dans sa longueur, enlaçant les deux murs opposés et conférant ainsi du caractère et une continuité à son espace commun. Ce meuble, construit avec des panneaux en contreplaqué de bois okoumé, comprend les deux lits escamotables d'une deuxième chambre dissimulée, l'accès à la buanderie, les éléments de base de la cuisine et une partie du mobilier du séjour et de la terrasse avec vue sur la mer.

La imagen de un desnudo femenino en una fotografía de Edward H. Weston inspira el trazado curvo de un mueble que recorre esta vivienda en sentido longitudinal, enlazando las dos fachadas opuestas y confiriendo carácter y continuidad a su área pública. Este mueble, construido con tableros DM forrados de madera de Okumen, integra las dos camas abatibles de una segunda habitación oculta, el acceso al lavadero, el equipo básico de cocina y parte del mobiliario del estar y de la terraza orientada al mar.

156

HOUSE WESTON

Antonio Maciá

LOCATION **Altea, Spain**   AREA **77,5 m² / 834 sq ft**   PHOTOS **© David Frutos**

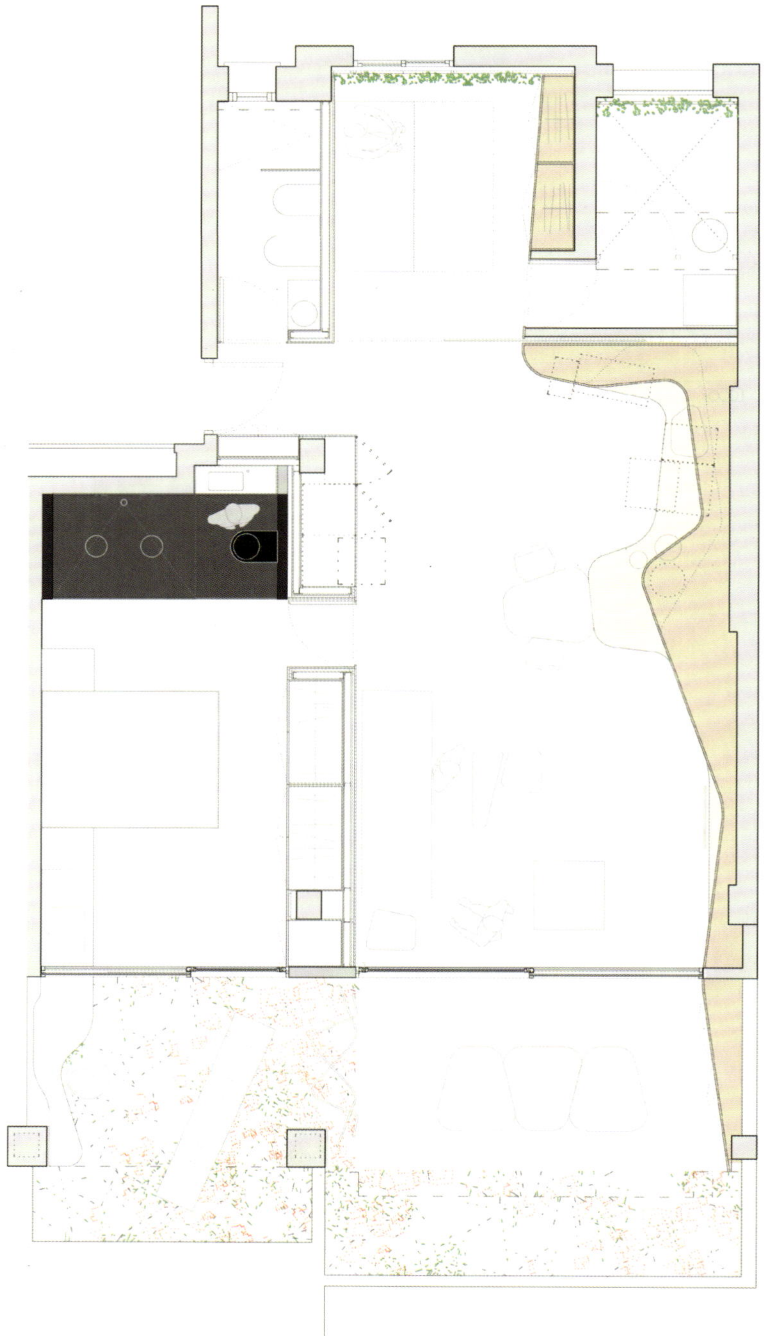

Floor plan

The room is divided lengthwise into two strips. The perpendicular lines of the narrower of the two, which holds the master bedroom, contrast with the curved cabinet that defines the space of the wider one.

Die Wohnung ist in zwei Längsstreifen aufgeteilt. Der rechtwinklige Charakter des schmäleren Streifens, wo das große Schlafzimmer untergebracht ist, dient als Kontrapunkt zu dem gebogenen Möbelstück, das den Raum des breiteren Streifens definiert.

La maison est divisée en deux espaces longitudinaux. Le caractère orthogonal du plus étroit qui comprend la chambre parentale sert de contraste au meuble incurvé qui définit l'espace le plus large.

La vivienda se divide en dos franjas longitudinales. El carácter ortogonal de la más estrecha, que alberga el dormitorio principal, sirve de contrapunto al mueble curvo que define el espacio de la más ancha.

A transparent glass enclosure surrounds the shower, which is in the bedroom area; a continuous mirror on the rear wall brings in views of the outdoors.

Ein durchsichtiger Glasabschluss fügt den Bereich der Dusche in den Bereich des Schlafzimmers ein. Ein durchgehender Spiegel, der als Hintergrund dient, sorgt dafür, dass die Landschaft draußen, in diesen Raum eindringt.

Une cloison en verre transparent sépare la douche de l'espace nuit de la chambre, avec un miroir continu en toile de fond qui permet au paysage extérieur de pénétrer cet espace.

Un cerramiento de vidrio transparente integra la zona de la ducha dentro del ámbito del dormitorio; un espejo continuo que actúa como fondo permite que el paisaje exterior penetre dentro este espacio.

A small, compartmentalized apartment, located in the city center, becomes a spacious urban loft. The design creates a volume of birch plywood constructed around the existing central core services and also builds into it a tiny box-style bedroom. This unit, with built-in cupboards in its walls, extends along the two contiguous open spaces, one designed as the living area, and the other as the kitchen/dining area.

Eine kleine und zerstückelte Wohnung, die im Stadtzentrum liegt, wird dank dieser Umgestaltung zu einem geräumigen städtischen Loft. Sein Design nutzt den bestehenden zentralen Kern der Funktionen, um ein Volumen aus Birkensperrholz zu bilden, in das ein Schlafzimmer in minimalen Maßen als Kasten eingegliedert wird. Dieses Volumen erstreckt sich zu den angrenzenden durchscheinenden Räumen hin, die als Wohnzimmer beziehungsweise Küche-Esszimmer in Form von in die Wände integrierten Schränken konzipiert sind.

Un petit appartement compartimenté, situé au cœur de la ville, a été transformé grâce à ce réaménagement en un loft urbain spacieux. Sa conception a su profiter du noyau central des services existants pour configurer un volume en contreplaqué de bouleau auquel s'intègre une chambre aux dimensions minimales en forme de caisson. Ce volume s'étend vers les deux espaces ouverts contigus, conçus respectivement comme un séjour et une cuisine-salle à manger en forme d'armoires intégrées aux murs.

Un pequeño y fragmentado apartamento, situado en el centro de la ciudad, se convierte gracias a esta remodelación en un espacioso loft urbano. Su diseño aprovecha el núcleo central de servicios existente para configurar un volumen de madera contrachapada de abedul, al que se incorpora un dormitorio de dimensiones mínimas a modo de caja. Este volumen se extiende hacia los dos espacios diáfanos contiguos, concebidos respectivamente como estar y cocina comedor, en forma de armarios integrados en las paredes.

162

AMSTERDAM URBAN LOFT

Bureau Fraai

LOCATION Amsterdam, The Netherlands   AREA 56 m² / 603 sq ft   PHOTOS © Wim Hanenberg

The openings in the wooden unit make for an interplay of visuals through the bedroom and toward the bathroom. This, along with the blue flooring used in all the rooms, adds continuity to the space.

Die Öffnungen des Volumens aus Holz ermöglicht ein Spiel der Augenlinien durch das Schlafzimmer und Richtung Bad, das, neben dem in allen Zimmern verwendeten blauen Bodenbelag, dem Raum des Lofts Kontinuität verleiht.

Les ouvertures du volume en bois permettent d'obtenir un jeu visuel grâce à la chambre et vers la salle de bains qui, avec le revêtement bleu utilisé dans toutes les pièces, offre une continuité à l'espace du loft.

Las aberturas del volumen de madera permiten un juego de visuales a través del dormitorio y hacia el baño que, junto al pavimento de color azul utilizado en todas las estancias, da continuidad al espacio de la casa.

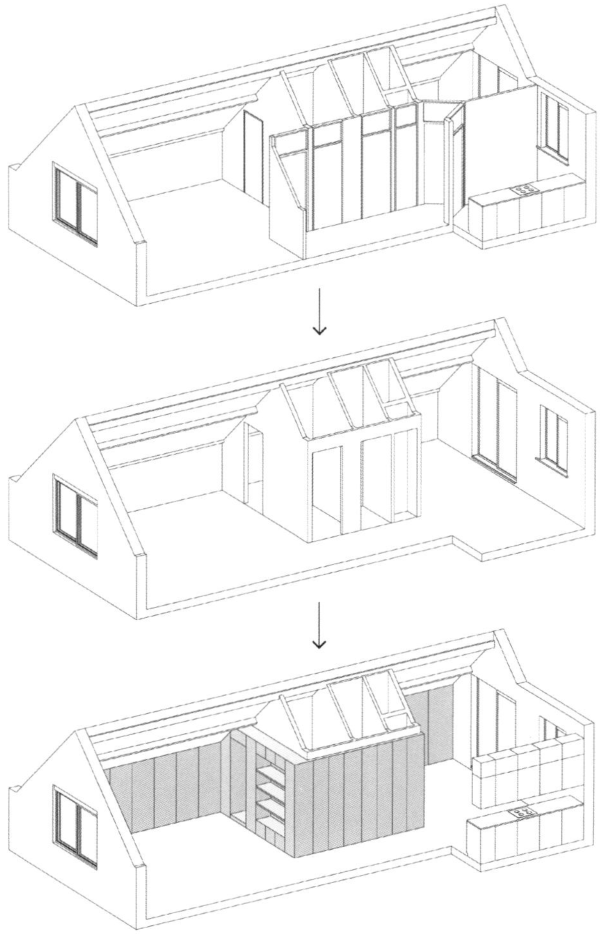

Axonometric view

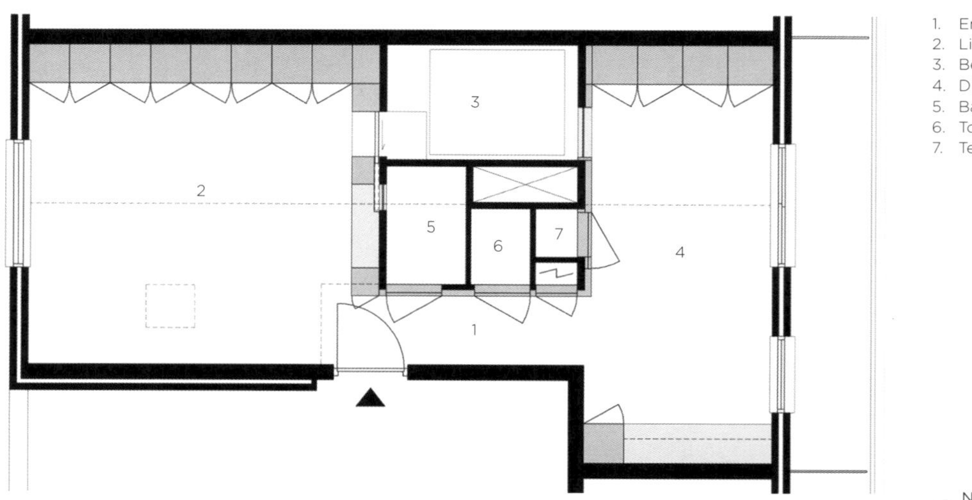

Floor plan

1. Entrance
2. Living room
3. Bedroom
4. Dining room
5. Bathroom
6. Toilet
7. Technical room

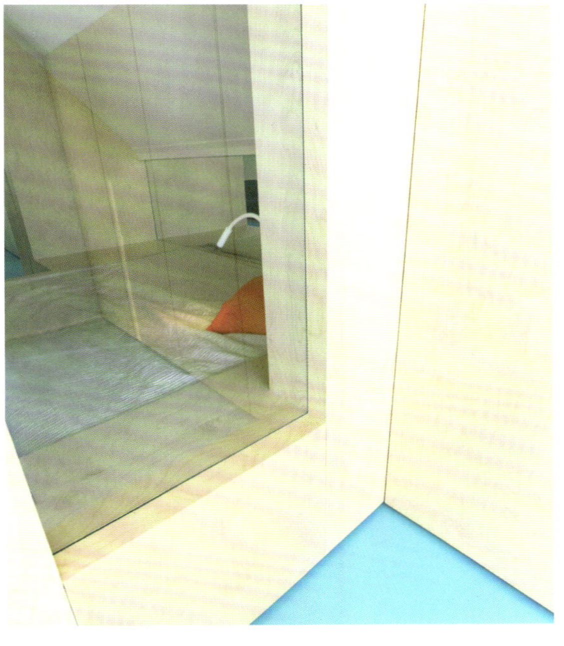

The design features a raised platform that is installed in the one room that makes up this apartment, which is used by its owner to live in during the work week. This multiplies the useable surface and organizes the limited space. The height of this platform makes it possible to create a front that integrates storage spaces and kitchen appliances, as well as to build an ample closet underneath it, complete with hangers and shelves, which can be accessed through a trap door under the dining table.

Die Gestaltung einer erhöhten Plattform innerhalb des einzigen Bereichs, der diese Wohnung bildet, welche von ihrem Eigentümer während der Arbeitstage als Unterkunft genutzt wird, vervielfacht die Nutzfläche und gliedert den kleinen Raum. Dank der Höhe dieser Plattform lässt sich eine Frontseite schaffen, in die Stauräume und die Kücheneinrichtung integriert werden, und ein geräumiger Schrank unter dessen Boden einbauen, der mit einer Garderobe und Regalen ausgestattet ist, zu denen man über eine Luke gelangt, die sich unter dem Esstisch befindet.

La conception d'une plateforme surélevée dans le cadre unique de cet appartement, utilisée par son propriétaire comme un logement pendant la semaine, multiplie la surface utile et organise l'espace réduit. La hauteur de cette plateforme permet de créer une façade sur laquelle s'intègrent des espaces de rangement et les éléments de cuisine et construire ainsi une grande armoire en dessous, avec des penderies et des étagères, accessible par une trappe située sous la table de la salle à manger.

El diseño de una plataforma elevada dentro del único ámbito que conforma este apartamento, utilizado por su propietario como alojamiento durante los días laborables, multiplica la superficie útil y organiza el reducido espacio. La altura de esta plataforma permite crear un frente en el que se integran espacios de almacenamiento y el equipo de cocina, y construir un amplio armario bajo su suelo, dotado de percheros y estanterías, al que se accede mediante una trampilla situada bajo la mesa de comedor.

168

MINI LOFT CREM'8

Silvana Citterio

LOCATION Milan, Italy AREA 13 m² / 140 sq ft PHOTOS © Silvana Citterio

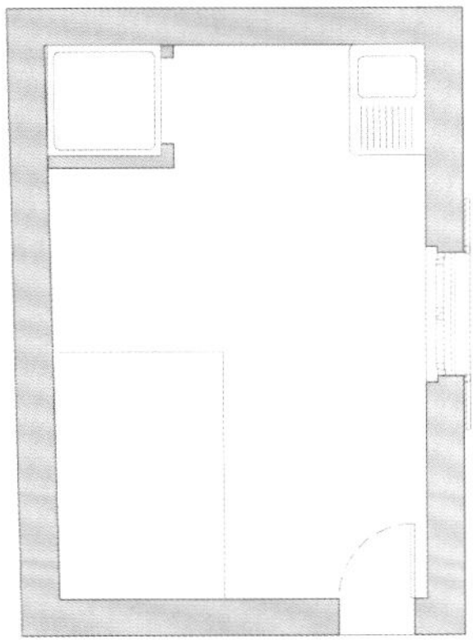

Existing conditions

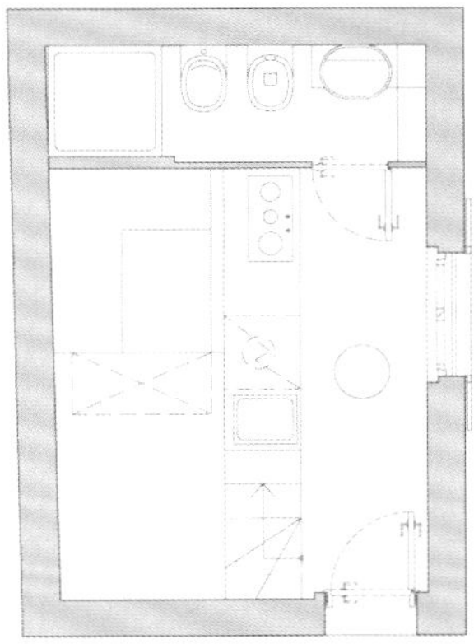

Project

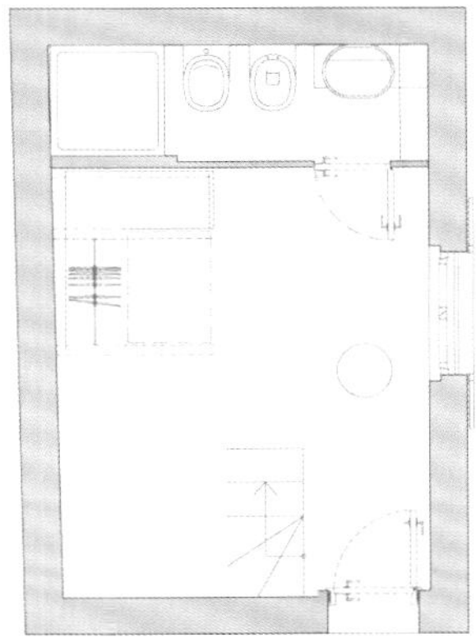

Furniture under the platform

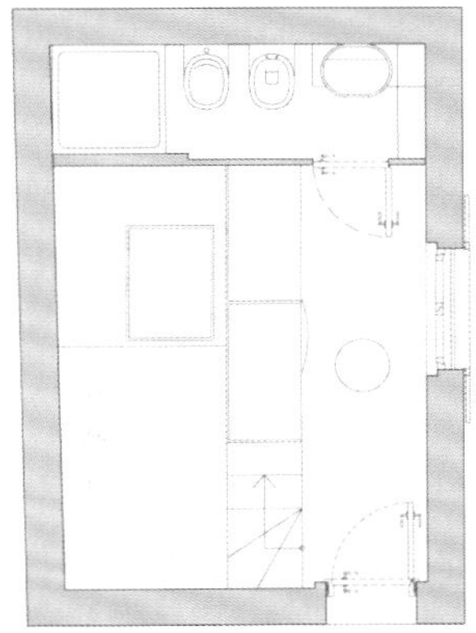

Platform

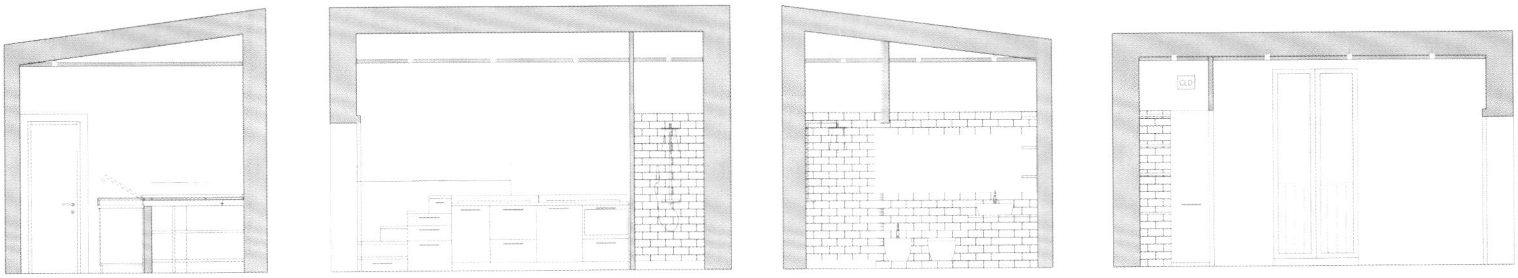

Sections

It is possible to hide the kitchen appliances to give a look of continuity to the elevated platform that holds the sleeping space and living/dining area. The bathroom is the only closed room in the house.

Der Bereich mit der Kücheneinrichtung kann verborgen werden, um der erhöhten Plattform, auf der sich Schlafzimmerbereich und Wohn-Essbereich befinden, Kontinuität zu verleihen. Das Bad bildet den einzigen geschlossenen Raum innerhalb der Wohnung.

L'espace cuisine peut être dissimulé pour ainsi donner de la continuité à la plateforme surélevée sur laquelle se trouvent la chambre et le séjour-salle à manger. La salle de bains est la seule pièce fermée de l'appartement.

La zona del equipo de cocina puede ocultarse para dar continuidad a la plataforma elevada, sobre la cual se sitúan las zonas de dormitorio y estar comedor. El baño constituye la única pieza cerrada dentro de la vivienda.

This project remodels a former carpentry shop into a small guest house. The layout consists of a lower floor, which is the living-dining area, an upper floor for the main bedroom, study, and bathroom, and a small multipurpose loft suspended under the sloping ceiling. The design exudes playfulness and relaxation as well as warmth, which is conveyed by the predominant use of wood.

Eine ehemalige Tischlerwerkstatt wird zum Gegenstand dieser Renovierung, die eine Unterkunft für gelegentliche Besucher schaffen soll. Die Raumaufteilung ist in ein Erdgeschoss gegliedert, das als Wohn-Essbereich dient, in eine obere Etage, auf der das große Schlafzimmer, Arbeitszimmer und Bad untergebracht sind, und in ein kleines multifunktionales Zwischengeschoss, dass im Raum unter der Dachschräge aufgehängt ist. Die Innenraumgestaltung strahlt dank der überwiegenden Verwendung von Holz Wärme aus, und vermittelt gleichzeitig eine spielerische und zwanglose Atmosphäre.

Un ancien atelier de menuiserie se transforme en un objet de réhabilitation destiné à créer un logement pour des visiteurs ponctuels. La répartition concerne le rez-de-chaussée destiné au séjour-salle à manger, un étage supérieur qui comprend une chambre parentale, un bureau et une salle de bains et, une petite mezzanine multifonctionnelle, suspendue dans le vide sous le plafond incliné. Le design intérieur diffuse de la chaleur grâce à la prédominance du bois tout en transmettant un air ludique et désinvolte.

Un antiguo taller de carpintería se convierte en objeto de esta rehabilitación, destinada a crear un alojamiento para visitantes ocasionales. La distribución se estructura en una planta baja destinada a estar-comedor, una planta superior que alberga el dormitorio principal, estudio y baño, y un pequeño altillo multifuncional, suspendido en el espacio bajo la cubierta inclinada. El diseño interior desprende calidez gracias al uso predominante de la madera, y a la vez transmite un aire lúdico y desenfadado.

174

SMALL TOWN HOUSE

Studiomama

LOCATION London, Great Britain AREA 35 m² / 367 sq ft PHOTOS © Ben Anders

The master bedroom, which is designed as a wooden "pod" and looks like a separate piece of furniture, offsets the height of the open space above.

Der Raum des großen Schlafzimmers ist als eine Art „Schote" konzipiert, die aus Holz gefertigt und wie ein unabhängiges Teil der Einrichtung betrachtet wird, um der großen Höhe des freien Raumes im ersten Stock entgegenzuwirken.

La pièce de la chambre parentale est conçue comme une « gaine » construite en bois et considérée comme une pièce indépendante du mobilier afin de contraster la hauteur sous plafond de l'espace libre du premier étage.

La pieza del dormitorio principal se concibe a modo de "vaina", construida en madera y tratada como una pieza autónoma del mobiliario, para contrarrestar la gran altura del espacio libre de la primera planta.

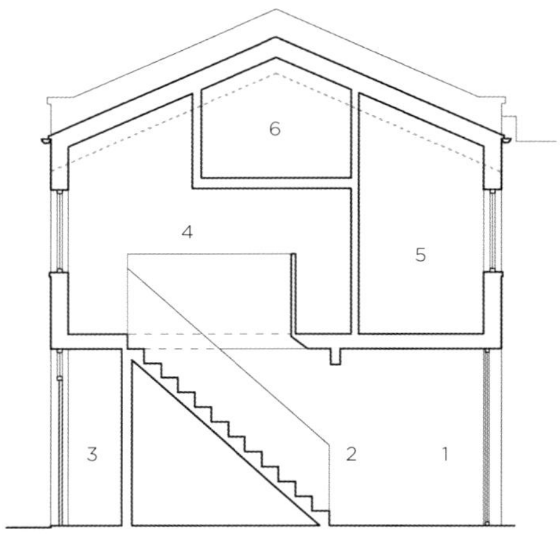

Section A-A

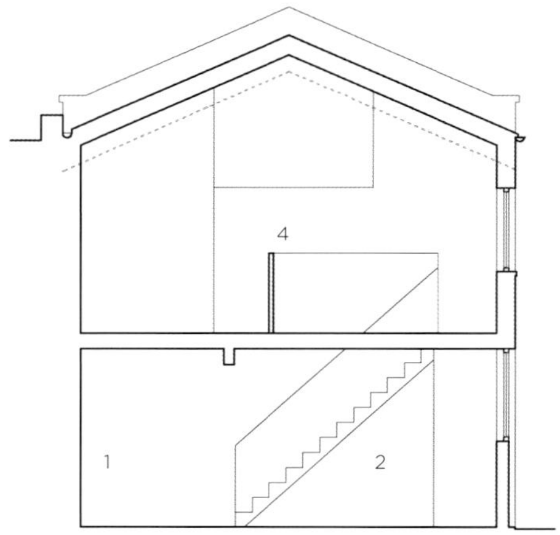

Section B-B

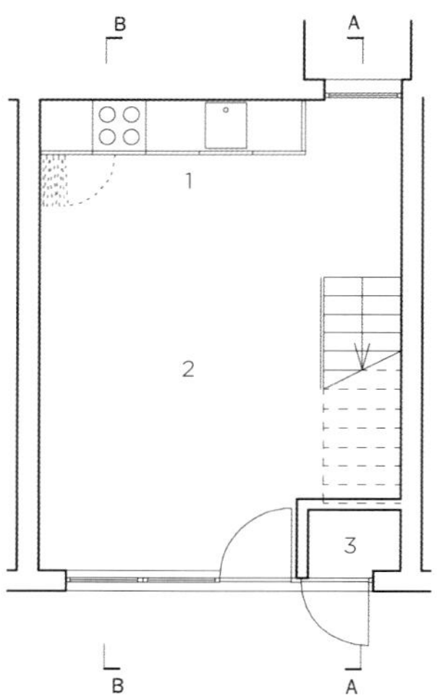

Ground floor plan

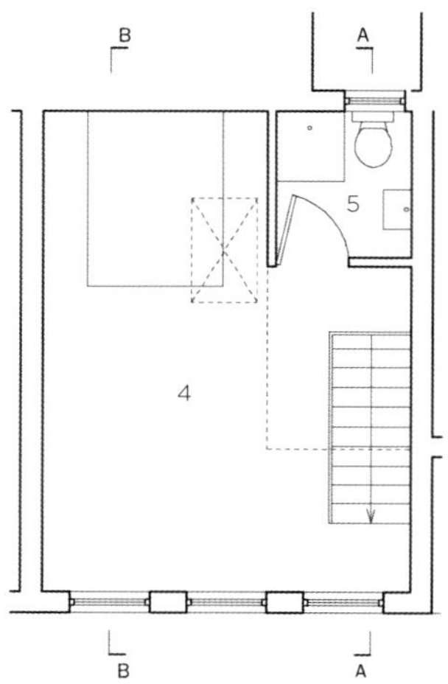

First floor plan

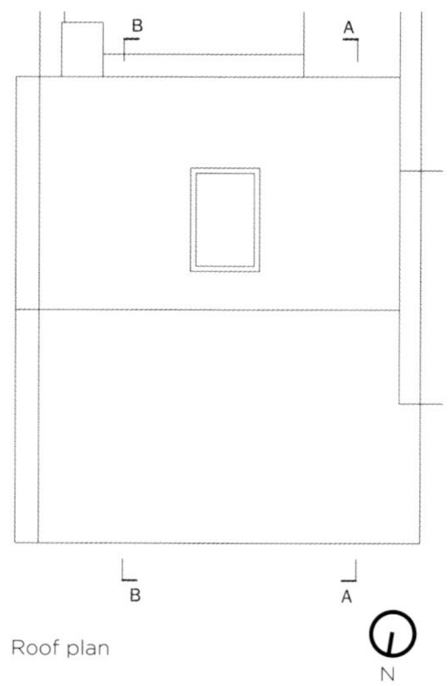

Roof plan

1. Kitchen
2. Living room
3. Bin store
4. Bedroom
5. Bathroom
6. Storage

A steep metal staircase with wooden steps leads to the loft located under the sloping roof; this can be used as bedroom or storage space.

Eine steile Metalltreppe mit Holzstufen führt zum Zwischengeschoss hinauf, das unter der Dachschräge liegt und bei Bedarf als Schlafzimmer oder Stauraum genutzt werden kann.

Un escalier raide à la structure métallique avec des marches en bois mène à la mezzanine sous-plafond incliné, qui peut servir de chambre occasionnelle ou d'espace de rangement.

Una empinada escalera de estructura metálica y peldaños de madera conduce al altillo situado bajo la cubierta inclinada, que puede ser utilizado como eventual dormitorio o como espacio de almacenamiento.

A large wooden prism, which appears to be just one more piece of furniture, rises up as an extension of the flooring, and presides over the space in this apartment. The bathroom is tucked inside it, and the sleeping place, accessed by an origami-like set of stairs, is up on top. The kitchen, the storage spaces, and a large floor-to ceiling bookcase connecting the two habitable levels, are positioned all around the perimeter, including the space under the windows.

Ein großes Holzprisma, das als ein weiteres Element in die Wohnungseinrichtung eingebunden ist und als Verlängerung des Bodenbelags dient, thront über dem Raum dieser Wohnung. Im Inneren des Prismas ist das Bad untergebracht, und darauf befindet sich das Schlafzimmer, in das man über eine Treppe im Origami-Look gelangt. Das Ausmaß der Wohnung, einschließlich der Bereiche, die unter den Fenstern liegen, konzentriert die Küche, die Stauräume und große Bücherregale, die sich vom Boden bis zur Decke erstrecken und beide Wohnebenen verbindet.

Une grande perspective en bois intégrée comme une pièce supplémentaire du mobilier en prolongement du mur, préside l'espace de cet appartement. À l'intérieur, la salle de bains au-dessus de laquelle se trouve la chambre, est accessible par un escalier en forme d'origami. Le périmètre de l'appartement, avec les espaces situés sous les fenêtres, comprend la cuisine, les espaces de rangement et une grande bibliothèque du sol au plafond qui relie les deux niveaux habitables.

Un gran prisma de madera integrado como una pieza más del mobiliario y que surge como prolongación del pavimento, preside el espacio que conforma esta vivienda. Su interior alberga el baño, y sobre él se sitúa el dormitorio, al que se accede por una escalera con aspecto de pieza de origami. El perímetro de la casa, incluidas las zonas situadas bajo las ventanas, concentra la cocina, los espacios de almacenamiento y una gran librería desarrollada de suelo a techo, que conecta los dos niveles habitables.

180

SMALL APARTMENT IN MOSCOW

Nowadays

LOCATION **Moscow, Russia** AREA **32 m² / 344 sq ft** PHOTOS **© Ilya Ivanov**

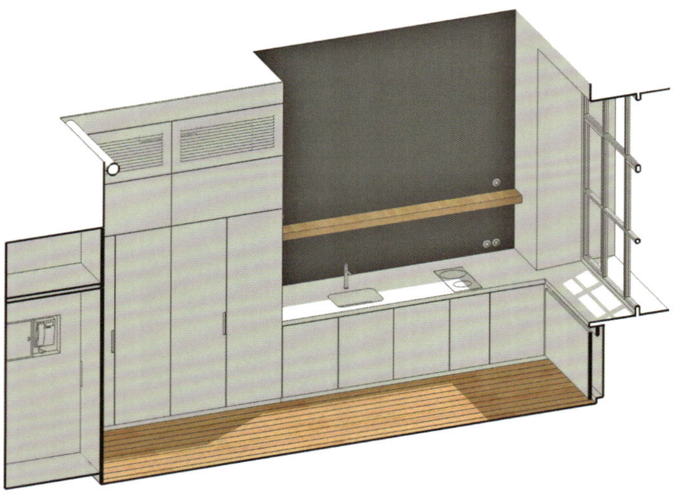

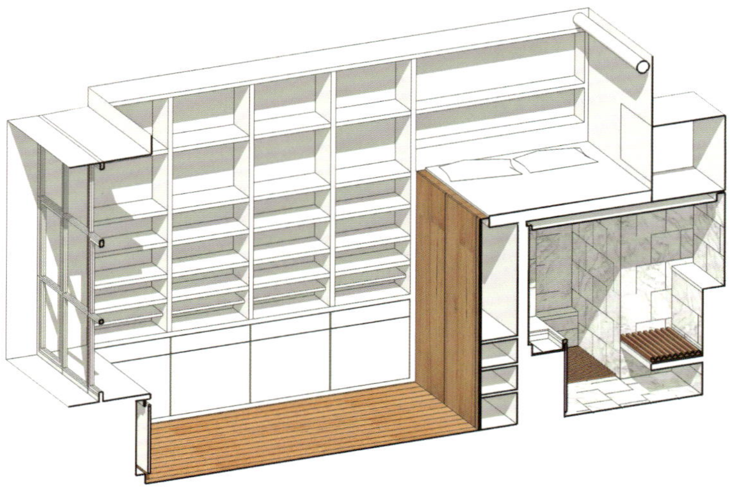

Axonometric sections

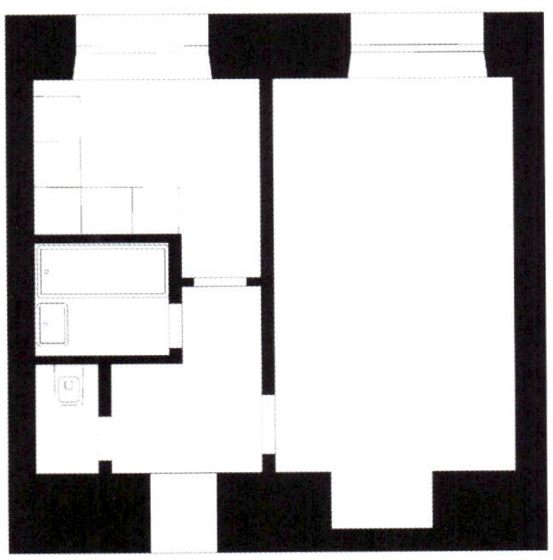

Existing plan

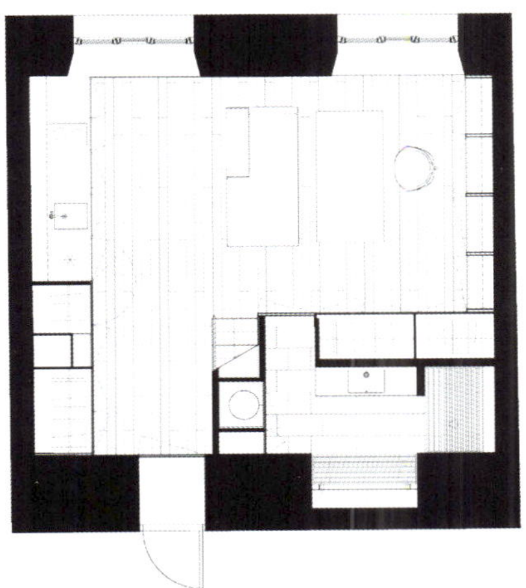

Floor plan

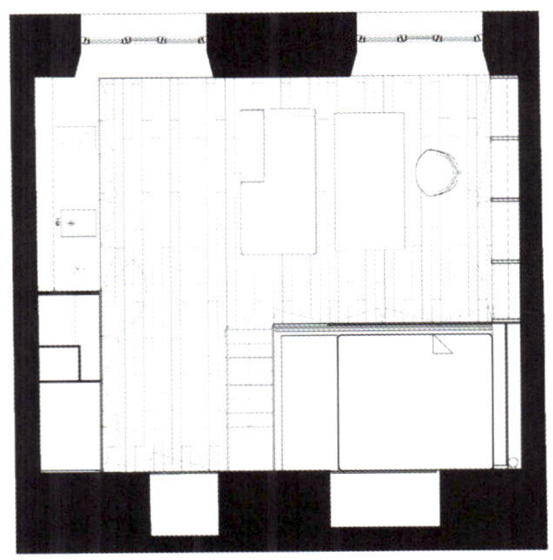

Mezzanine

Like the main room, the bathroom features an elegant combination of timber set off against the color white. The judicious placement of the fixtures makes the interior seem larger than it actually is.

Die Gestaltung des Bades verwendet die gleiche elegante Kombination aus Holz und der Farbe Weiß wie der Hauptraum. Die intelligente Ausrichtung seiner Elemente trägt dazu bei, dass der Innenraum größer wirkt, als er tatsächlich ist.

Le design de la salle de bains reprend la même combinaison élégante en bois et de couleur blanche que celle de la pièce principale. L'organisation intelligente de ses pièces rend l'intérieur plus grand que ce qu'il en paraît.

El diseño del baño utiliza la misma elegante combinación de madera y color blanco que la estancia principal. La inteligente organización de sus piezas hace que el interior se perciba más grande de lo que realmente es.

The layout of this lightly-used apartment brings the functional areas together into one third of the available surface, situated in a band running lengthwise along one side, which also holds the sleeping space. This creates a spacious living-dining area, (except for the bathroom), which, since there are no walls, can use glass dividers to remain open to everything else.

Die Strategie, die zur Neuaufteilung dieser Wohnung zur gelegentlichen Nutzung eingesetzt wird, konzentriert die technischen Bereiche auf ein Drittel der vorhandenen Fläche, die einen Längsstreifensäumen, der auch den als Schlafzimmer gedachten Bereich umfasst. Dadurch entsteht ein geräumiger Wohn-Essbereich, zu dem sich alle Bereiche der Wohnung hin öffnen, mit Ausnahme der Toilette, dank der Abwesenheit von Wänden oder des Vorhandenseins von trennenden Glaspaneelen.

La stratégie utilisée dans la nouvelle répartition de cet appartement à usage occasionnel se focalise sur les zones techniques d'un tiers de la surface disponible, situées le long d'une frange longitudinale qui comprend aussi un espace réservé à la chambre. On crée ainsi un espace séjour-salle à manger qui donne sur tous les autres espaces de l'appartement, excepté les toilettes, grâce à l'absence de cloisons ou à la présence de panneaux séparateurs en verre.

La estrategia utilizada en la redistribución de este apartamento de uso ocasional concentra las zonas técnicas en un tercio de la superficie disponible, situadas a lo largo de una franja longitudinal que contiene también la zona destinada a dormitorio. De esta manera se crea un amplio espacio de estar-comedor hacia el que se abren todos los ámbitos de la casa, a excepción de la pieza del aseo, gracias a la ausencia de cerramientos o a la existencia de paneles separadores de vidrio.

184

GENEVE FLAT

FREAKS Architects

LOCATION Geneva, Switzerland AREA 35 m² / 377 sq ft PHOTOS © David Foessel

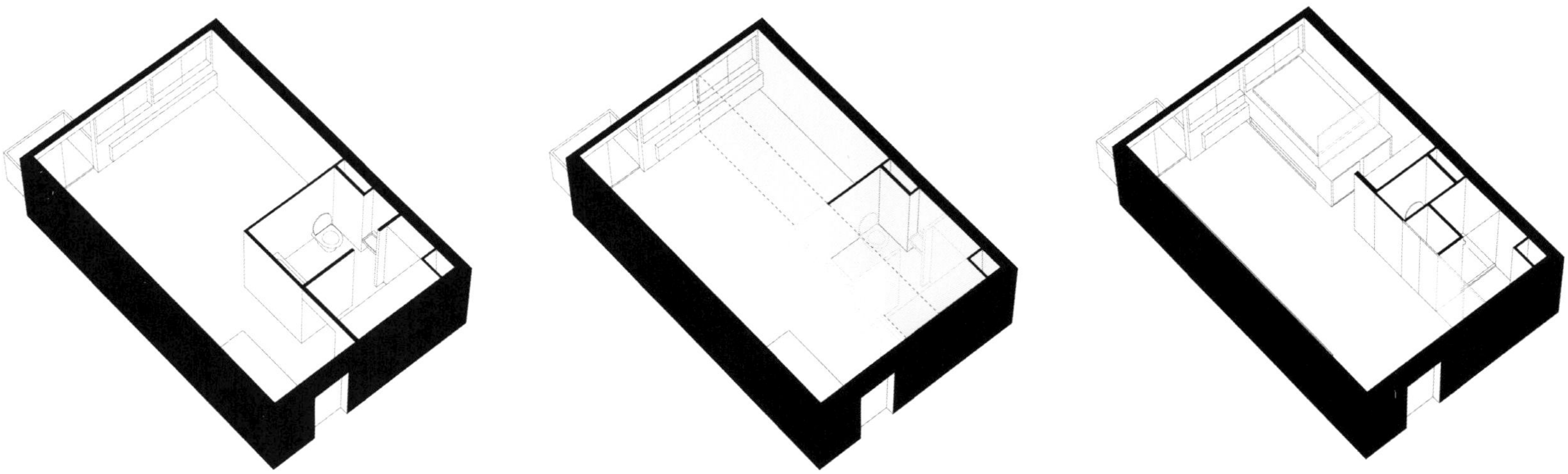

Axonometric view

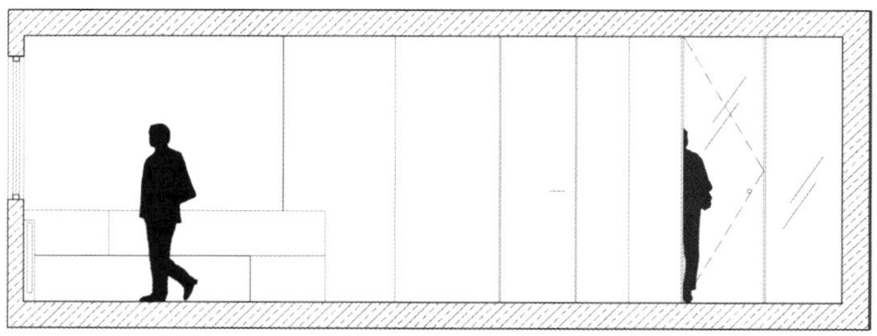

Section

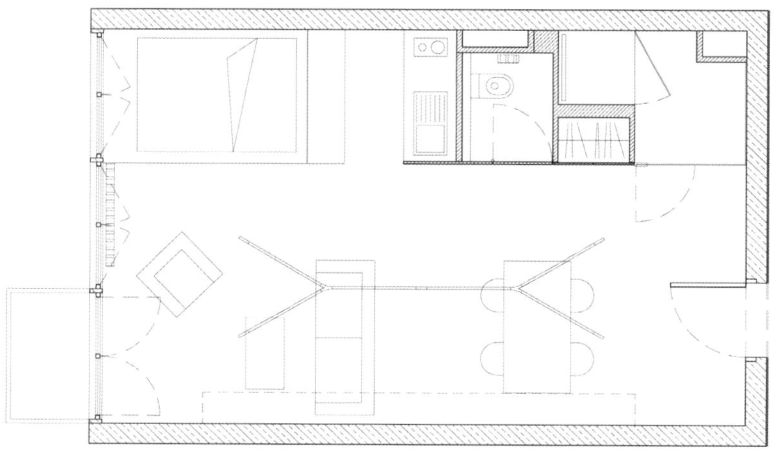

Floor plan

0 1 2m N

The one continuous space has a minimalist look, with only the dark flooring serving as a contrast to the dominant white tones of the walls and furniture.

Die Wohnung bildet einen durchgehenden Raum mit minimalistischem Ambiente, in dem nur der dunkle Bodenbelag als Kontrapunkt zu den an allen Wandflächen und bei den Möbeln vorherrschenden Weißtönen fungiert.

Le logement comprend un espace continu et conçu sur un air minimaliste dans lequel seul le revêtement de couleur sombre contraste avec les tons blancs dominants de tous les murs et du mobilier.

La vivienda constituye un espacio continuo y de aire minimalista, en el que solamente el pavimento de color oscuro actúa como contrapunto a los tonos blancos dominantes en todos los paramentos y en el mobiliario.

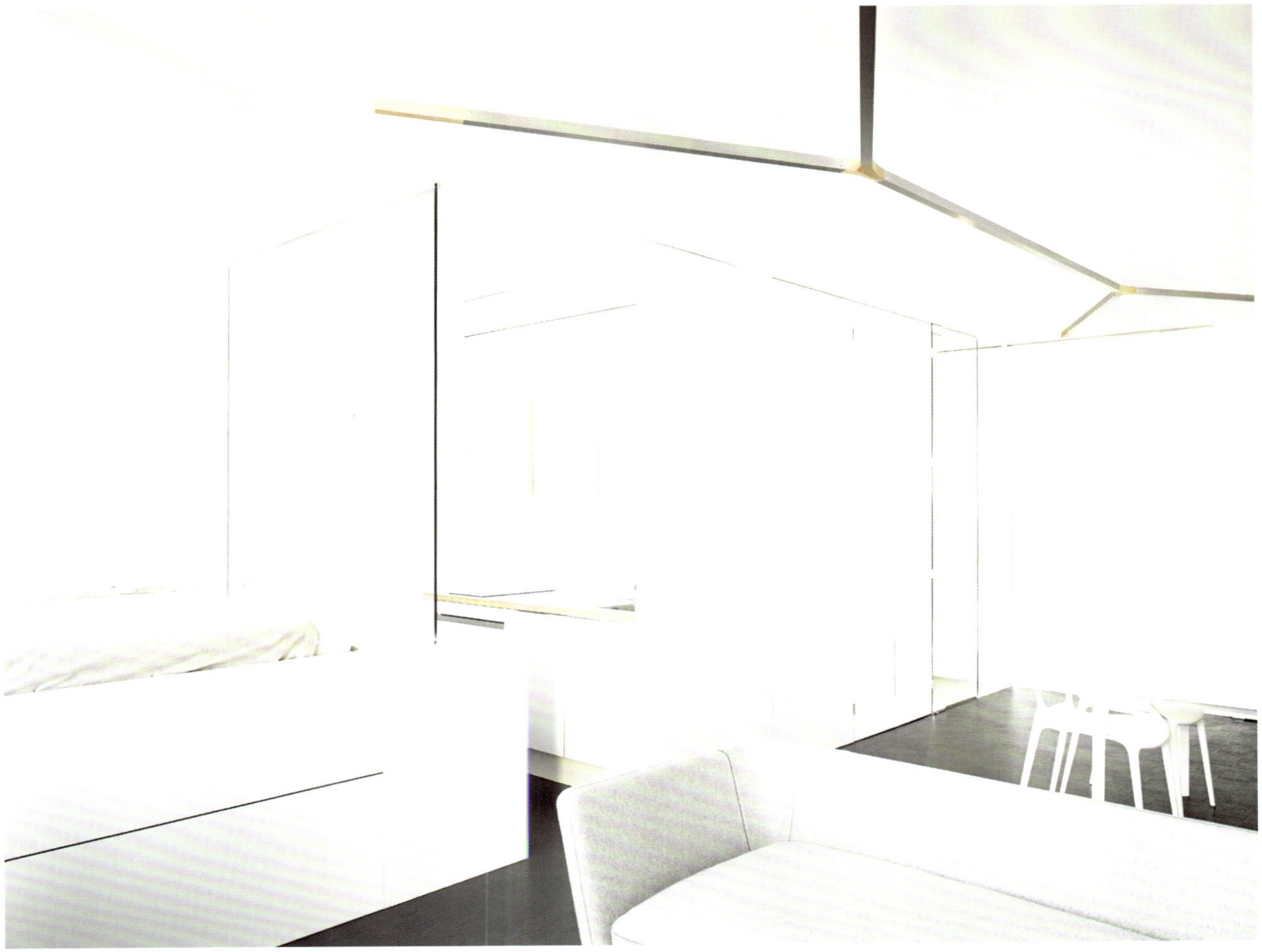

The transformation of this attic in a traditional Victorian building eliminates the existing interior partitions and accesses the space under the roof. This creates an open plan double-height home, also used as a workshop. A loft, open to the lower floor becomes the bedroom. Within the abstract and functional design of the project, the neutral-colored surfaces become canvases readied for a lifestyle in constant change.

Die Umwandlung dieses Dachgeschosses, das in einem traditionellen Gebäude im viktorianischen Stil liegt, entfernt die vorhandenen Trennwände im Inneren und bezieht den Raum, der unter dem Dach liegt, mit ein. Dadurch entsteht ein Wohnraum mit einem einzigen Bereich auf doppelter Höhe, der auch als Arbeitszimmer dient, in dem ein zur unteren Ebene offenes Zwischengeschoss das Schlafzimmer beherbergt. Innerhalb der abstrakten und funktionellen Konzeption des Projektes stellen die Flächen in neutralen Farbtönen eine Art Leinwände dar, die ein Leben im ständigen Wandel täglich neu bemalt.

La transformation de cet appartement situé au dernier étage d'un édifice traditionnel victorien a retiré les cloisons intérieures existantes pour en faire un espace sous-plafond. On créé ainsi un appartement d'une seule ambiance à double hauteur qui sert également d'atelier dans lequel se trouve une mezzanine ouverte sur l'étage inférieur avec chambre. Dans le cadre du design abstrait et fonctionnel du projet, les surfaces sur tons neutres représentent des pans construits pour une vie en constant changement.

La transformación de este ático situado en un tradicional edificio de estilo victoriano elimina las particiones interiores existentes e incorpora el espacio situado bajo cubierta. Se crea así una vivienda de un único ambiente a doble altura, también utilizado como taller, en el que un altillo abierto hacia la planta inferior alberga el dormitorio. Dentro de la concepción abstracta y funcional del proyecto, las superficies de tonos neutros representan lienzos preparados para una vida en constante cambio.

188

LIVING WORKSHOP

Ullmayersylvester architects Ltd.

LOCATION **London, Great Britain** AREA **53,5 m² / 575 sq ft** PHOTOS **© Kilian O'Sullivan**

THE HARE WITH AMBER EYES
inside

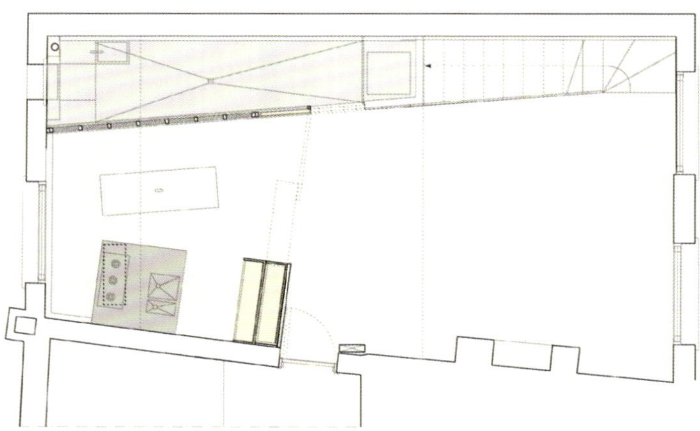

Floor plan

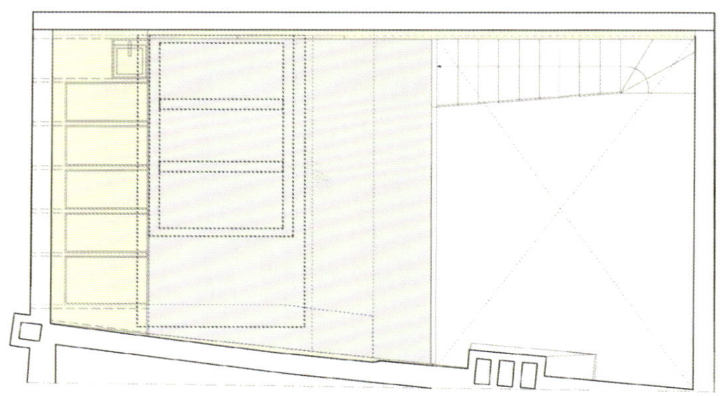

Mezzanine

A slanting line outlines the volume that contains the bathroom, thus setting off the funnel-shaped geometry of the original floor and opening up the spaces so that they appear larger.

Die das Volumen definierende geneigte Leitlinie, welche die das Bad umfasst und die Treppe einbindet, spielt mit der Geometrie in Form eines Trichters der ursprünglichen Ebene, um die Räume zu öffnen, damit sie größer wirken.

La directrice inclinée qui détermine le volume de la salle de bains et intègre l'escalier, joue avec la géométrie en forme d'entonnoir de l'étage d'origine pour ouvrir des espaces de sorte à paraître plus grands.

La directriz inclinada que define el volumen que contiene el baño y e integra la escalera, juega con la geometría en forma de embudo de la planta original para abrir los espacios, de manera que parezcan más grandes.

Here the layout of a semi-detached house is modified by relocating the kitchen and bath areas to a more central position, and moving the living room to the rear, thus opening it up to the garden. Positioning the service core on a lower level than the other rooms made it possible to create a loft. This, open to the main room and lit by a skylight, holds a study and an extra bedroom.

Dieses Projekt verändert die Raumaufteilung einer Doppelhaushälfte durch die Neuanordnung der Bereiche Küche und Bad an einer zentraleren Position innerhalb der Ebene, sowie des Wohnzimmers, das in den hinteren Teil des Hauses verlagert wird, der zum Garten hin offen ist. Die Positionierung der Kernleistungen auf einer niedrigeren Ebene hinsichtlich der übrigen Wohnräume ermöglicht die Platzierung eines Zwischengeschosses, das mit dem Wohnzimmer verknüpft ist. Durch ein Dachfenster erhält das Zwischengeschoss Tageslicht und dient bei Bedarf ein Arbeitszimmer und ein Schlafzimmer.

Ce projet modifie la répartition d'une maison mitoyenne en réaménageant les espaces cuisine et salle de bains dans une position plus centrale à l'étage, ainsi que le séjour, déplacé à l'arrière de la maison et ouvert sur le jardin. L'emplacement du cœur des services à une cote inférieure par rapport aux autres pièces permet de créer une mezzanine, connectée au séjour et éclairée grâce à une ouverture zénithale qui abrite un bureau et une chambre d'appoint.

Este proyecto modifica la distribución de una vivienda pareada mediante la reubicación de las zonas de cocina y de baño a una posición más central dentro de la planta, así como de la sala de estar, trasladada a la parte posterior de la casa y abierta hacia el jardín. La colocación del núcleo de servicios a una cota inferior respecto del resto de estancias permite ubicar un altillo, vinculado a la sala de estar e iluminado mediante una abertura cenital, que alberga un estudio y un dormitorio ocasional.

194

TAMARAMA SEMI-D

David Langston-Jones

LOCATION **Sydney, Australia** AREA **72 m² / 775 sq ft** PHOTOS **© Anthony Browell**

The sculptural stairway to the loft sits next to the module containing the kitchen appliances. The bathroom flooring extends out to the utility area, which is on the same level.

Die skulpturartige Treppe, die auf die Zwischengeschossebene hinaufführtsteht neben dem Möbelstück, das die Kücheneinrichtung einbindet. Der Bodenbelag im Bad erstreckt sich zum Bereich des Flurs hin, der sich auf der gleichen Ebene befindet.

L'escalier sculptural d'accès à la mezzanine se trouve à proximité du meuble des éléments de cuisine. Le revêtement de la salle de bains s'étend vers la zone de dégagement située à la même cote.

La escultural escalera de acceso al nivel del altillo se sitúa junto al mueble que integra el equipo de cocina. El pavimento del baño se extiende hacia la zona del distribuidor situada a la misma cota de nivel.

Between the two opaque horizontal bands that hold the fireplace and the television, is a window, which frames the view of the garden. The sheet metal finishes used in several areas of the house give unity to the whole.

Ein Fenster, das sich zwischen zwei undurchlässigen Streifen befindet, in denen Kamin und Fernseher untergebracht ist, rahmt den Blick Richtung Garten ein. Die Oberflächen aus Metallplatten, die in den verschiedenen Bereichen des Hauses zum Einsatz kommen, geben dem Ganzen eine Einheit.

Une fenêtre située entre deux bandes opaques qui accueillent la cheminée et la télévision, offre une vue sur le jardin. Les finitions en planche métallique, utilisées dans différentes parties de la maison procurent une uniformité à l'ensemble.

Una ventana situada entre dos franjas opacas, que albergan la chimenea y la televisión, enmarca la vista hacia el jardín. Los acabados en plancha metálica utilizados en diferentes zonas de la casa dan unidad al conjunto.

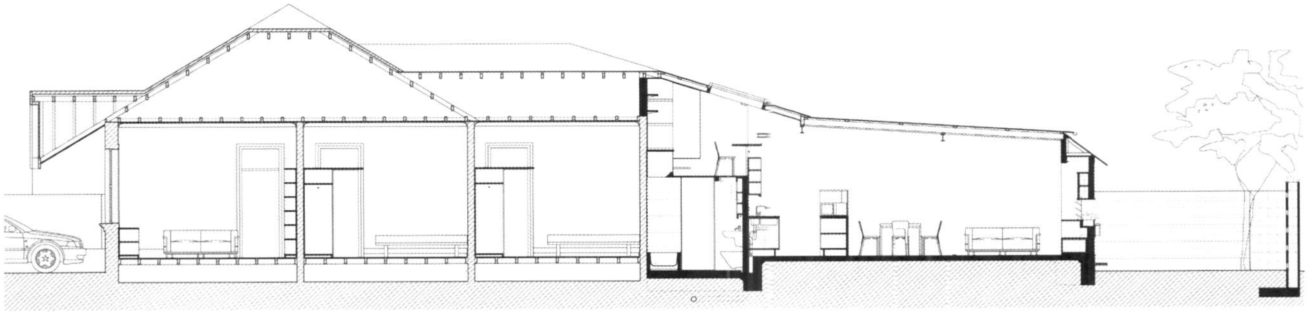

Longitudinal section

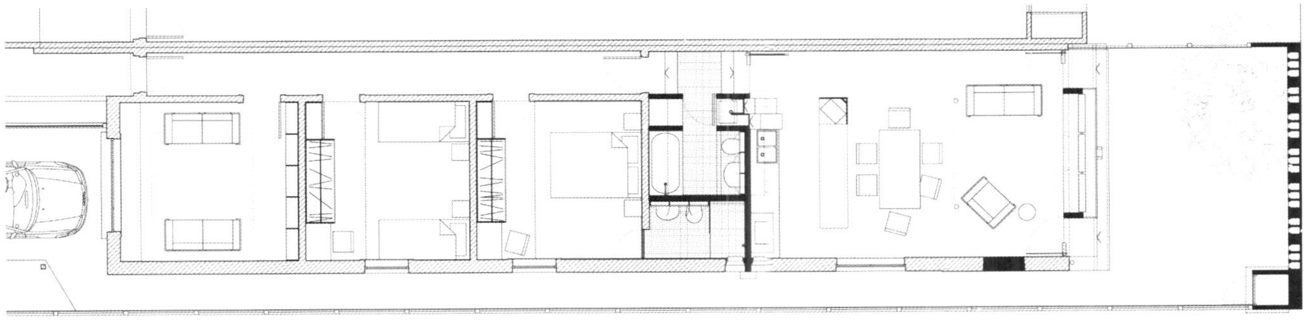

Ground floor plan

0 1 2m

N

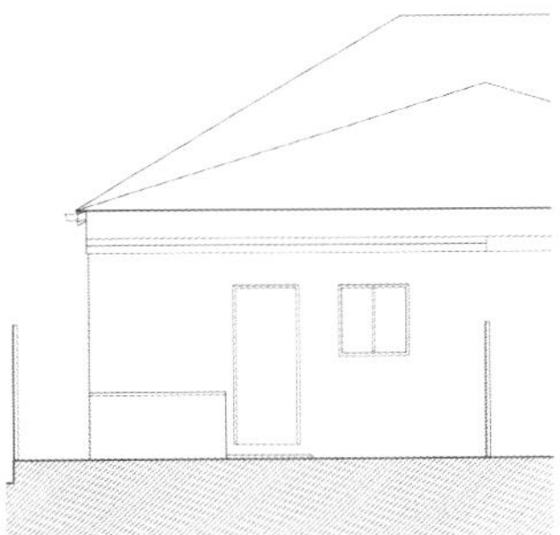

Existing east elevation to garden

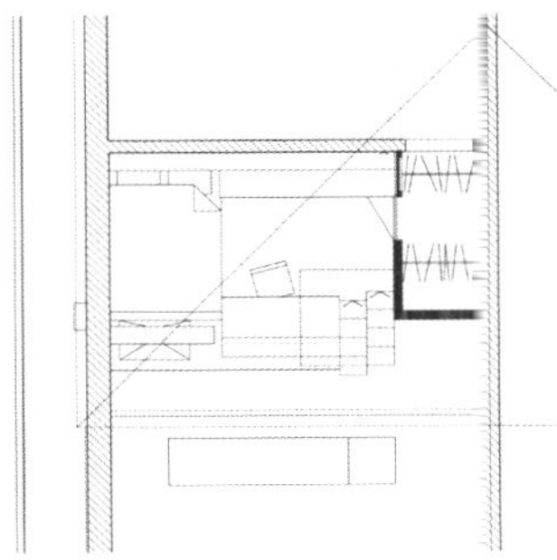

As-built mezzanine plan

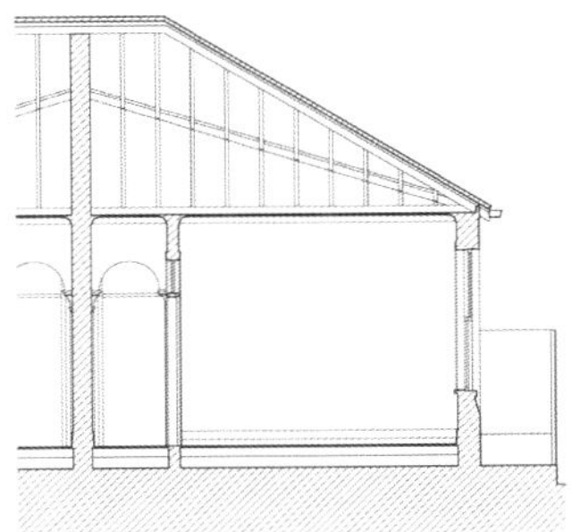

As-built section through third bedroom

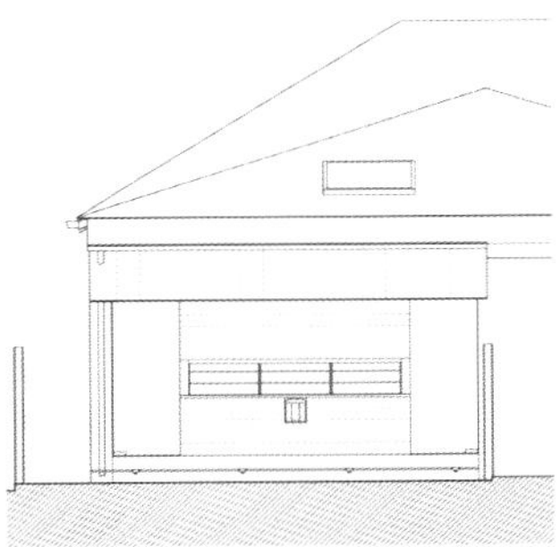

As-built east elevation to garden

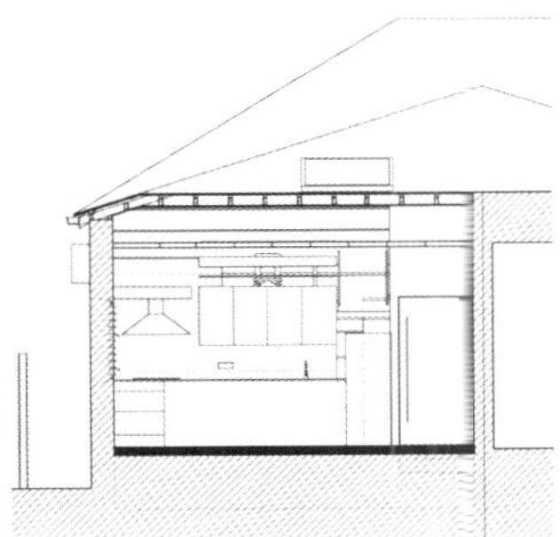

As-built section through living area

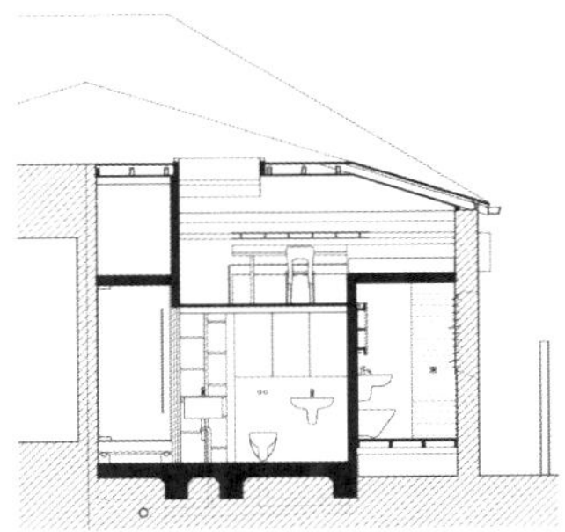

As-built section through
bathrooms & mezzanine

0 1 2m

The owners of this typical apartment in the "Eixample" zone of Barcelona wished to keep the bedrooms within existing walls, and devote the rest of the space to a living room, kitchen, dining room, and study. The renovation keeps the two original bedrooms and then creates one continuous space that includes the remaining required functions. The kitchen is conceived as a free-standing piece of furniture with an overhead loft that can be used as a study or guest room.

Der Ausgangspunkt dieses Umbaus einer typischen Wohnung im Eixample-Viertel Barcelonas war der Wille der Kunden, die beiden bestehenden Räume Richtung Fassade beizubehalten und den restlichen Raum als Wohnzimmer, Küche, Esszimmer und Arbeitszimmer zu nutzen. Der Eingriff lässt die beiden Zimmer unverändert, wodurch ein durchgehender Raum entsteht, der die restlichen der erforderlichen Funktionen abdeckt und in dem die Küche als freistehendes Möbelstück behandelt wird, auf dem sich ein Zwischengeschoss befindet, das als Arbeitszimmer oder Gästezimmer benutzt werden kann.

Le point de départ de ces travaux d'un appartement typique de l'Eixample barcelonais fut la volonté des clients de conserver les deux chambres au niveau de la façade existante et réserver le reste de l'espace au salon, la cuisine, la salle à manger et le bureau. L'intervention conserve les deux chambres et créé un espace continu qui comprend les autres fonctions exigées et dans lequel la cuisine est comme un meuble dépourvu, au-dessus de laquelle se trouve une mezzanine qui peut servir de bureau ou de chambre d'amis.

El punto de partida de esta reforma de un típico piso del Eixample barcelonés fue la voluntad de los clientes de mantener las dos habitaciones en fachada existentes y destinar el resto del espacio a salón, cocina, comedor y estudio. La intervención conserva las dos habitaciones y genera un espacio continuo que contiene el resto de funciones requeridas y en el que la cocina se trata como un mueble exento, sobre el cual se sitúa un altillo que puede utilizarse como estudio o como cuarto de invitados.

200

DWELLING IN THE EIXAMPLE

Anna & Eugeni Bach

LOCATION Barcelona, Spain AREA 70 m² / 753 sq ft PHOTOS © Eugeni Bach

Because of the significant height of the apartment, there can be a loft over the independent kitchen module. The wooden roof beams extend above it, thereby giving continuity to the main space.

Dank der großen Raumhöhe der Wohnung lässt sich auf dem freistehenden Modul der Küche ein Zwischengeschoss platzieren, über dem sich die Decke mit Holzbalken erstreckt, die dem Hauptbereich Kontinuität verleiht.

La hauteur sous plafond du logement permet d'installer une mezzanine sur le module indépendant de la cuisine, au-dessus duquel se trouvent des poutres en bois apparentes qui assurent la continuité de l'espace principal.

La gran altura libre de la vivienda permite situar un altillo sobre el módulo independiente de la cocina, por encima del cual se extiende el techo de vigas de madera que da continuidad al ámbito principal.

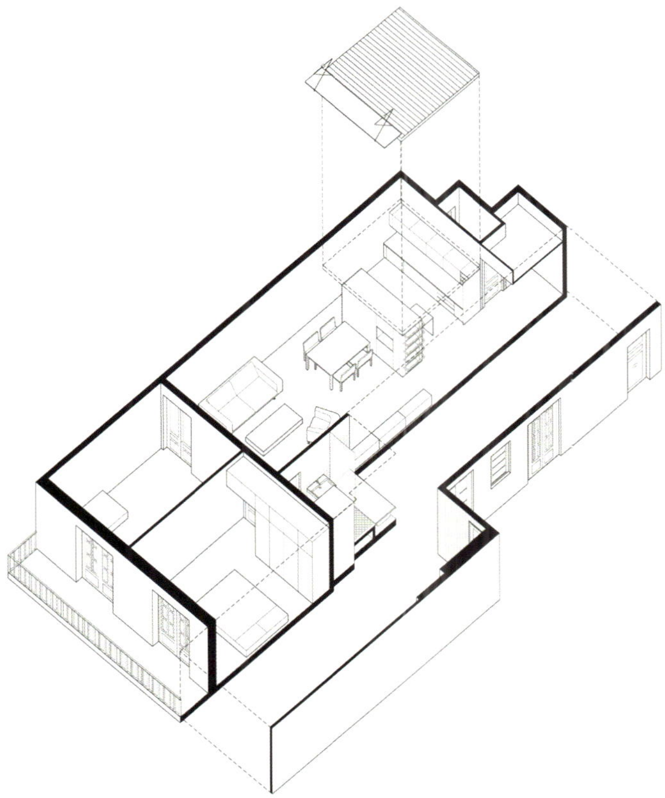

Axonometric view

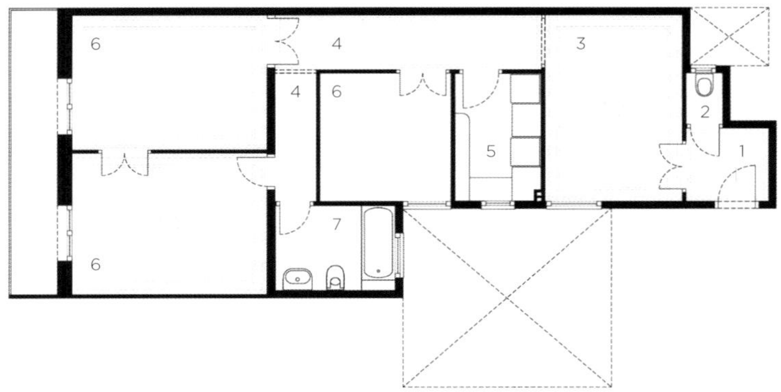

1. Hall
2. Toilet
3. Dining
4. Corridor
5. Kitchen
6. Bedroom
7. Bathroom

Original floor plan

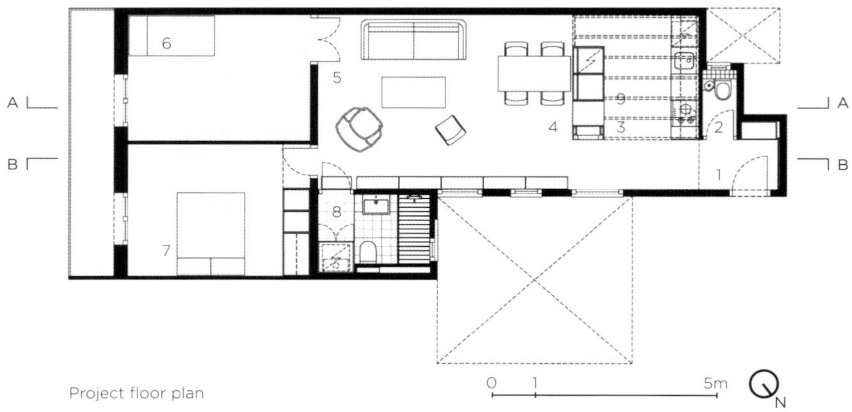

1. Hall
2. Toilet
3. Kitchen
4. Dining
5. Living
6. Bedroom
7. Main Bedroom
8. Bathroom
9. Studio-Mezzanine

Project floor plan

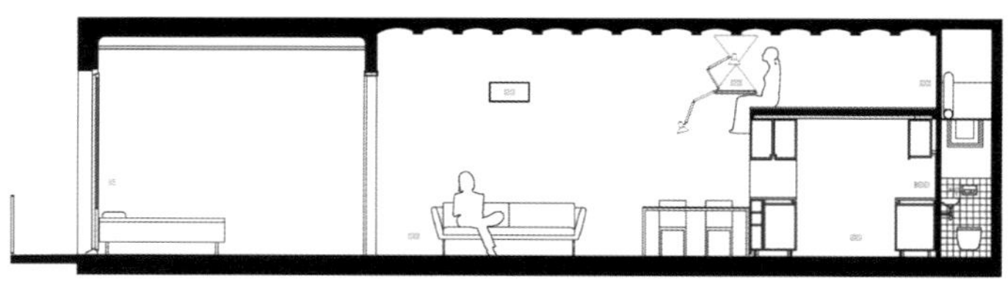

Section A

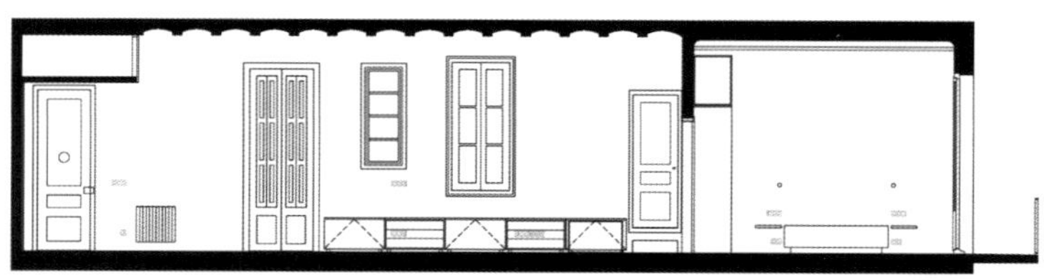

Section B

The renovation elevates the original bathroom, which is now accessed by two steps. This allows a tub and a shower to be installed in the same position, and creates storage space under the floor.

Die Renovierung verwandelt das ursprüngliche Bad in ein erhöhtes Zimmer mit zwei Zugangsstufen, wodurch sich Badewanne und Dusche in der gleichen Stelle platzieren lassen und unter dem Boden Stauraum schaffen.

Les travaux ont transformé la salle de bains initiale en une pièce suré evée avec deux marches pour y accéder, ce qui permet de placer une baignoire et une douche au même niveau et créer ainsi un espace de rangement en dessous.

La reforma convierte el baño original en una pieza elevada, con dos escalones en su acceso que permiten situar una bañera y una ducha en la misma posición y que crean un espacio de almacenamiento bajo su suelo.

This project was a renovation of the upper floor of a former granary, previously used as a stable, then a guest house, and now being reconverted into a home. Uncovering and refurbishing the wooden beams supporting the sloping roof creates a very high interior space. A main element of the layout is an independent unit containing the kitchen and the bathroom. The rest of the floor space is taken up by a living area, two bedrooms, and a loft.

Dieses Projekt zeigt den Umbau der oberen Etage einer alten Scheune, die einst als Stall und Gästehaus genutzt wurde und nun wieder in Wohnraum umgewandelt wird. Bei diesem Eingriff werden die Holzträgerbalken der Dachschräge saniert, um einen sehr hohen Raum zu erzeugen. Das Hauptelement der Raumaufteilung bildet ein unabhängiges Volumen, das Küche und Bad umfasst. Wohnbereich, zwei Schlafzimmer und ein Zwischengeschoss belegen die übrige Grundfläche.

Ce projet prévoit la rénovation de l'étage supérieur d'une ancienne grange, utilisée autrefois comme étable et maison d'invités et, aujourd'hui transformée en maison. L'intervention permet de mettre en relief et de restaurer les poutres structurelles en bois du toit incliné afin de conférer un espace sous haut plafond. Le principal élément de la répartition est un volume indépendant qui comprend la cuisine et la salle de bains. Le reste de l'étage est composé d'un séjour, de deux chambres et d'une mezzanine.

Este proyecto contempla la reforma de la planta superior de un antiguo granero, anteriormente utilizado como establo y como casa de invitados, y ahora reconvertido en vivienda. La intervención descubre y rehabilita las vigas de madera estructural del techo inclinado para generar un espacio de gran altura. El principal elemento de la distribución lo constituye un volumen independiente que contiene la cocina y el baño. El resto de la planta se compone de una zona de estar, dos dormitorios y un altillo.

208

HISTORIC BARN

Richardson Architects

LOCATION Marin County, USA AREA 93 m² / 1,000 sq ft PHOTOS © Jeff Zaruba

The design of the cube as an autonomous room provides the sloping wooden roofline with continuity, thereby contributing to the feeling of spaciousness that it shares with living/dining area.

Die Gestaltung des Würfelelements als unabhängiges Element verleiht der Holzdachschräge Kontinuität und trägt, genau wie der Wohn-Essbereich, dazu bei, das Gefühl von Geräumigkeit zu steigern.

La conception de l'élément cubique en tant que pièce indépendante va dans la continuité du toit incliné en bois contribuant ainsi à augmenter la sensation de grandeur de l'espace partagé avec le séjour-salle à manger.

El diseño del elemento cúbico como pieza autónoma da continuidad al techo inclinado de madera, contribuyendo a aumentar la sensación de amplitud del espacio que comparte con la zona de estar comedor.

The strategic position of the bedroom space is the key to the layout of this apartment. As the bed revolves, different room environments are created around it. This is because it is located at the center of one continuous space, and at right angles to its surroundings. When it is positioned to be open to the other rooms, the bedroom looks rather unusual, but it allows the scant sunlight to penetrate into the living room.

Der Aufbau dieser Wohnung beruht auf der strategischen Position des Schlafzimmers. Die verschiedenen Bereiche entstehen darum dank dessen Position im Zentrum eines durchgehenden Raumes und der Drehbewegung seiner Ebene im Hinblick auf die umgebende Senkrechte. Eine Konfiguration, die zu den übrigen Wohnräumen hin offen ist, verleiht dem Schlafzimmer einen außergewöhnlichen Charakter und lässt das wenige Sonnenlicht einfallen, das Richtung Wohnbereich in die Wohnstätte eindringt.

La composition de cet appartement repose sur la position stratégique de la chambre. Les différents espaces sont créés autour de celle-ci grâce à son emplacement au cœur d'un espace continu et au mouvement de rotation de son niveau par rapport à l'enveloppe orthogonale. Une configuration ouverte sur les autres pièces conférant ainsi à la chambre un caractère un peu habituel et en la transformant en un émetteur de faible lumière du soleil qui pénètre l'appartement pour se rendre dans le séjour.

La composición de este apartamento se fundamenta en la estratégica posición de la pieza del dormitorio. Los diferentes ámbitos se generan en torno a él gracias a su ubicación en el centro de un espacio continuo y al movimiento de rotación de su planta con respecto de la envolvente ortogonal. Una configuración abierta hacia el resto de las estancias confiere al dormitorio un carácter poco habitual y le convierte en transmisor de la escasa luz solar que penetra en la vivienda hacia la zona del estar.

212

PARLAMENT 29

Miel Arquitectos & Studio P10

LOCATION Barcelona, Spain AREA 48 m² / 517 sq ft PHOTOS © Mila Belyaeva

The sleeping space is designed as a sort of nest made of oak, elevated above floor level. There is a guest bed underneath it and an air conditioning unit above it.

Als „Nest" aus Eichenholz konzipiert, ist das Schlafzimmer über der Ebene des Bodens erhöht, unter dem sich ein Bett für Gäste verbirgt und über dem die Klimaanlage platziert wird.

La chambre est conçue comme un « nid » en chêne, surélevé par rapport au niveau du sol, sous lequel se cache un lit d'amis et sur lequel se trouve l'installation de la climatisation.

La pieza del dormitorio se concibe como un "nido" de madera de roble, elevado sobre el nivel del suelo, bajo el cual se esconde una cama para invitados y sobre el cual se sitúa la instalación de aire acondicionado.

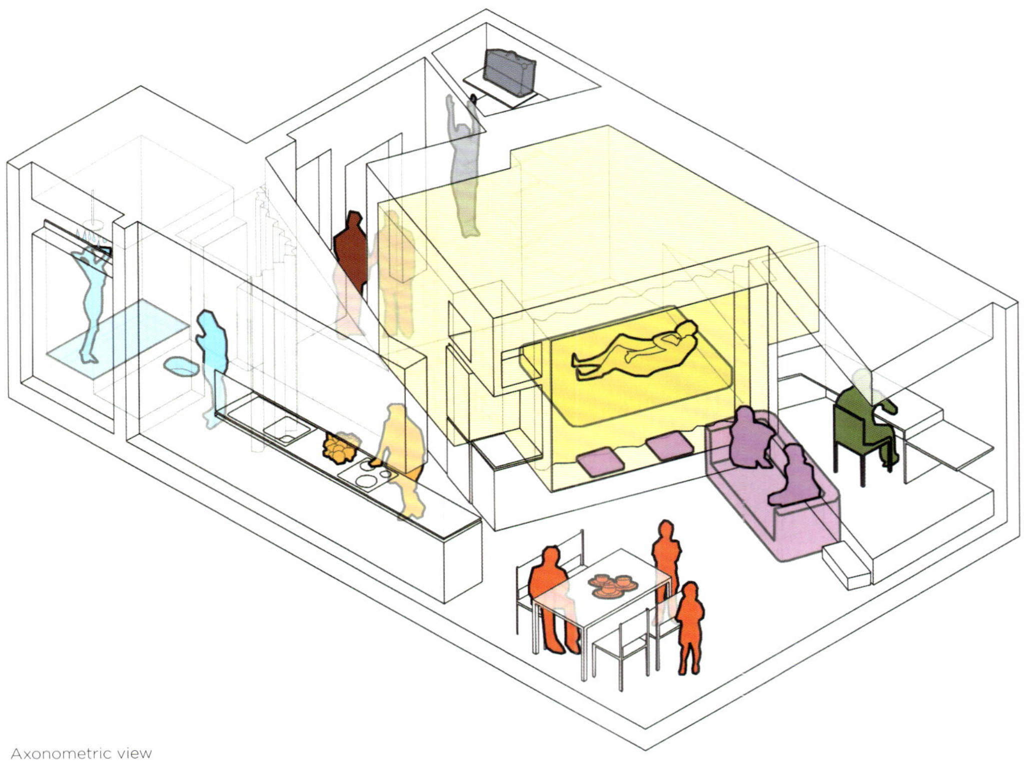

Axonometric view

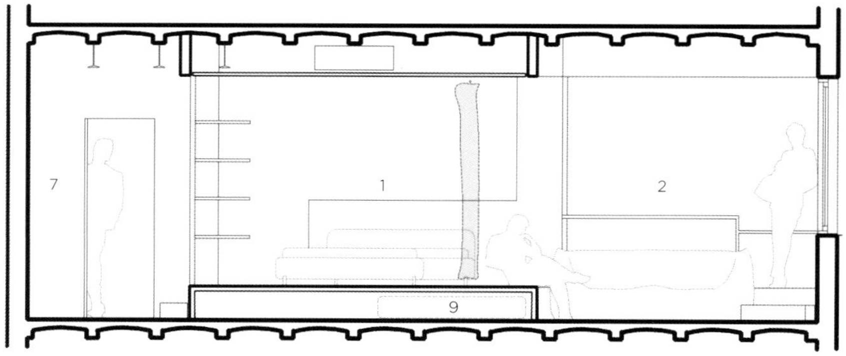

Longitudinal section

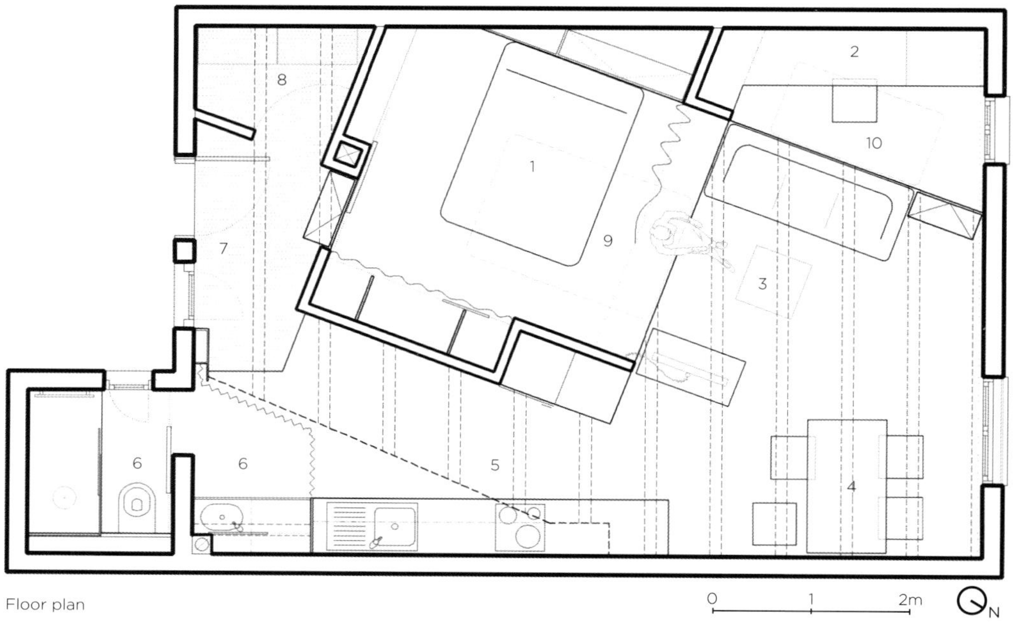

1. Bedroom
2. Studio
3. Living room
4. Dining room
5. Kitchen
6. Bathroom
7. Entry hall
8. Storage
9. Guest bed
10. Concealed storage

Floor plan

The black and white tiles in the bathroom and kitchen act as a poetic counterpoint to the overall design of the dwelling, which combines light wood tones and white walls that distribute the limited amount of sunlight.

Die weißen und schwarzen Fliesen in Bad und Küche werden zu einem poetischen Kontrapunkt zum Gesamtentwurf der Wohnstätte, die den Einsatz von Holz mit senkrechten weißen Wandflächen kombiniert, die das wenige Sonnenlicht verbreiten.

La faïence blanche et noire de la salle de bains et la cuisine deviennent un contraste poétique à la conception générale de l'appartement, qui combine l'utilisation du bois et les parements verticaux blancs qui diffusent les rares rayons du soleil.

Las baldosas blancas y negras del baño y la cocina devienen un contrapunto poético al diseño general de la vivienda, que combina el uso de la madera con paramentos verticales blancos que propagan la escasa luz del sol.

In the remodeling plan, this apartment is made up of two independent studios, each with a bathroom, that share a commonly accessed central area containing the kitchen and dining room. The idea is to balance the privacy of each studio against the requirements of the common space. The wall systems are designed to allow light to enter the central area, but they also provide the option to completely isolate each small abode.

Der Plan für den Umbau dieser Wohnung setzt sich aus zwei unabhängigen mit Bad ausgestatteten Studios zusammen, die sich den Eingangsbereich teilen, der im Zentrum der Ebene liegt, die Küche und Esszimmer umfasst. Das Projekt wirft das Thema der Balance zwischen der Privatsphäre in beiden Studios und den Anforderungen des Gemeinschaftsbereichs auf. Die Gestaltung des Wandsystems ermöglicht den Einfall von Tageslicht in den zentralen Bereich der Wohnung, bietet jedoch gleichzeitig die Möglichkeit, beide Bereiche vollständig zu isolieren.

Le programme de rénovation de cet appartement comprend deux studios indépendants équipés d'une salle de bains avec une partie commune, située au centre de l'étage avec cuisine et salle à manger. Le projet prévoit un équilibre entre les espaces privatifs de chaque studio et les besoins de l'espace commun ; la conception du système de cloisonnage permet à la lumière naturelle de pénétrer la partie centrale de l'étage, tout en offrant la possibilité d'isoler complètement chaque habitacle.

El programa de la reforma de este piso se compone de dos estudios independientes dotados de baño, que comparten una zona común de acceso situada en el centro de la planta, que contiene la cocina y el comedor. El proyecto plantea el tema del equilibrio entre las privacidades de cada estudio y las necesidades del espacio comunitario; el diseño del sistema de cerramientos permite que la luz natural llegue a la zona central del piso, pero a la vez da la opción de aislar completamente cada habitáculo.

218

SALVA 46

Miel Arquitectos & Studio P10

LOCATION **Barcelona, Spain** AREA **65 m² / 700 sq ft** PHOTOS **© Asier Rua**

A fixed shelving unit separates the entryway from the kitchen. It is set along the dividing line between the parquet industrial flooring and the original refurbished encaustic tiles.

Ein fest eingebauter Regalschrank trennt Zugangsbereich und Küche. Seine Leitlinie wird auf der Trennlinie zwischen dem Boden aus Industrieparkett und dem restaurierten Originalzementfliesenboden platziert.

Un meuble-étagère fixe sépare l'accès et la cuisine. Sa directrice se situe sur la ligne de division entre le sol du parquet industriel et la mosaïque hydraulique d'origine du sol récupérée.

Un mueble estantería fijo separa el ámbito de acceso y la cocina. Su directriz se sitúa sobre la línea divisoria entre el suelo de parquet industrial y el recuperado mosaico hidráulico original del piso.

NERUDA

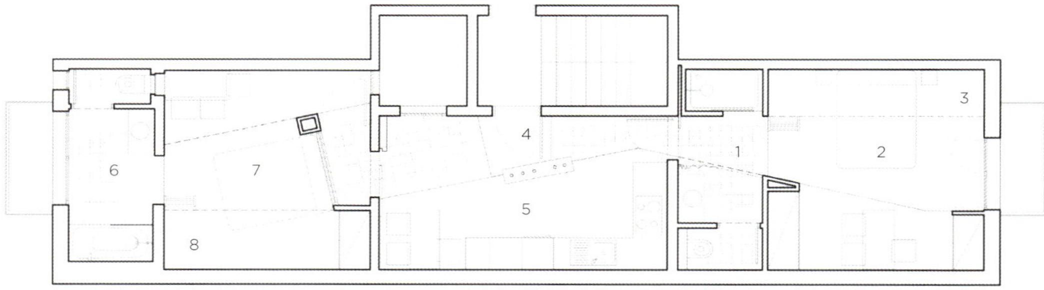

Floor plan

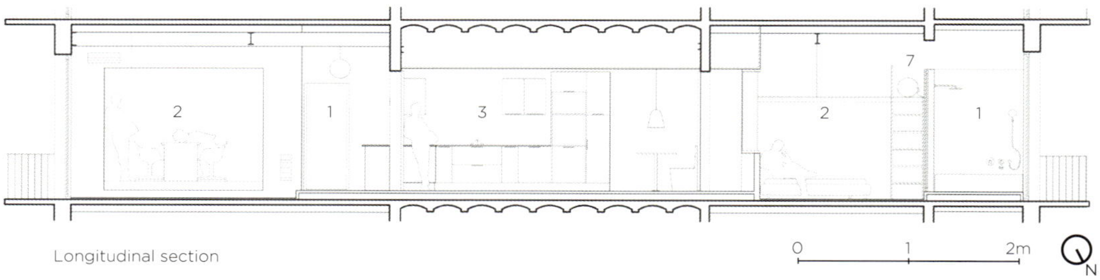

Longitudinal section

1. Bathroom 1
2. Study 1
3. Multifuctional space 1
4. Entrance
5. Dining room/Kitchen
6. Bathroom 2
7. Study 2
8. Multifunctional space 2

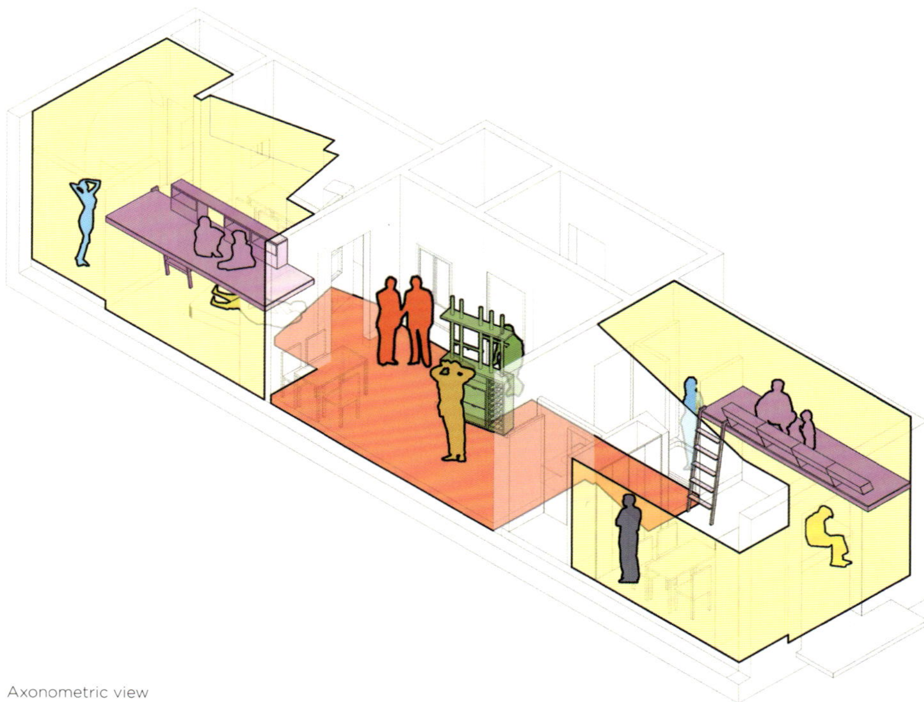
Axonometric view

The 3.40-meter ceiling height allows space for a small multipurpose loft over the beds in each studio. Their banisters are designed as bookcases and shelves that face both sides.

Durch die lichte Höhe von w 3,40 Metern lässt sich ein kleines Mehrzweckzwischengeschoss über den Betten beider Studios schaffen. Dessen Geländer werden als Bücherwände und Regale entworfen, die nach beiden Seiten ausgerichtet sind.

Une hauteur sous-plafond de 3,40 mètres permet de créer une petite mezzanine polyvalente sur les lits de chacun des studios. Ses barrières sont conçues comme des bibliothèques et étagères orientées des deux côtés.

Una altura libre de 3,40 metros permite crear un pequeño altillo polivalente sobre las camas de cada uno de los estudios. Sus barandillas se diseñan como librerías y estantes orientados hacia ambos lados.

This apartment was remodeled as a short-term residence for visitors to Budapest. It is a functional open space centered around an elevated plywood platform; this holds a double bed and storage spaces, and continues on in the design of the kitchen counter. The bathroom, which is the only closed room, receives natural light from a translucent glass window next to the bedroom.

Die Umgestaltung dieser Wohnung ist auf die Nutzung von Wohnraum für Kurzzeitaufenthalte für Reisende gedacht, welche die ungarische Hauptstadt besuchen. Hier handelt es sich um einen offenen und funktionellen Funktionsraum, in dem eine erhöhte Plattform aus Sperrholz das Herz bildet, auf der ein Doppelbett und Stauraum untergebracht sind, und die sich in der Holztafel der Küche fortsetzt. Das Bad ist der einzige geschlossene Raum der Wohnung undwird dank eines durchscheinenden Glasfensters, das neben bei dem Schlafzimmer liegt, mit Tageslicht versorgt.

La transformation de cet appartement est destinée à des séjours de courte durée, pour les voyageurs de passage dans la capitale hongroise. Il s'agit d'un espace ouvert et fonctionnel dans lequel la pièce principale est une plateforme surélevée en contreplaqué sur laquelle se trouve un lit double et des espaces de rangement, venant en continuité du plan de travail de la cuisine. La salle de bains, l'unique pièce fermée de l'appartement, reçoit la lumière naturelle grâce à une fenêtre en verre transparent située à proximité de la chambre.

La transformación de este apartamento se orienta hacia un uso de estancias de corta duración, destinado a viajeros de paso por la capital húngara. Se trata de un espacio abierto y funcional, en el que la pieza central es una plataforma elevada de madera contrachapada que alberga una cama doble y espacios de almacenaje, y que tiene continuidad en el tablero de la cocina. El baño, la única estancia cerrada del piso, recibe luz natural gracias a una ventana de vidrio translúcido situada junto al dormitorio.

224

AIR B N'P HOME

Position Collective

LOCATION **Budapest, Hungary** AREA **30 m² / 323 sq ft** PHOTOS **© Balázs Glódi**

A modular plywood panel with a system of adjustable shelves links the bedroom and kitchen areas. The objects on these shelves become decorative items for the apartment.

Ein modulares Paneel aus Sperrholz mit einem System verstellbarer Borde verknüpft den Schlafzimmerbereich mit der Küche. Die dort platzierten Gegenstände werden zu Dekorationselementen der Wohnung.

Un panneau modulaire en contreplaqué avec un système d'étagères graduelles enlace les espaces chambre et cuisine. Les objets se trouvant là-bas deviennent des éléments de décoration de l'appartement.

Un panel modular de madera contrachapada con un sistema de estantes graduables enlaza las zonas de dormitorio y cocina. Los objetos allí depositados se convierten en elementos de la decoración del apartamento.

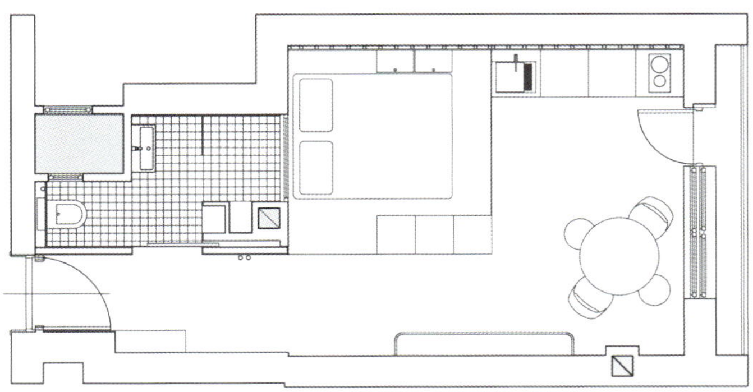

Floor plan

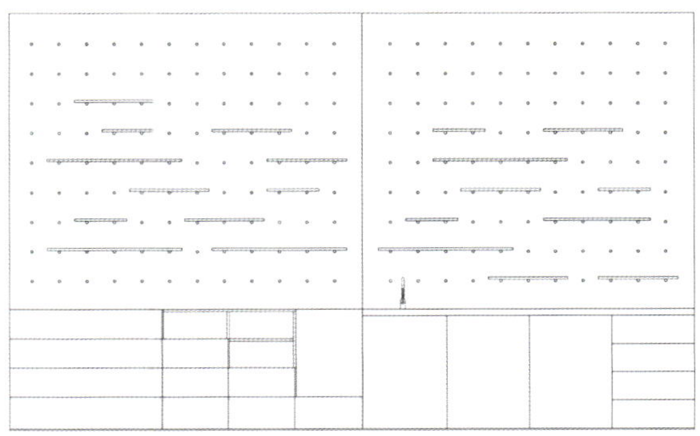

Pegboard elevation

The twelve rectangular apartments that comprise this building are designed with the kitchen, bathroom, sleeping, and storage spaces alongside a compact wooden unit that is attached to the longest of the perimeter walls. This layout, which groups and overlaps furniture and ancillary spaces, takes advantage of the three meters of height inside the homes to create an expansive and dynamic central area, oriented toward the large picture windows along the facade.

Die Gestaltung des Innenraums von 12 rechteckig geschnittenen Wohnungen, aus denen dieses Gebäude besteht, organisiert die Bereiche von Küche, Bad, Schlafzimmer und Stauraum entlang eines Kompaktmodularmöbelstücks, angelehnt an die längste perimetrale Wand. Diese gruppierte und überlagerte Anordnung von Einrichtung und Nebenräumen profitiert von den 3 Metern lichter Höhe im Innenbereich der Wohnungen und schafft einen geräumigen und dynamischen Hauptbereich, der zu den großen Fenstern der Fassade ausgerichtet ist.

La conception intérieure des douze appartements de forme rectangulaire de cet édifice organise les espaces de cuisine, salle de bains, chambre et rangement le long d'un meuble modulaire compact, adossé au mur périphérique de longueur supérieure. Cette disposition regroupée et superposée du mobilier et des espaces annexes bénéficie de trois mètres de hauteur sous plafond des logements et crée un cadre principal vaste et dynamique qui donne sur les grandes baies vitrées de la façade.

El diseño interior de los doce apartamentos de forma rectangular que conforman este edificio organiza los espacios de cocina, baño, dormitorio y almacenamiento a lo largo de un mueble modular compacto, adosado a la pared perimetral de mayor longitud. Esta disposición agrupada y superpuesta del mobiliario y de los espacios auxiliares se beneficia de los tres metros de altura libre interior de las viviendas, y crea un ámbito principal amplio y dinámico que se orienta hacia los grandes ventanales de la fachada.

228

QUINTANA 4598

IR Arquitectura

LOCATION **Buenos Aires, Argentina** AREA **33 m² / 355 sq ft** PHOTOS **© Federico Cairoli**

There are two types of apartments in the building. In the smaller ones, the cabinet with the bed is perpendicular to the facade that opens to the outside; in the larger ones, it is parallel to it.

Das Gebäude beherbergt zwei Arten von Wohnungen. In der kleineren Variante steht das Containermöbelstück senkrecht zur Fassade, welche die Öffnung zur Außenseite umfasst, während er in der größeren parallel platziert wird.

L'édifice offre deux typologies d'appartement. Dans la plus petite, le meuble container est placé perpendiculairement à la façade qui comprend l'ouverture à l'extérieur, tandis que dans la plus grande, il est situé en parallèle.

El edificio alberga dos tipologías de apartamento. En la más pequeña, el mueble contenedor se sitúa perpendicularmente a la fachada que contiene la abertura al exterior, mientras que en la mayor se sitúa en paralelo.

Section

Floor plan

Axonometric view

There are two main approaches to the layout of this home. The first orients the living room, kitchen, and bedrooms toward the natural light of the main facade; the second is the transversal axis formed by a continuous bookcase that crosses the house, interrupted only by the vestibule and the entry to the kitchen, and separates the public and private areas. A made-to-measure adjustable cabinet, used in every room, increases the overall functionality of the design.

Zwei Hauptstrategien prägen die Raumaufteilung dieser Wohnung: Die erste orientiert Wohnzimmer, Küche und Zimmer zum natürlichen Licht der Hauptfassade hin. Bei der zweiten trennt eine Querachse, die sich in einem durchgehenden Bücherregal materialisiert, das die Wohnung durchkreuzt und nur im Flug und im Zugang zur Küche abgeändert wird, den gemeinsam genutzten Bereich vom privaten. Das wandelbare eigens dafür entworfene Mobiliarwird in allen Wohnräumen eingesetzt und bereichert die Funktionalität des Ganzen.

Deux principales stratégies configurent la répartition de cette maison : la première concerne le séjour, la cuisine et les chambres qui reçoivent la lumière naturelle de la façade principale et la deuxième se focalise sur un axe transversal, concrétisé par une bibliothèque continue qui traverse la maison et qui est seulement modifiée au niveau de l'entrée et de l'accès à la cuisine, sépare l'espace commun de la partie nuit. Le mobilier changeant conçu sur mesure et utilisé dans toutes les pièces enrichit la fonctionnalité de l'ensemble.

Dos estrategias principales configuran la distribución de esta vivienda: la primera orienta la sala de estar, la cocina y las habitaciones hacia la luz natural de la fachada principal; en la segunda, un eje transversal, materializado en una librería continua que atraviesa la casa y que solo es alterada en el recibidor y en el acceso a la cocina, separa la parte pública de la privada. El mobiliario cambiante diseñado a medida y utilizado en todas las estancias enriquece la funcionalidad del conjunto.

234

DWELLING SANTO DOMINGO

PLP Atelier

LOCATION Ourense, Spain AREA 90 m2 / 969 sq ft PHOTOS © Héctor Santos-Díez

Doctor
JOSE LORENTE
OCULISTA

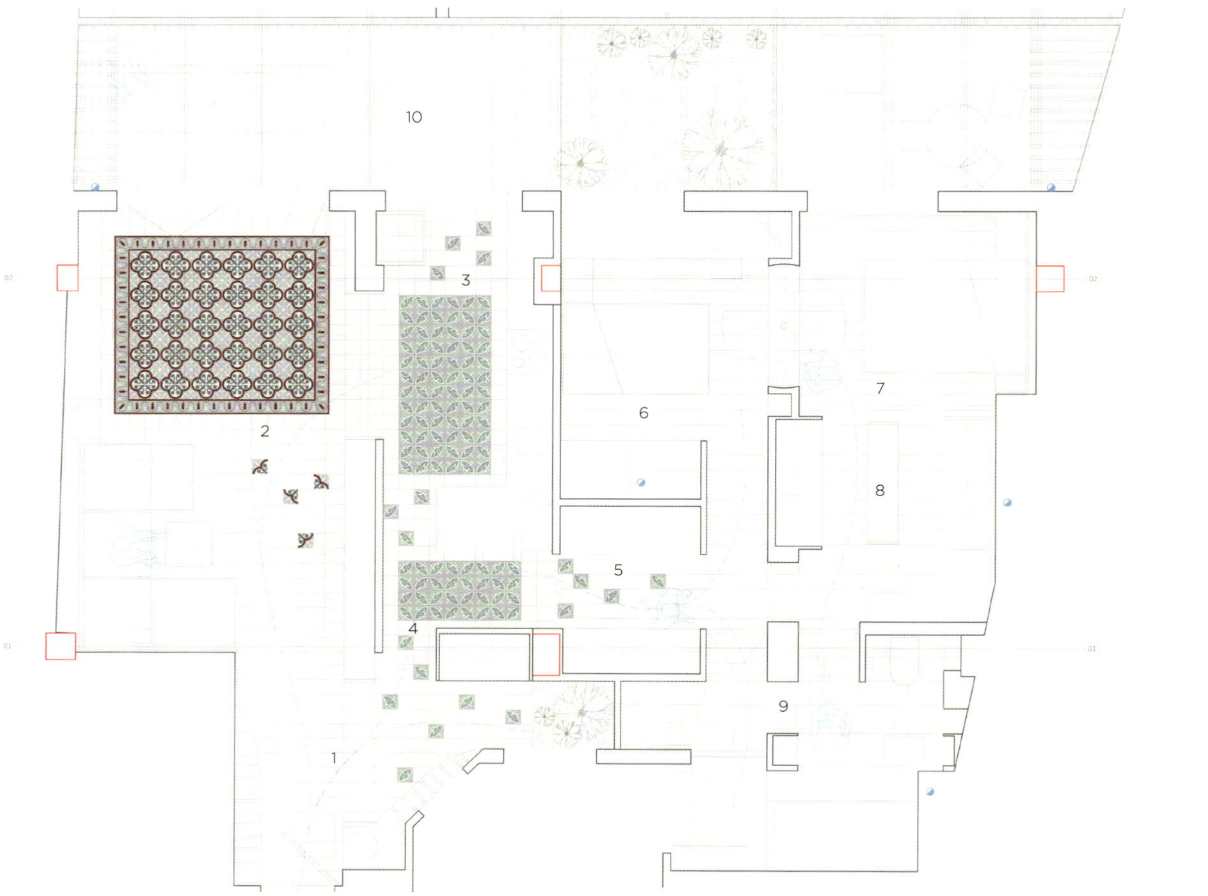

Floor plan

1. Drawing room
2. Living/Dining
3. Kitchen
4. Lobby kitchen
5. Hall
6. Guest Bedroom/Study
7. Bedroom
8. Dressing room
9. Bathroom
10. Terrace

There are two corridors, flanked here and there by benches that emerge from the vestibule, one leading to the public, and one to the private, zones of the house. There is a false third corridor that ends in a light-filled courtyard brightened by a mirror.

Vom Flur aus beginnen zwei Rundgänge, flankiert von durchgehenden Bänken, die in die gemeinsam genutzten bzw. privaten Bereiche der Wohnung führen. Ein dritter jedoch falscher Rundgang endet in Lichthof, der mit einem Spiegel ausgestattet ist.

Depuis l'entrée partent deux couloirs, flanqués de bancs discontinus qui mènent respectivement à une partie commune et à un espace privé de la maison. Un faux troisième couloir donne sur une cour de lumière avec un miroir.

Desde el recibidor parten dos recorridos, flanqueados por bancos discontinuos, que conducen respectivamente a las zonas pública y privada de la casa. Un falso tercer recorrido acaba en un patio de luz dotado de un espejo.

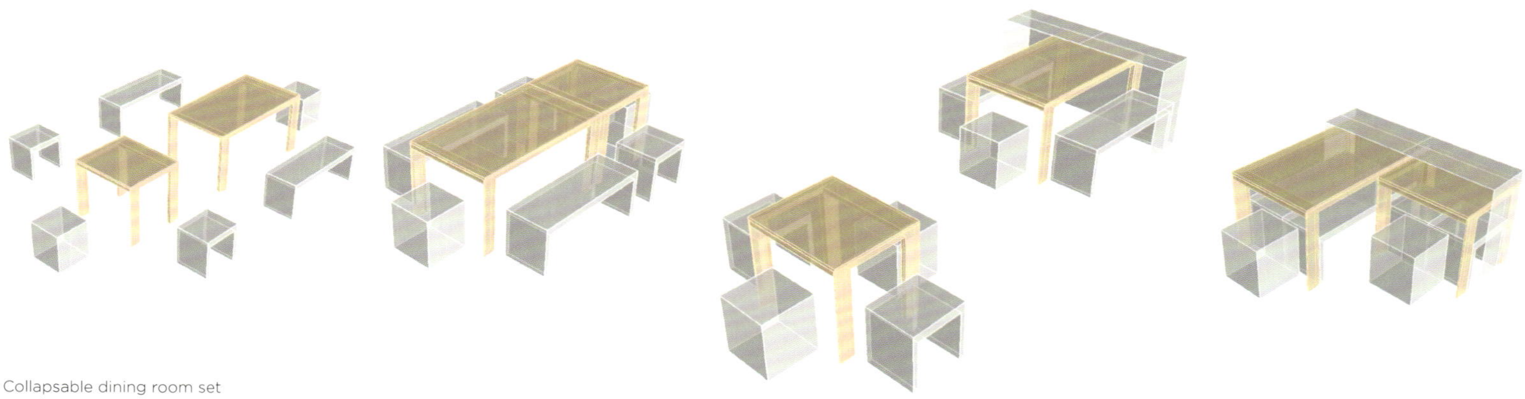

Collapsable dining room set

The patterns on the hydraulic mosaic floor tiles, designed especially for this project and featured in the common areas, appear to dwindle in number on the corridors that lead to the more private zones of the house.

Die Bereiche mit einem Bodenbelag aus Zementfliesen, die eigens für das Projekt entworfen und in den Gemeinschaftsbereichen verlegt wurden, werden im Verlauf der Rundgänge, die in die privateren Bereiche der Wohnung eindringen, immer schwächer.

Les zones de revêtement à mosaïque hydraulique, conçues spécialement pour le projet et situées dans les parties communes, se diluent au fil des parcours qui pénètrent dans les parties les plus intimes de la maison.

Las áreas de pavimento de mosaico hidráulico, diseñado especialmente para el proyecto y situadas en las zonas comunes, se van diluyendo a lo largo de los recorridos que se adentran en las zonas más privadas de la casa.

The master bedroom connects with a neighboring room through a revolving shelf built into the wall. This room can be used a study or bedroom, as needed.

Durch ein integriertes, drehbares Bücherregal in der Wand ist das große Schlafzimmer mit einem angrenzenden Zimmer verbunden. Dieser Wohnraum kann je nach Anforderung an die Funktion als Arbeits- oder Schlafzimmer genutzt werden.

La chambre parentale est reliée à une pièce contiguë par une étagère giratoire intégrée au mur. Cette pièce peut servir de bureau ou de chambre selon les besoins fonctionnels.

El dormitorio principal se conecta con una estancia contigua mediante una estantería giratoria integrada en el muro. Esta estancia puede ser utilizada como estudio o como dormitorio según las necesidades funcionales.

It is the time factor that will determine the planning for this project, which involves remodeling an apartment that will, in a few years, be enlarged to double its current size. It is the future uses that influence the layout, which is designed bearing in mind that later its elements will be reused and its functions will be reassigned. Thus, the living room and bedroom are planned with their final dimensions, and the current office is laid out and equipped with a view to its future role as the dressing room for the master bedroom.

Der Faktor Zeit bestimmt die Fragestellung dieses Projektes, das sich mit der Renovierung einer Wohnung beschäftigt, die sich in wenigen Jahren in eine Wohnung mit der doppelten Fläche verwandeln wird. Die künftigen Nutzungen bedingen die Raumaufteilung, die im Hinblick auf die Wiederverwendung ihrer Elemente und der Neuzuordnung ihrer Funktionen entworfen wurde. Auf diese Weise werden Wohn- und Schlafzimmer mit den endgültigen Maßen geplant, und das derzeitige Büro wird so konfiguriert und ausgestattet, um als Ankleidezimmer des großen Schlafzimmers zu fungieren.

Le facteur temps détermine l'approche de ce projet qui aborde les travaux d'un appartement qui, dans quelques années, deviendra un appartement avec une superficie double. Les futures fonctions conditionnent la répartition des espaces, conçus en pensant à la réutilisation de ses éléments et la réaffectation de ses fonctions. De cette manière, le séjour et la chambre sont envisagés avec leurs dimensions définitives et l'actuel bureau est configuré et offre des vues du fait d'être le dressing de la chambre parentale.

El factor tiempo determina el planteamiento de este proyecto, que aborda la reforma de un piso que en pocos años se convertirá en uno con el doble de superficie. Los futuros usos condicionan la distribución de los espacios, diseñados pensando en la reutilización de sus elementos y la reasignación de sus funciones. De esta manera, el estar y el dormitorio se proyectan con sus dimensiones definitivas, y el actual despacho se configura y se equipa con vistas a ser el vestidor del dormitorio principal.

244

HOUSE QUINTELA

Castroferro Arquitectos

LOCATION **Vigo, Spain** AREA **55 m² / 592 sq ft** PHOTOS **© Héctor Santos-Díez**

SAMSUNG

A strip that will become storage space in the future, now holds enough kitchen appliances to meet the needs of the initial apartment. A system of folding panels hides it and integrates into the living area.

Im Einklang mit den Bedürfnissen der Ausgangswohnung enthält ein Streifen, der künftig als Stauraum gedacht ist, die Kücheneinrichtung. Ein System aus Faltpaneelen verbirgt diese und bindet sie dadurch in die Gesamtheit des Wohnzimmers ein.

Un passage destiné à un futur espace de rangement comprend les éléments de cuisine selon les besoins de l'appartement d'origine. Un système de panneaux pliables le cache et l'intègre dans l'ensemble du séjour.

Una franja destinada a futura zona de almacenaje contiene un equipo de cocina acorde a las necesidades del piso inicial. Un sistema de paneles plegables la oculta y la integra en el conjunto de la sala de estar.

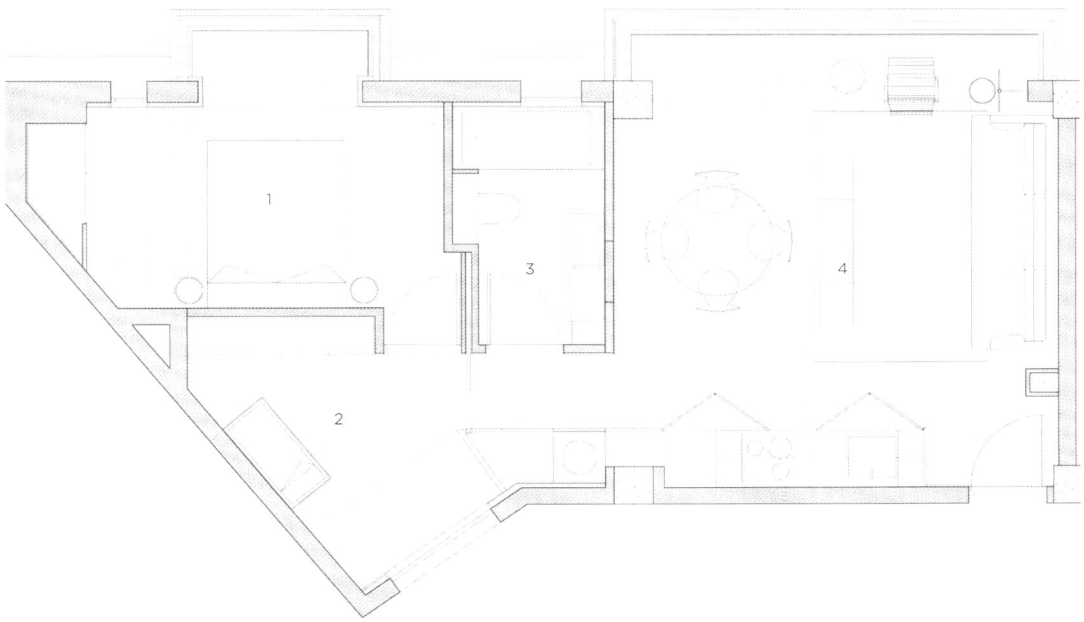

1. Bedroom
2. Study
3. Bathroom
4. Living room

Floor plan

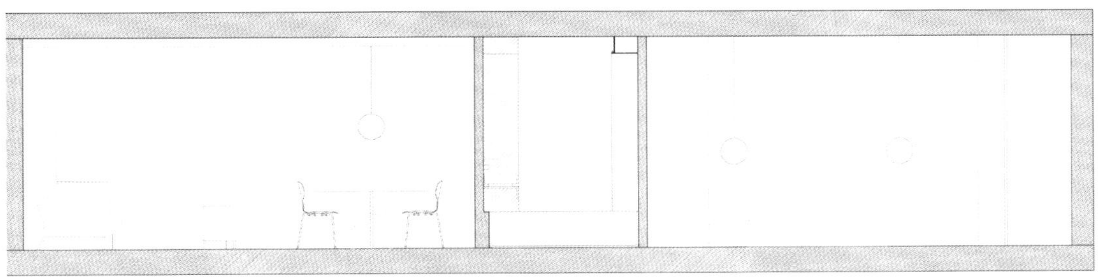

Section A

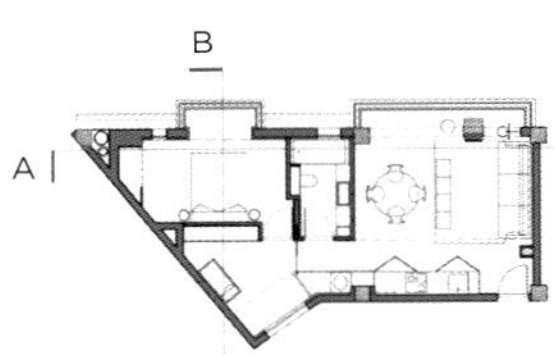

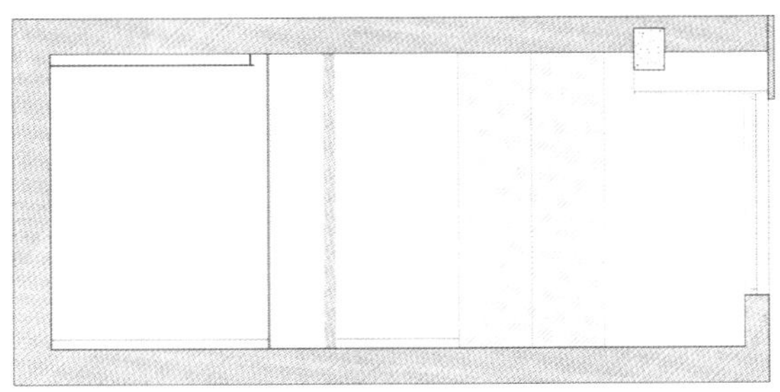

Section B

The decor uses smooth simple surfaces that can flexibly respond to future requirements; they are painted white, and oak is used in the parquet floor and in the natural veneer on the walls.

Die Innenraumgestaltung verwendet glatte und einfache Oberflächen, die für künftige Anforderungen flexibel gestaltet, in weiß gestrichen und aus Eichenholz gefertigt sind - in Form von Parkett am Boden und Furnierholz an den Wänden.

Le design intérieur utilise des surfaces lisses et simples, modulables pour les futures exigences, revêtues de peinture blanche et en chêne en forme de parquet au sol et en tôle naturelle au mur.

El diseño interior utiliza superficies lisas y simples, flexibles a los futuros requerimientos, revestidas de pintura blanca y de madera de roble en forma de parqué en los suelos y de chapa natural en las paredes.

The objective of the project was to create a second bedroom while simultaneously obtaining more common space. This was done by designing a wooden floor-to-ceiling unit that houses the two small rooms, and includes a tall narrow side cabinet that separates the private from the public zones and can be accessed from both. Inspired by Japanese tradition, there are sliding panels that can open the main bedroom into the living areas.

Zielsetzung des Projekts war, einen zweiten Raum im Haus einzurichten und gleichzeitig eine größere Fläche für die gemeinsam genutzten Bereiche zu gewinnen. Hierfür wurde ein Container in voller Höhe aus Holz gestaltet und erbaut, in dem zwei Schlafzimmer auf minimaler Fläche sowie Stauraum untergebracht, wodurch der private Bereich von den gemeinsam genutzten Bereichen getrennt wird und von beiden zugänglich ist. Inspiriert von der japanischen Tradition, lässt sich das große Schlafzimmer durch bewegliche Paneele zum Wohnbereich hin öffnen.

L'objectif du projet a été de créer une deuxième chambre dans l'appartement tout en obtenant plus de surface pour les espaces de vie. Pour cela, on a conçu un container sur toute la hauteur, construit en bois qui comprend deux chambres d'une surface minimale et une bande de rangement qui sépare l'espace privatif de l'espace commun et accessible depuis les deux espaces. Inspirés de la tradition japonaise, des panneaux amovibles permettent d'ouvrir la chambre parentale sur les espaces de vie.

El objetivo del proyecto fue implantar una segunda habitación en la vivienda y, al mismo tiempo, obtener mayor superficie para los espacios de convivencia. Para ello, se diseñó un contenedor a toda altura construido en madera, que alberga dos dormitorios de superficie mínima y que incluye una franja de almacenaje que separa la zona privada de la pública y es accesible desde ambas. Inspirados en la tradición japonesa, unos paneles móviles permiten abrir el dormitorio principal hacia las zonas de estar.

252

FLINDERS LANE APARTMENT

Clare Cousins Architects

LOCATION **Melbourne, Australia** AREA **75 m² / 807 sq ft** PHOTOS **© Lisbeth Grosmann**

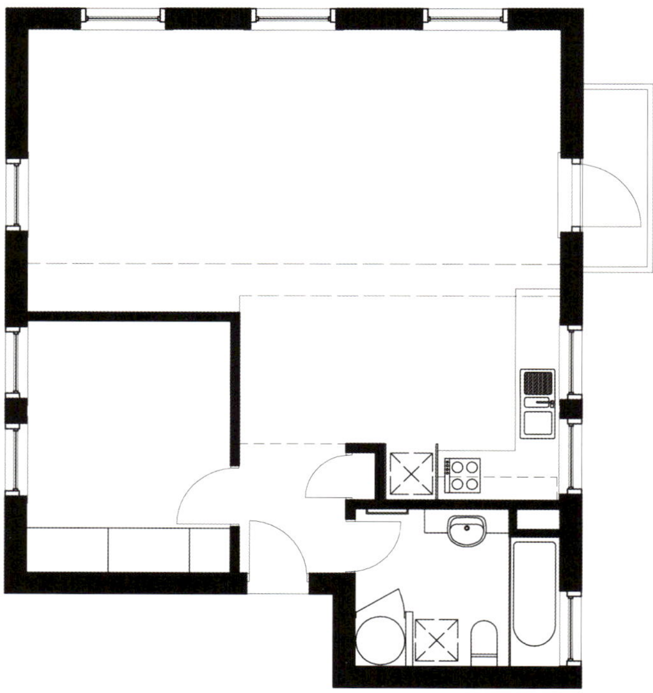

Existing floor plan

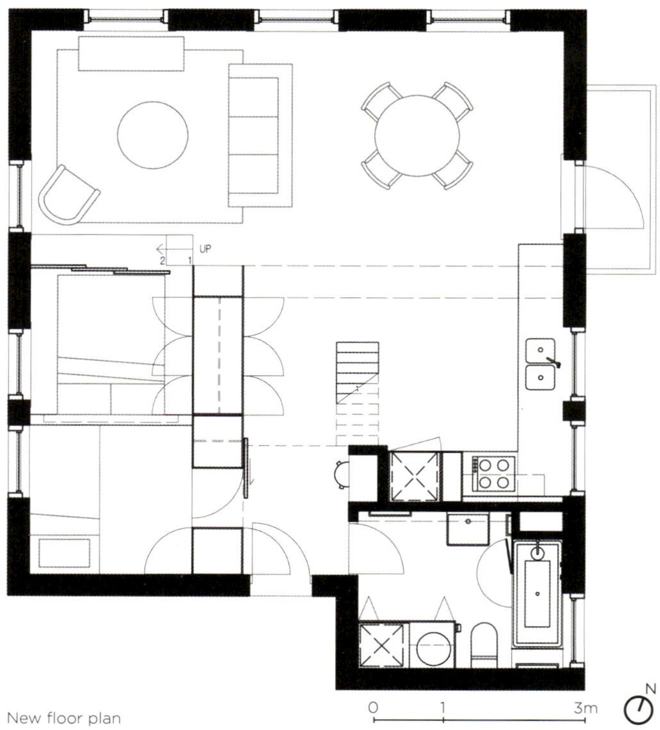

New floor plan

The careful design of the spaces in the abode increases the useable surface in the common areas. A loft over the entryway can be used as either a guest room or a storage space.

Die sorgfältige Gestaltung der Räume des Hauses erhöht die Nutzfläche in den Gemeinschaftsbereichen. Ein Zwischengeschoss über dem Eingangsbereich dient als mögliches Schlafzimmer für Gäste sowieals Stauraum.

Le design soigné des espaces de l'appartement augmente la surface utile des parties communes. Une mezzanine située au niveau de l'accès sert d'éventuelle chambre d'amis et d'espace de rangement.

El cuidado diseño de los espacios de la vivienda incrementa la superficie útil de las zonas comunes. Un altillo situado sobre la zona de acceso es utilizado como eventual dormitorio de invitados y espacio de almacenaje.

This housing prototype is a mobile module suitable for any type of site. It is the result of a very eco-friendly industrialized manufacturing process. Its floor plan, in the form of a flattened ellipse, contains three different areas; there is a double-height central space that connects the two other living spaces; a technical module on one end, with the bathroom and other installations; and a storage area at the opposite end.

Dieser Prototyp eines Hauses ist ein transportfähiges Modul, das für jeden Standort geeignet ist. Es ist das Ergebnis eines industrialisierten Herstellungprozesses, der den Kriterien der Nachhaltigkeit gegenüber sensibel ist. Sein Grundriss in Form einer abgeflachten Ellipse umfasst drei verschiedene Bereiche: Ein zentraler Raum mit doppelter Höhe, der die bewohnbaren Räume vereint, ein technisches Modul, an einem der Enden, welches Bad und Installationen beinhaltet, und Stauraum am gegenüberliegenden Ende.

Ce prototype de maison constitue un module transportable adéquat pour tout type d'emplacement. C'est le fruit d'un procédé de fabrication industrialisée sensible aux critères de durabilité. Son niveau en forme elliptique aplatie comprend trois espaces distincts : un espace central à double hauteur qui réunit les pièces habitables, un module technique situé à une de ses extrémités avec salle de bains et installations et, un espace de rangement situé à l'opposé.

Este prototipo de vivienda constituye un módulo transportable apto para cualquier tipo de emplazamiento, y es el resultado de un proceso de fabricación industrializada sensible a criterios de sostenibilidad. Su planta de forma elíptica achatada contiene tres zonas diferenciadas: un espacio central de doble altura que reúne las estancias habitables, un módulo técnico situado en uno de sus extremos, que contiene el baño y las instalaciones, y una zona de almacenamiento situada en el extremo opuesto.

256

MACHINE HOME

Ad-hoc

LOCATION **Murcia, Spain** AREA **40 m² / 430 sq ft** PHOTOS **© David Frutos**

The lofts, on either side of the generous space over the house's central living area, contain the sleeping spaces, accessed by two extension ladders.

Im Zwischengeschoss zu beiden Seiten der großen Öffnung, die über dem Hauptraum des Hauses thront, sind die Schlafbereiche vorgesehen, zu denen die Bewohner über die beiden ausklappbaren Leitern gelangen.

Au niveau de la mezzanine, des deux côtés du vaste vide qui préside l'espace principal de la maison, se trouve la chambre, accessible par deux échelles rabattables.

En la planta altillo, a ambos lados del amplio hueco que preside el espacio principal de la casa, se disponen las zonas de dormitorio, a las que se accede mediante dos escaleras de mano abatibles.

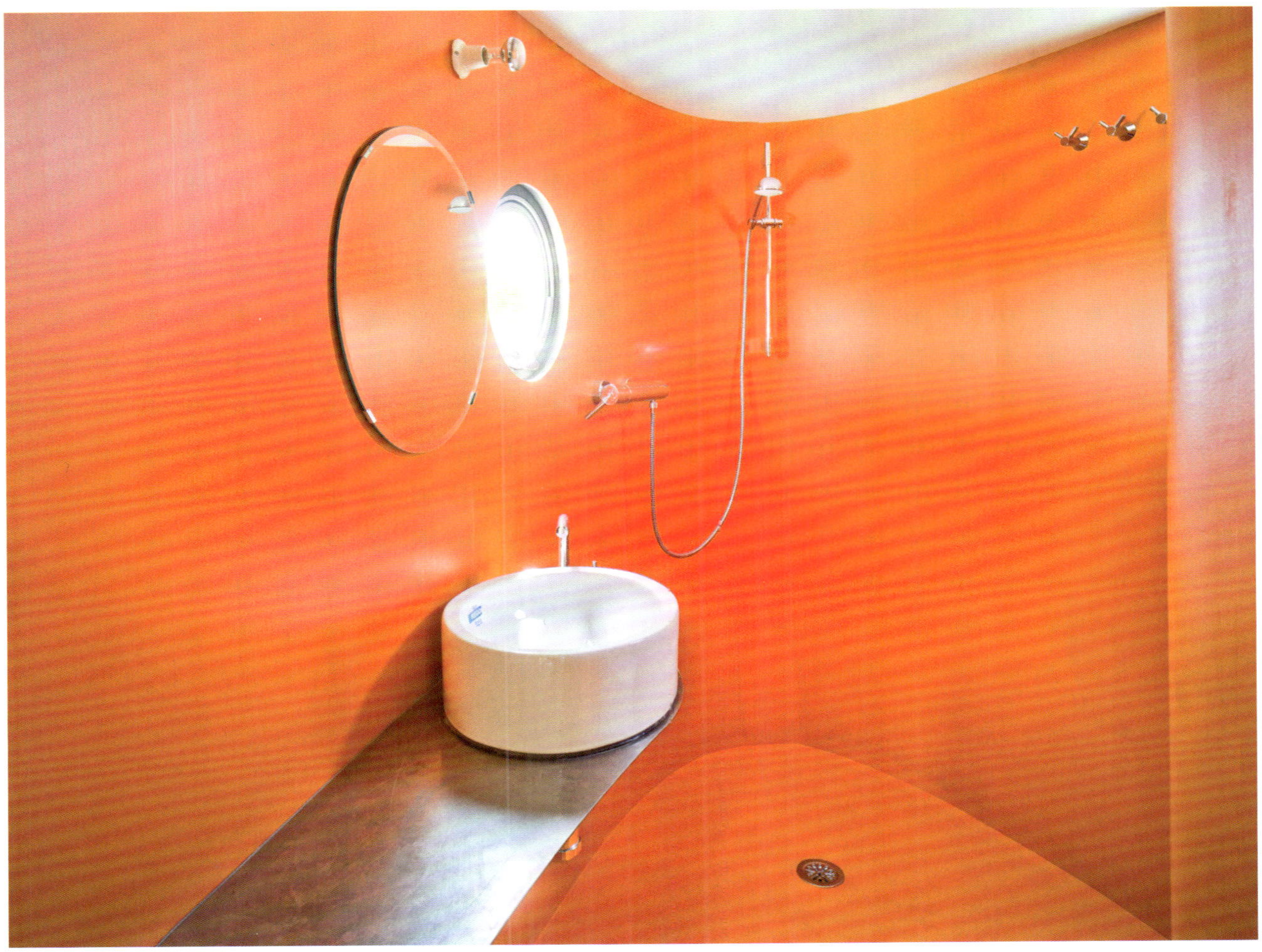

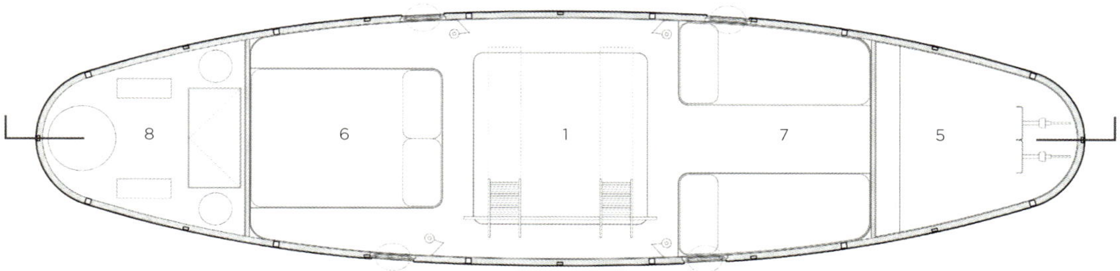

Mezzanine

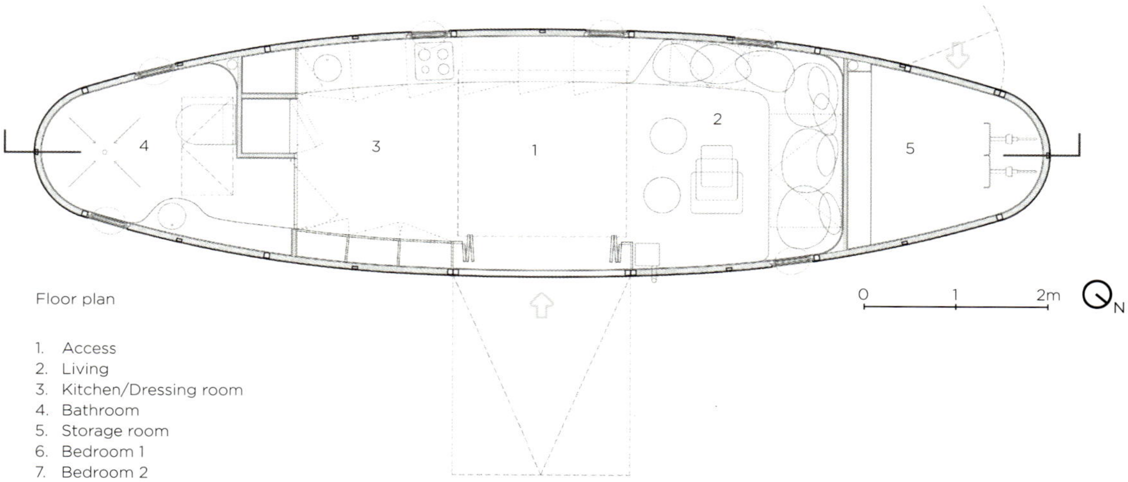

Floor plan

1. Access
2. Living
3. Kitchen/Dressing room
4. Bathroom
5. Storage room
6. Bedroom 1
7. Bedroom 2
8. Facilities

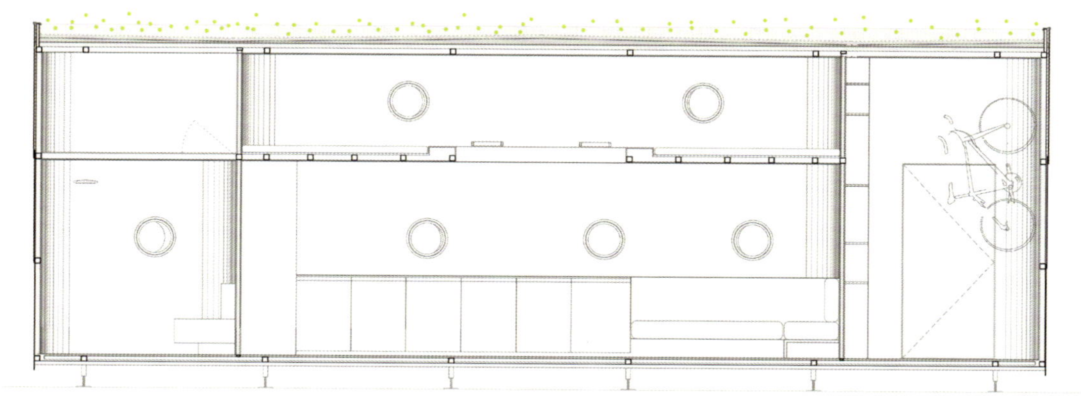

Section

The renovation plan for this typical Genoese "tower house" involves four small floors, connected by a steep, narrow, staircase. The two upper floors are larger and hold the most important areas of the house, the living/dining room and the bedroom. These two environments are connected by a two-story space that faces the building's front wall, and is divided by horizontal suspended net, accessible from the upper floor.

Der Umbau dieses typischen „Turmhauses" in Genua entfaltet seine Ziele auf vier kleinen Ebenen, die durch eine enge und steile Treppe verbunden sind. Das Herzstück des Hauses liegt auf den beiden oberen Etagen mit einer größeren Fläche, wo sich Wohnzimmer-Küche und Schlafzimmer befinden. Diese beiden Bereiche sind durch einen Raum mit doppelter Höhe verbunden, der zur Fassade des Zuganges ausgerichtet und durch ein aufgehängtes horizontales Netz geteilt ist, das von der oberen Etage aus zugänglich ist.

Les travaux de cette typique « maison tour » génoise disposent de leur programme sur quatre niveaux limités, reliés entre eux par un escalier étroit et raide. Le cœur de la maison réside dans les deux niveaux supérieurs, d'une superficie plus importante, dans lesquels se trouvent le séjour-cuisine et la chambre. Ces deux espaces sont reliés par un espace à double hauteur, orienté vers la façade d'accès et divisé par un réseau horizontal suspendu, accessible depuis le niveau supérieur.

La reforma de esta típica "casa torre" genovesa desarrolla su programa a lo largo de cuatro reducidas plantas, conectadas por una estrecha y empinada escalera. El núcleo principal de la vivienda se encuentra en las dos plantas superiores, de mayor superficie, en las que se sitúan la sala de estar cocina y el dormitorio. Estos dos ámbitos se relacionan a través de un espacio a doble altura orientado hacia la fachada de acceso y dividido por una red horizontal suspendida, accesible desde la planta superior.

262

FISHERMAN HOUSE

Gosplan Architects

LOCATION Genova, Italy AREA 35 m² / 377 sq ft PHOTOS © Anna Positano

A wooden cabinet was designed to span this two-story space and work as both a safety precaution for the empty stairwell and a storage unit for the kitchen.

Im Erdgeschoss wurde zur Durchquerung des Raumes mit doppelter Höhe ein Einrichtungsgegenstand aus Holz entworfen, der als Stauraum für die Küche dient und gleichzeitig der Leere der Treppe entgegenwirkt.

Au niveau du rez-de-chaussée, traversant l'espace à double hauteur, on a conçu un meuble en bois qui sert de rangement pour la cuisine tout en servant de protection contre le vide de l'escalier.

En la planta principal, atravesando el espacio a doble altura, se diseñó un mueble construido en madera que sirve de almacenaje para la cocina y al mismo tiempo actúa como protección hacia el vacío de la escalera.

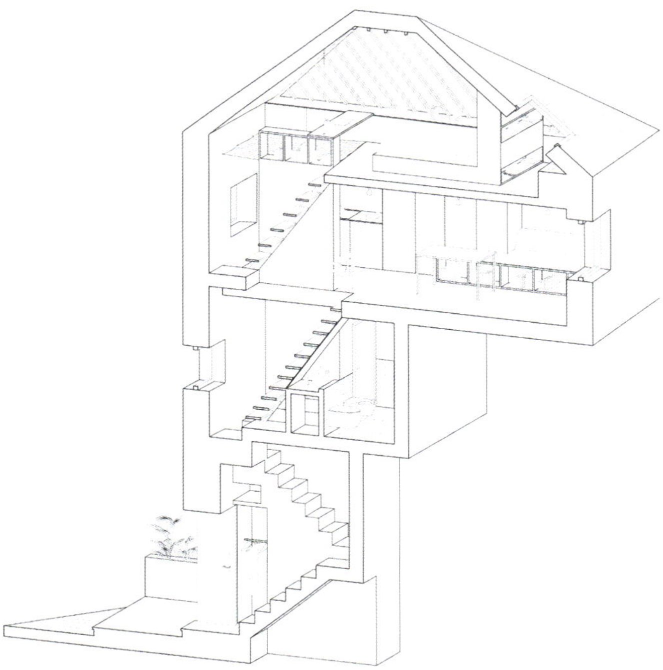

Axonometric section

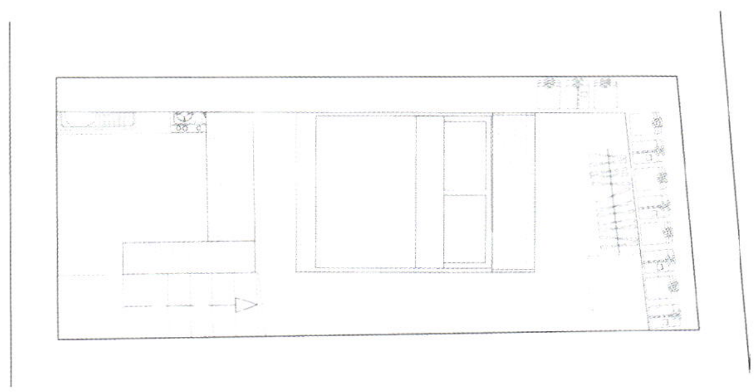

Third floor plan

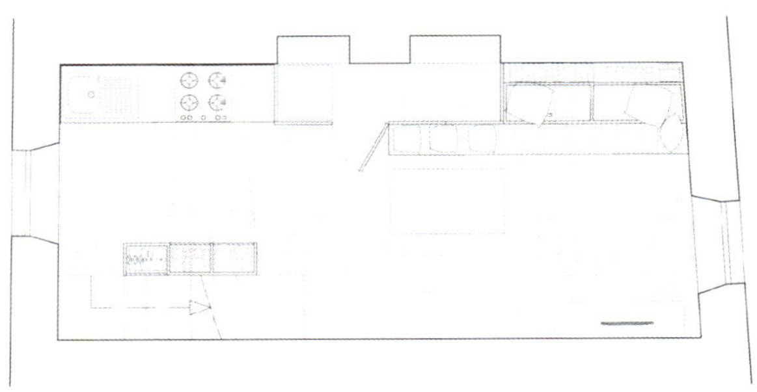

Second floor plan

The top floor holds the main bedroom, where a hidden space in back holds clothing and personal belongings. A folding writing table was designed to fit next to the free space above the kitchen.

In der oberen Etage befindet sich das große Schlafzimmer, an dessen Rückseite sich ein Raum zum Aufbewahren von Kleidung und Geräten verbirgt. Neben dem Leerraum über der Küche wurde ein klappbarer Schreibtisch platziert.

À l'étage supérieur se trouve la chambre parentale dont la partie arrière cache un dressing et des effets personnels. À proximité du vide, au-dessus de la cuisine, un bureau rabattable a été conçu.

En la planta superior se sitúa el dormitorio principal, en cuya parte posterior se esconde un espacio para guardar ropa y enseres. Junto al vacío sobre la cocina se ha diseñado una mesa de escritorio abatible.

A newly constructed building, designed as a community environment with multiple living spaces, serves as the site for this type of micro-housing. The interior of each unit contains one single space for the living, study, and storage areas; the sleeping area is located in a loft over the bathroom. There is a community kitchen in the center of each floor of the building; this also functions as a meeting and social space.

Ein als Gemeinschaftsumfeld konzipierter Neubau, ausgestattet mit mehreren Räumen für das Zusammenleben, dient als Rahmen dieser Art von Mikro-Wohnung. Der Innenraum jeder Einheit besteht aus einem einzigen Raum, der als Wohn- und Studierzimmer soweit als Stauraum vorgesehen ist. Über dem Bad ist in einem Zwischengeschoss das Schlafzimmer untergebracht. In einem Raum in der Mitte jeder Etage des Gebäudes befindet sich eine Gemeinschaftsküche, die auch als Versammlungsort und Treffpunkt fungiert.

Un édifice récemment construit, conçu comme un cadre communautaire avec divers espaces de convivialité, sert de cadre à cette typologie de micro-maison. L'intérieur de chaque unité est composé d'un espace unique, destiné au séjour, au bureau et à un espace de rangement, avec au-dessus de la salle de bains, une mezzanine où se trouve la chambre. Une pièce située au centre de chacun des étages du bâtiment comprend une cuisine commune qui sert également de lieu de réunion et de point de rencontre.

Un edificio de nueva construcción, concebido como un entorno comunitario dotado de múltiples espacios de convivencia, sirve de marco a esta tipología de microvivienda. El interior de cada unidad está formado por un único espacio, destinado a estar, estudio y zona de almacenamiento; sobre la pieza del baño, un altillo aloja el dormitorio. Una estancia situada en el centro de cada una de las plantas del edificio alberga una cocina comunitaria, que actúa también como lugar de reunión y punto de encuentro.

268

YOBI APARTMENTS

Neiman Taber Architects

LOCATION Seattle, USA AREA 13 m² / 140 sq ft PHOTOS © William Wright Photography

The spatial continuity between the bedroom and the lower level, and the greater headroom in the loft, help make the home seem larger.

Die räumliche Kontinuität zwischen dem Schlafzimmer und der unteren Ebene zusammen mit der größeren lichten Höhe, die im Bereich des Zwischengeschosses vorgesehen ist, trägt dazu bei, das Gefühl von Geräumigkeit der Wohnung zu steigern.

La continuité spatiale entre la chambre et le niveau inférieur, reliée à la hauteur sous plafond la plus élevée qui est prévue dans la zone de la mezzanine, contribue à augmenter la sensation de grandeur de la maison.

La continuidad espacial entre el dormitorio y el nivel inferior, unida a la mayor altura libre que se ha previsto en la zona del altillo, contribuye a aumentar la sensación de amplitud de la vivienda.

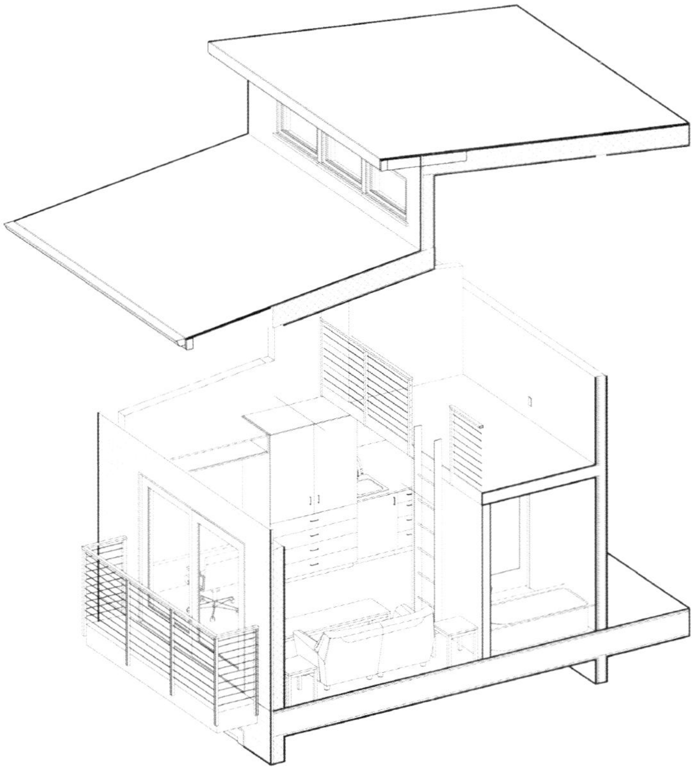

Axonometric view

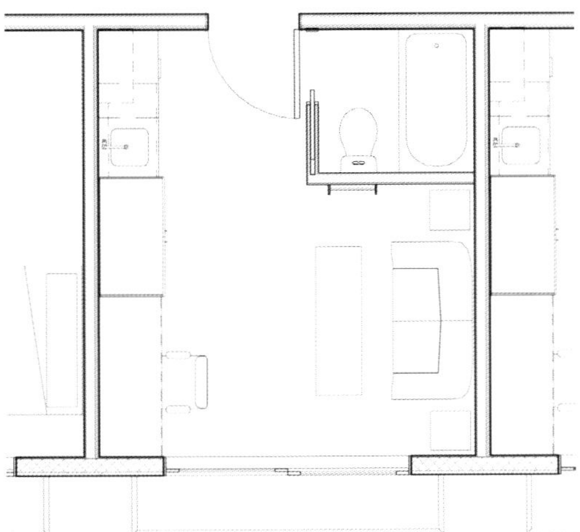

Floor plan

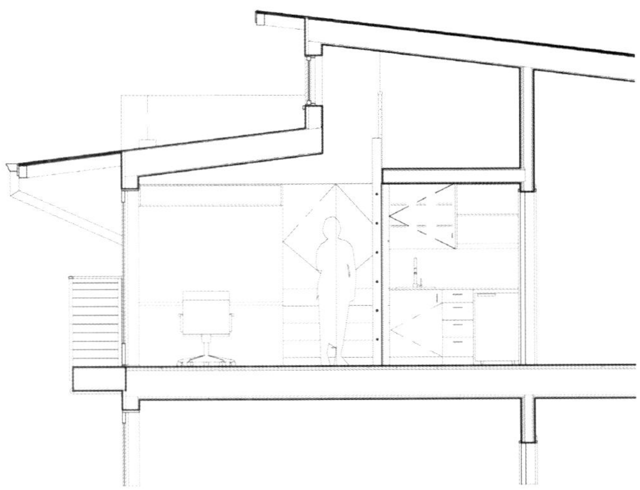

Section

The planner for this project has successfully incorporated all the functions of a home into the barely thirteen square meters of this tiny rectangular space. The kitchen, bath, and storage space form a core grouping at one end of the rectangle. Over this is a loft that serves as the bedroom. The rest of the home consists of an open space of minimalist design, with a light color scheme opening up the space.

Bei diesem Eingriff gelingt es dem Designer, die Funktionen einer Wohnung auf einerrechteckigen Fläche von nur 13 Quadratmetern unterzubringen. Sein Ansatz platziert an einem der beiden Enden des Rechtecks einen Kern, der die Bereiche Küche, Bades und Ablage zusammenfasst, auf dem ein Zwischengeschoss errichtet wird, das als Schlafzimmer dient. Die übrige Wohnung besteht aus einem einzigen Raum, geprägt durch minimalisches Design und helle Töne, die dazu beitragen, dem Raum Weite zu geben.

Dans cette intervention, le concepteur a réussi à intégrer le programme fonctionnel d'un appartement dans les rares treize mètres carrés d'un minuscule espace rectangulaire. Son approche repose sur une extrémité du rectangle, un espace central qui regroupe la cuisine, la salle de bains et des rangements au-dessus desquels se trouve une mezzanine qui fait office de chambre. Le reste de l'appartement est composé d'un espace unique au design minimaliste avec des tons clairs qui confèrent de la grandeur à l'espace.

En esta intervención, el proyectista consigue incorporar el programa funcional de una vivienda en los escasos trece metros cuadrados de un minúsculo espacio de forma rectangular. Su planteamiento sitúa en uno de los extremos del rectángulo un núcleo que agrupa las zonas de cocina, baño y almacenaje, sobre las que se eleva un altillo que funciona como dormitorio. El resto de la vivienda está constituido por un único ambiente, de diseño minimalista y tonos claros que contribuyen a dar amplitud al espacio.

272

13 SQ M

Szymon Hanczar

LOCATION **Wrocław, Poland** AREA **13 m² / 140 sq ft** PHOTOS **© Jedrzej Stelmaszek**

The functional core was carefully designed to meet the basic requirements of a home, and it fits into the whole as if it were one more item of furniture.

Das gepflegte Design des kleinen Kerns, der die Funktionsbereiche umfasst, ist optimiert, um die grundlegenden Anforderungen an eine Wohnstätte zu erfüllen und wird wie ein weiteres Möbelstück in die Gesamtheit eingebunden.

Le design soigné du petit espace central qui comprend les zones fonctionnelles est optimisé afin de répondre aux besoins de base d'un appartement et s'intègre à l'ensemble comme une pièce supplémentaire.

El cuidado diseño del pequeño núcleo que contiene las zonas funcionales está optimizado para satisfacer las necesidades básicas de una vivienda y se integra en el conjunto como una pieza más del mobiliario.

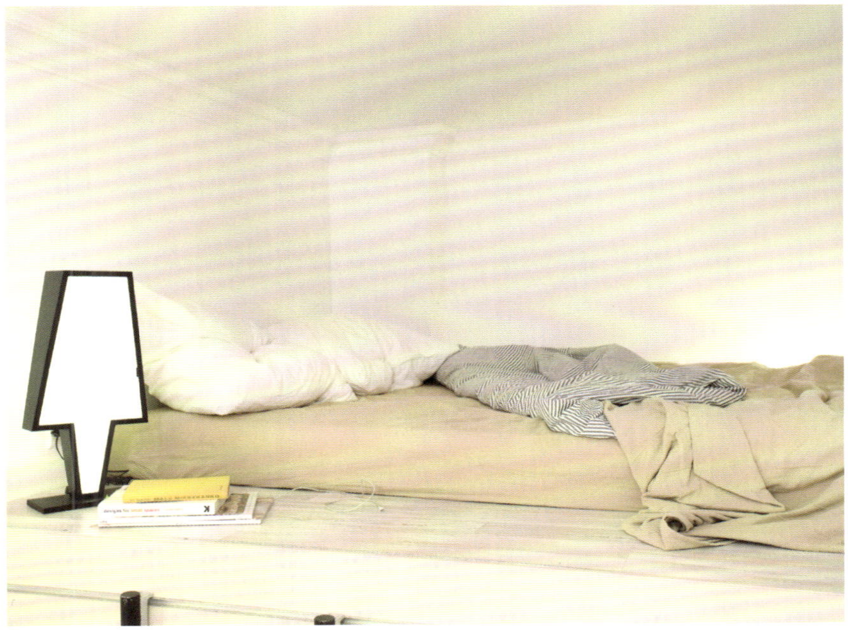

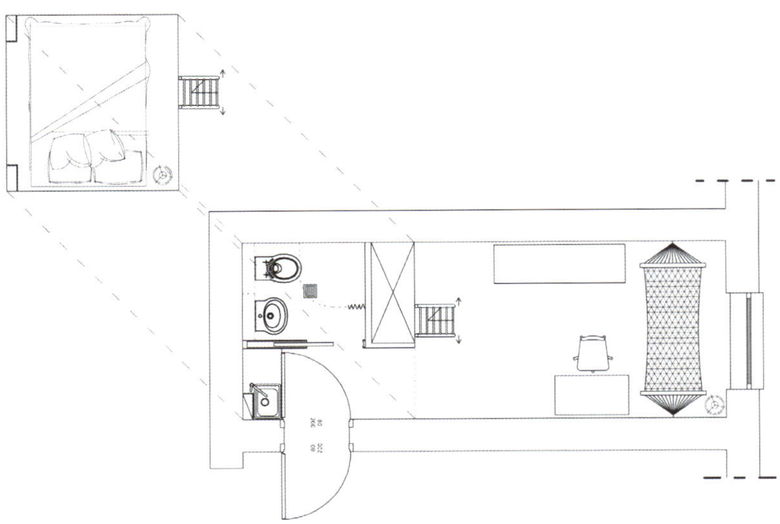

Floor plan

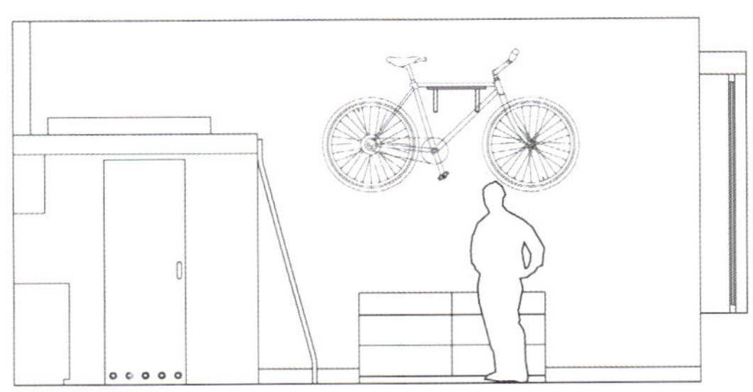

Section

This project originated with the owner's wish to provide her home with an open, multi-functional space that could work as a classroom as well as a room for guests. The elevated platform, inspired by Japanese tradition, contains two double beds and storage spaces, so that the room is both distinctive and convertible. A sliding cabinet can divide the space into two separate areas.

Dieses Projekt entstand durch den Wunsch der Eigentümerin, Ihre Wohnung mit einem offenen Multifunktionsraum auszustatten, der sowohl als Unterrichtsraum als auch als Gästezimmer dienen kann. Das Anlegen einer erhöhten Plattform, inspiriert durch die japanische Tradition, die in ihrem Inneren mit zwei Doppelbetten und Stauräume beherbergt, ermöglicht einen andersgeartetenund umwandelbaren Bereich. Dank eines mit einem Verschiebemechanismus ausgestatteten Containermöbelstücks lässt sich dieser Bereich in zwei voneinander unabhängige Bereiche aufteilen.

Ce projet est né de la volonté de la propriétaire d'aménager dans son bien un espace ouvert et multifonctionnel qui peut servir aussi bien de salle de cours que de chambre d'amis. La création d'une plateforme surélevée inspirée de la tradition japonaise, comprenant deux lits doubles et des espaces de rangement, permet de disposer d'un cadre spécifique et convertible. Un meuble container, équipé d'un système de déplacement, permet de diviser cet espace en deux zones indépendantes.

Este proyecto nace de la voluntad de la propietaria de dotar a su vivienda de un espacio abierto y multifuncional, que pudiese funcionar tanto de aula como de habitación de invitados. La creación de una plataforma elevada inspirada en la tradición japonesa, que alberga en su interior dos camas dobles y espacios de almacenamiento, permite disponer de un ámbito diferenciado y convertible. Un mueble contenedor, dotado de un sistema de desplazamiento, permite dividir este ámbito en dos zonas independientes.

276

CHANGEABLE SCENE

Studioata

LOCATION Salamanca, Spain AREA 50 m² / 538 sq ft PHOTOS © Vicente de la Calle, Eduardo Núñez López, Studioata

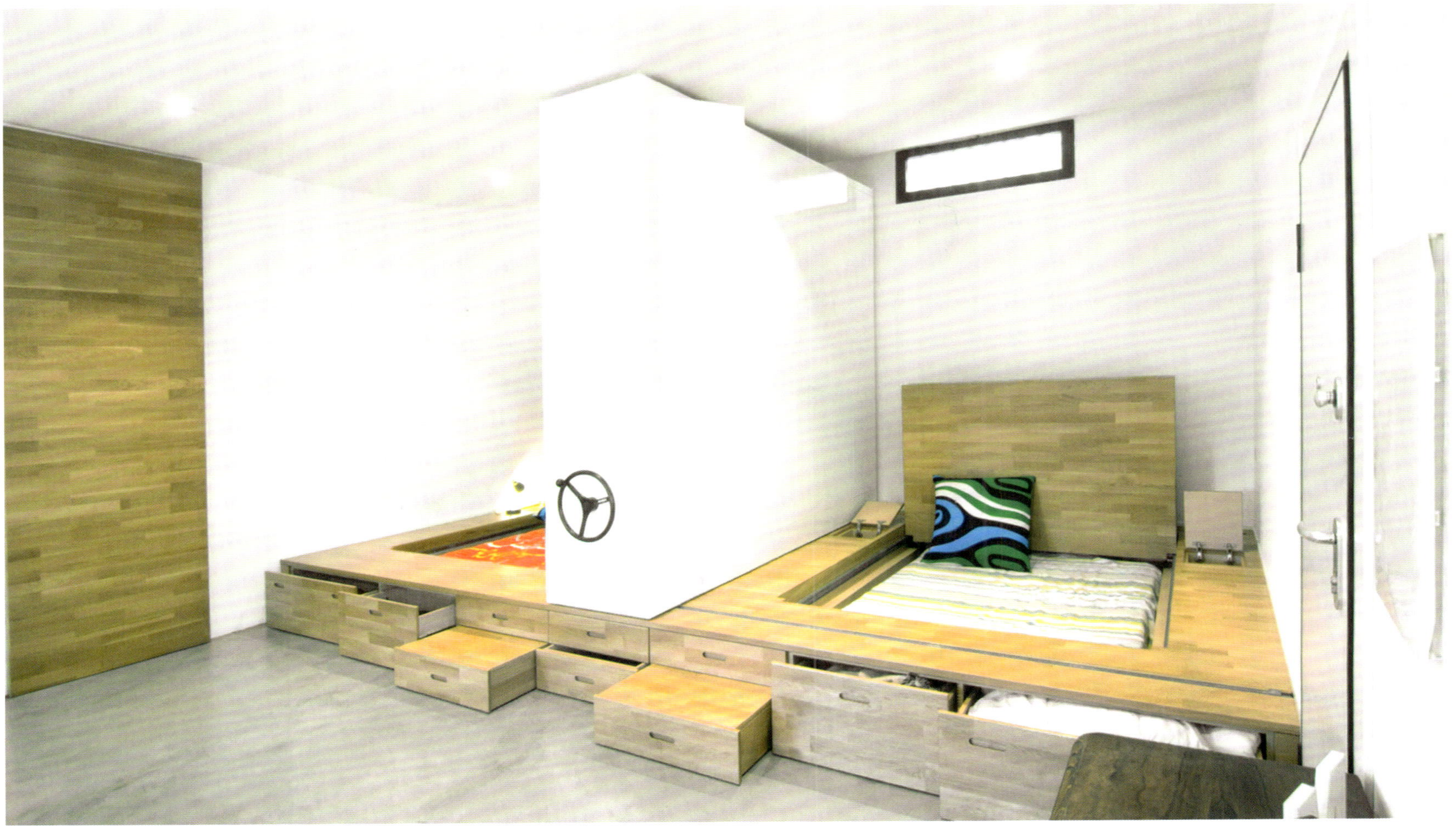

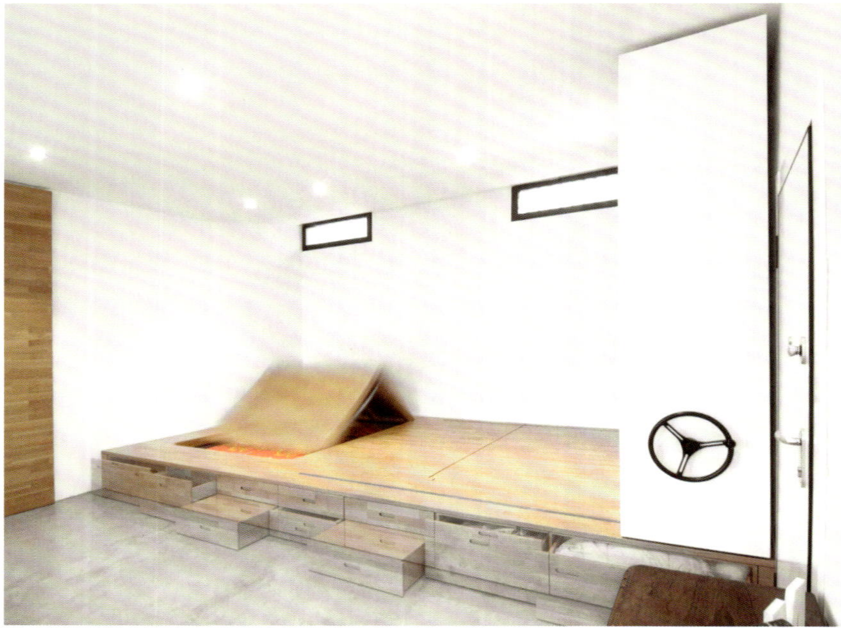

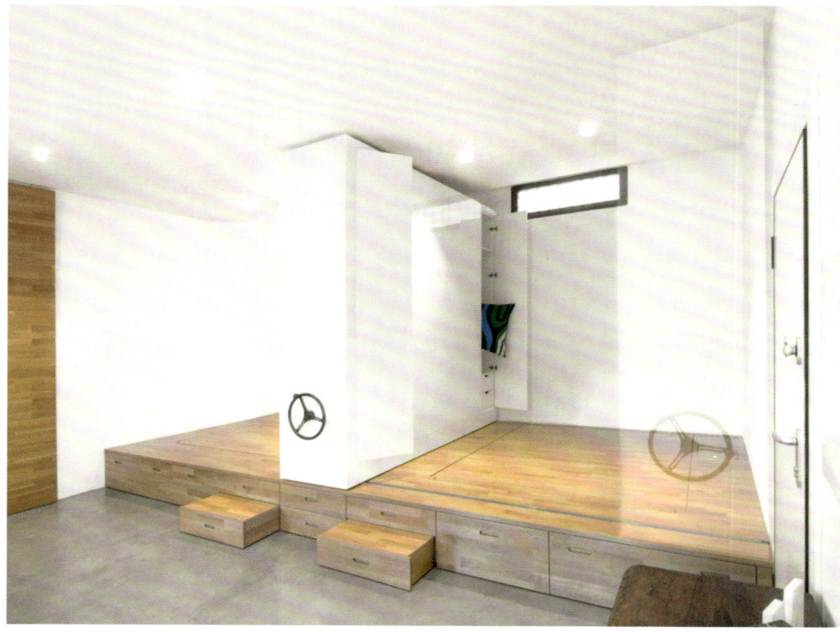

By moving the sliding cabinet and opening or closing the beds, it becomes possible to create configurations for a variety of uses, such as a massage studio, classroom, living room, guest room, etc.

Durch die Verschiebung des trennenden Möbelstücks und die Möglichkeit, die Betten zu öffnen, lassen sich verschiedene Konfigurationen der Nutzung erzeugen: Massageraum, Unterrichtsraum, Wohnzimmer, Schlafzimmer für Gäste, etc.

Le déplacement du meuble séparateur et la possibilité d'ouverture des lits permettent de créer diverses configurations d'utilisation : salle de massages, salle de cours, séjour, chambre d'amis, etc.

El desplazamiento del mueble separador y la posibilidad de abertura de las camas permite generar diversas configuraciones de usos: sala de masajes, aula para clases, sala de estar, dormitorio de invitados, etc.

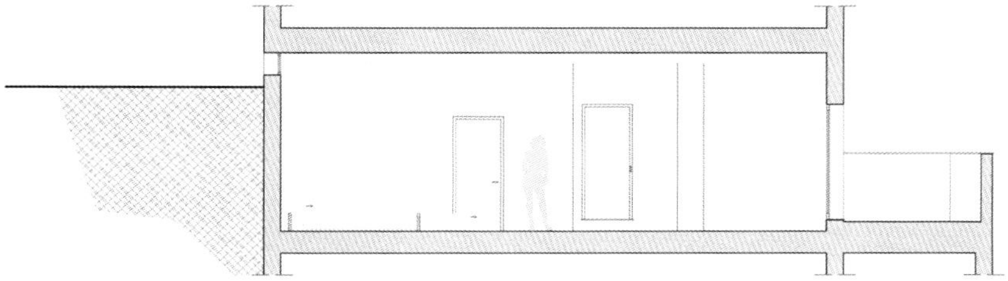

Section A-A

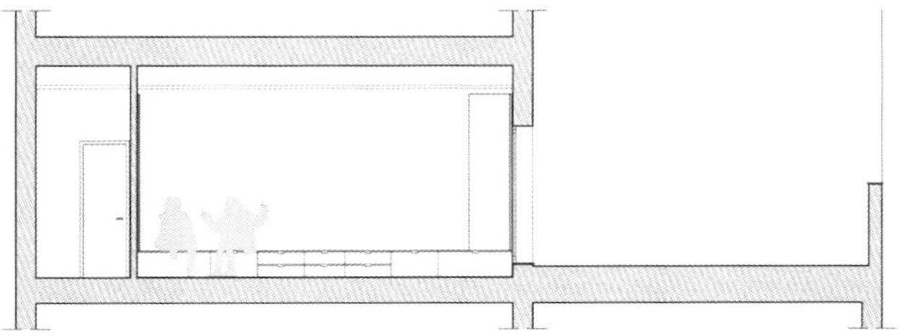

Section B-B

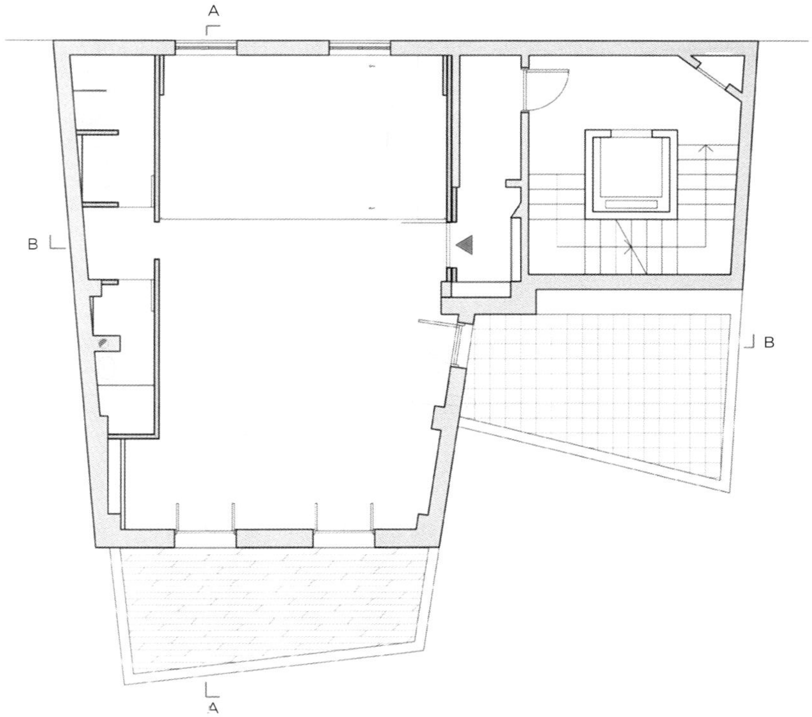

Floor plan

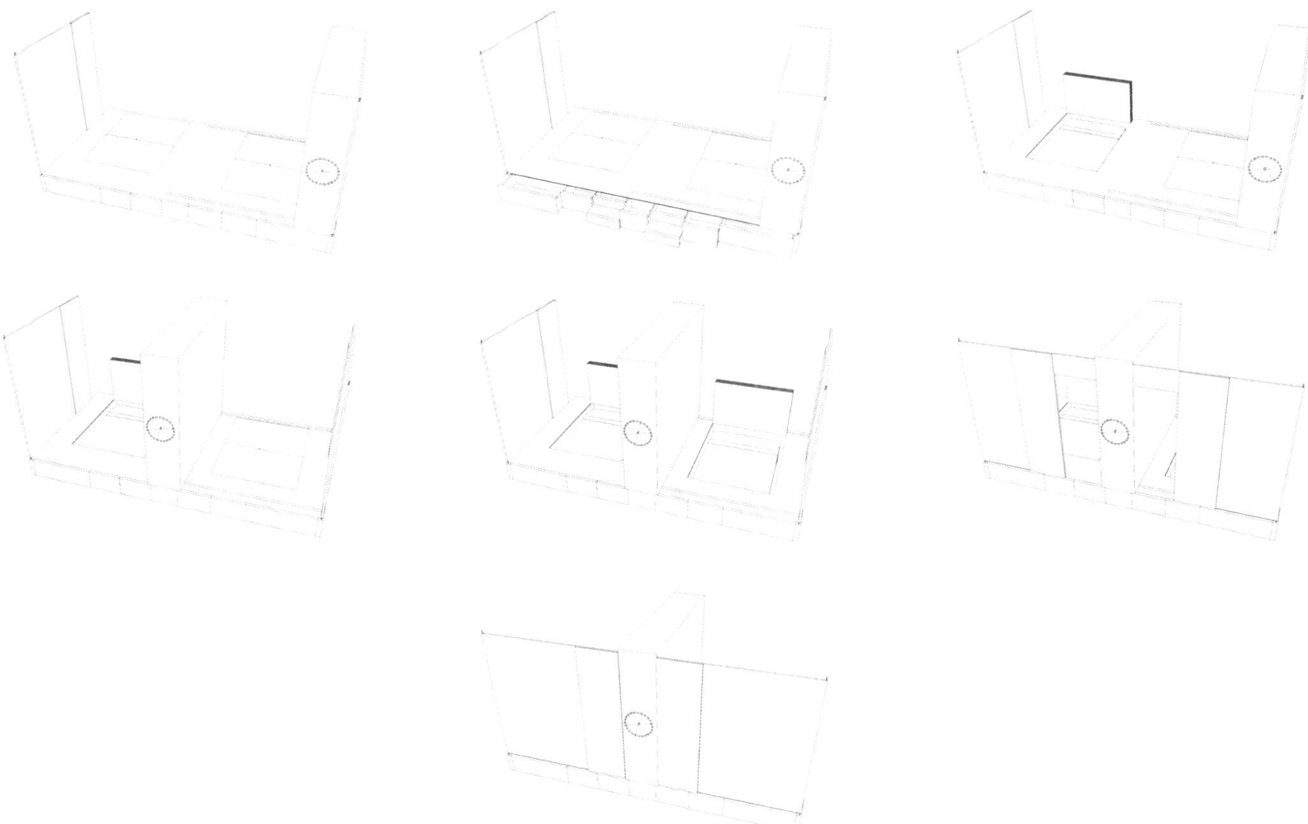

Diagram of storage opportunities in built-in sleeping platform

In this apartment renovation, the interior space was organized by building in two functional strips. The first separates the main hall from the bath and entryway, and contains the kitchen appliances; the other is formed by shelving and a staircase, which leads up to a loft that was refurbished during the remodeling to provide a place for the bedroom. This stairway is unique in that it has rows of small cupboards that run across the entire structure.

Beim Umgestaltungsprojekt dieser Wohnung wird durch Einfügen von zwei Funktionslinien der Innenraum gegliedert. Die erste Linie trennt den Hauptraum von Bad und Eingang und umfasst die Kücheneinrichtung. Einige Regale und die Treppe bilden die zweite Linie, die zu einem Zwischengeschoss hinaufführt, das während des Umbaus wiedergewonnen wurde und wo sich nun das Schlafzimmer befindet. Diese Treppe bildet ein einzigartiges Element, dessen Gestaltung eine Reihe kleiner Wandschränke einbindet, welche sich über die gesamte Wand erstrecken.

Le projet de transformation de cet appartement est d'organiser un espace intérieur grâce à l'intersection de deux couloirs fonctionnels. Le premier sépare la pièce principale de la salle de bains et de l'entrée et comprend les éléments de la cuisine ; le deuxième est composé d'étagères et d'un escalier qui permet d'accéder à la mezzanine, récupéré au cours des travaux, où se trouve la chambre. Cet escalier est un élément singulier dont la conception comprend une série de petites armoires tout le long du mur.

El proyecto de transformación de este apartamento organizó el espacio interior mediante la inserción de dos franjas funcionales. La primera separa la sala principal del baño y de la entrada, y contiene el equipo de cocina; la segunda está formada por unas estanterías y por una escalera que accede a un altillo recuperado durante la reforma, en el que se sitúa el dormitorio. Esta escalera constituye un elemento singular, cuyo diseño integra una serie de pequeños armarios que se extienden por toda la pared.

280

APARTMENT C

SCHEMAA

LOCATION Paris, France   AREA 57 m² / 614 sq ft   PHOTOS © Fred Toulet

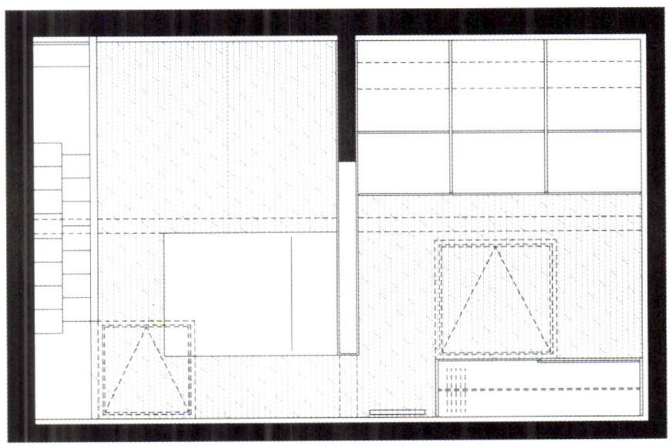

Upper floor plan

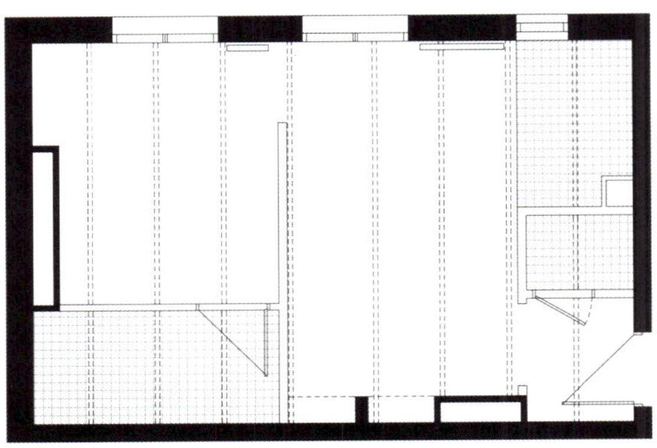

Existing plan

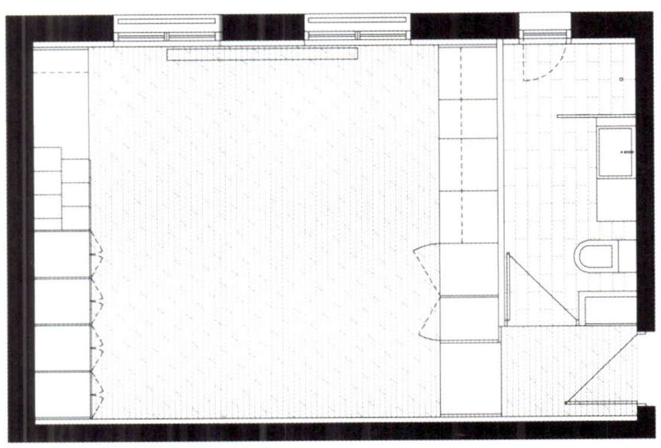

Lower floor plan

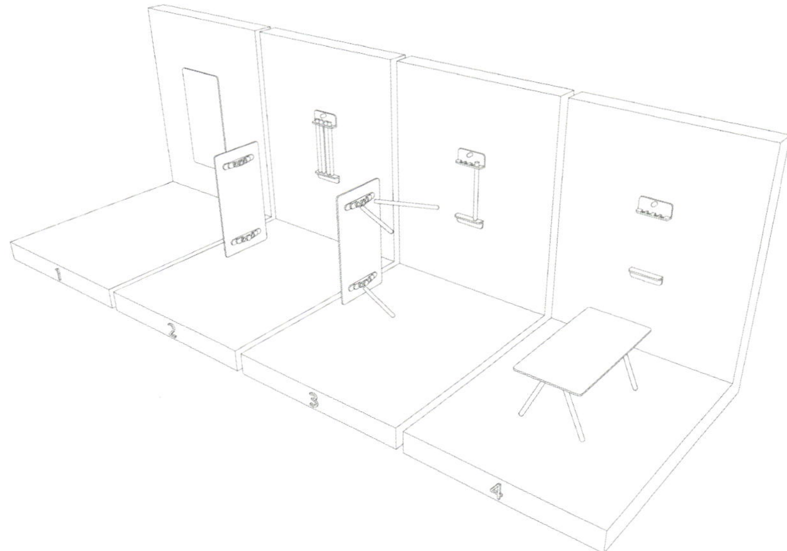

The dining-room table can be taken apart to create more space in the main room. Pieces of the table can be hung on hooks between the two existing windows, adding to the overall symmetrical effect.

Der Tisch im Esszimmer kann auseinandergebaut werden, um im Hauptraum Platz zu gewinnen. Seine Bestandteile werden an Haken aufgehängt, die zwischen den beiden vorhandenen Fenstern angebracht sind, wodurch der symmetrische Aufbau des Ganzen unterstrichen wird.

La table de salle à manger peut être démontée pour gagner de l'espace dans la pièce principale. Ses composants sont placés sur des crochets situés entre les deux fenêtres existantes mettant ainsi en valeur la composition symétrique de l'ensemble.

La mesa de comedor puede ser desmontada para ganar espacio en la sala principal. Sus componentes se colocan sobre unos ganchos situados entre las dos ventanas existentes, resaltando la composición simétrica del conjunto.

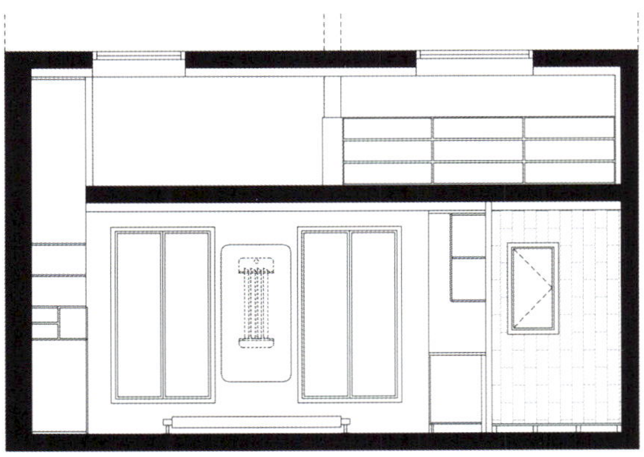

Sections

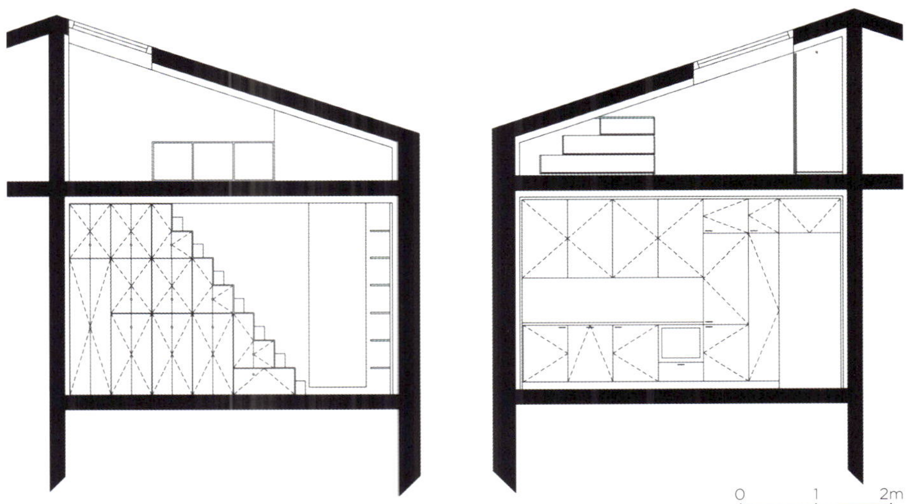

A nest-like loft, planned as a bedroom, presides over the continuous space of this apartment, and frees up useful space underneath, where there is a storage area. The renovation sets off different areas by using wooden frames, whose form is repeated in the shape of the window, and that stand out against the overall white background of the wall and ceilings. The two existing windows bring in the outdoor courtyard as one more living space in the home.

Ein als Schafzimmer dienendes Zwischengeschoss beherrscht als eine Art Nest den durchgehenden Raum dieser Wohnung und erzielt unter dieser Ebene eine Nutzfläche, auf der Ablageflächen angebracht sind. Der Eingriff definiert die verschiedenen Bereiche durch den Einsatz von Holzeinfassungen, die sich auch in der Form der Fenster wiederholen und sich vor dem weißen Gesamthintergrund abheben, den Wände und Decken bilden. Die beiden vorhandenen Fenster schließen den äußeren Innenhof als einen weiteren Raum der Wohnung an.

Une mezzanine aménagée en chambre sous forme de nid domine l'espace continu de ce loft et libère de l'espace utile sous son niveau où se trouvent des rangements. L'intervention permet de déterminer les divers espaces grâce à l'utilisation de délimitations en bois qui rappellent aussi le contour des fenêtres et qui se distinguent sur le fond blanc général des murs et plafonds. Les deux fenêtres intègrent la cour extérieure comme un espace supplémentaire du loft.

Un altillo destinado a dormitorio preside a modo de nido dominante el espacio continuo de este apartamento y rescata superficie útil bajo su planta, donde se ubica una zona de almacenaje. La intervención define los diferentes ámbitos mediante la utilización de enmarcados de madera que se repiten también en el contorno de las ventanas y que destacan sobre el fondo blanco general que constituyen paredes y techos. Las dos ventanas existentes incorporan el patio exterior como otro espacio más de la vivienda.

286

LOFT JERTE

Beriot, Bernardini Arquitectos

LOCATION **Madrid, Spain** AREA **30 m² / 323 sq ft** PHOTOS **© Yen Chen**

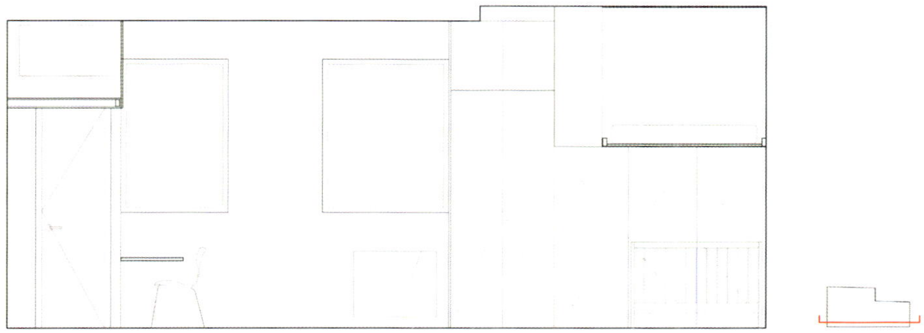

Longitudinal section

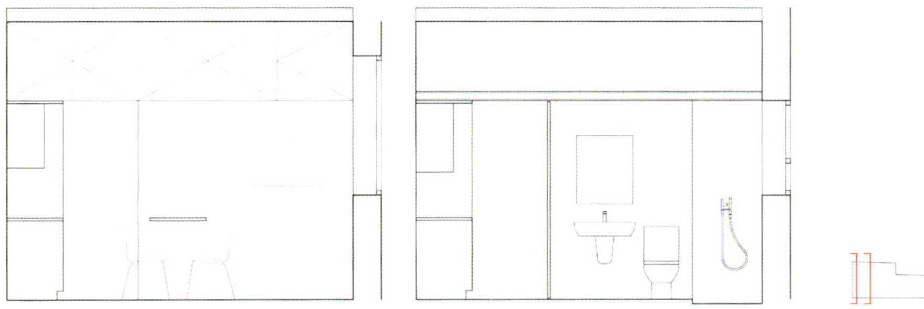

Cross section

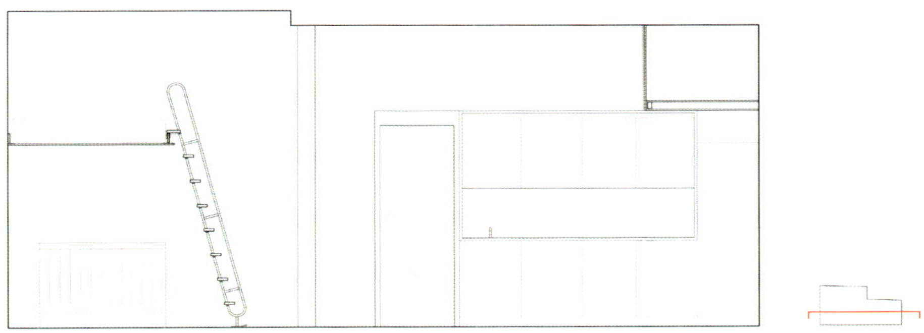

Cross section

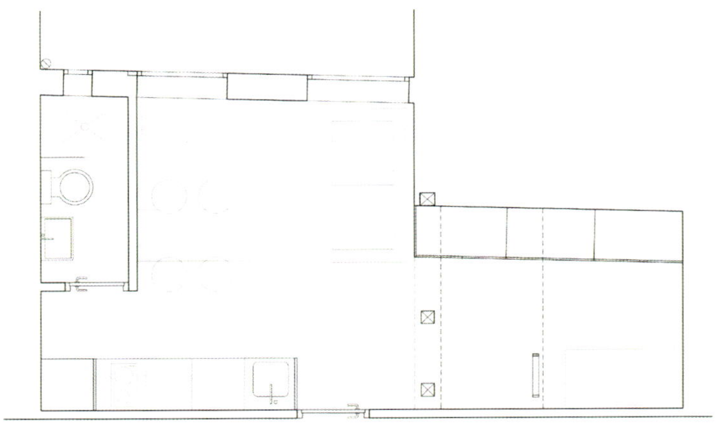

Main floor plan

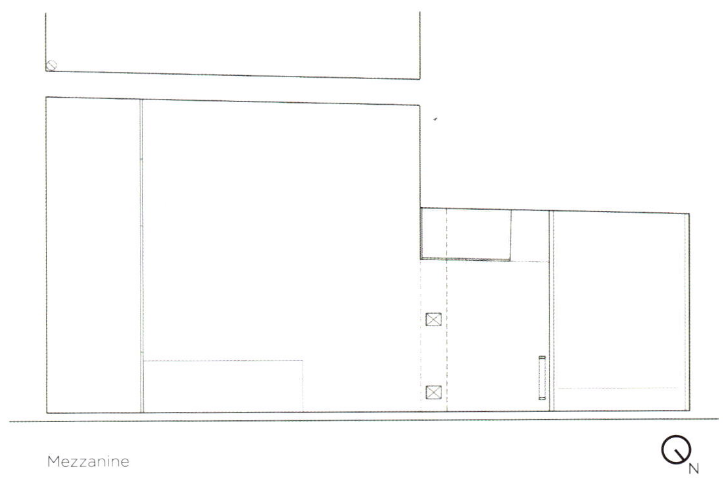

Mezzanine

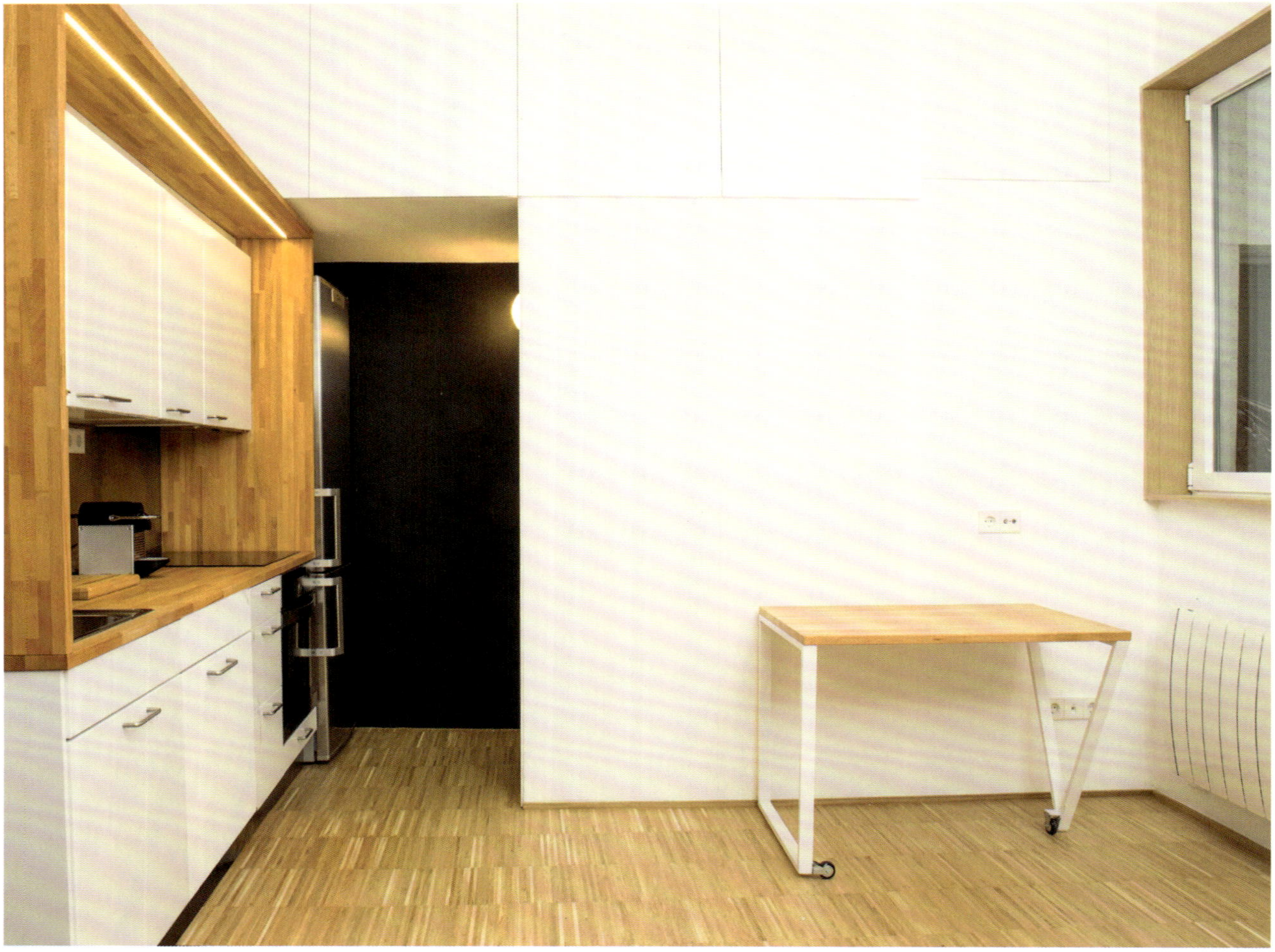

The kitchen is designed as a piece of furniture that references the wooden trim used throughout. The position of an adjacent pivoting table, anchored to the wall, can be adapted to different functional requirements.

Die Küche wird als ein Element des Mobiliars konzipiert, das mit den Holzoberflächen der Wohnung spielt. Daneben passt ein an der Wand befestigter drehbarer Tisch seine Position an die verschiedenen funktionellen Anforderungen an.

La cuisine est conçue comme un élément du mobilier qui joue sur les finitions en bois du loft. À proximité, une table pivotante fixée au mur s'adapte aux divers besoins fonctionnels.

La cocina se proyecta como un elemento del mobiliario que juega con los acabados de madera de la vivienda. Junto a ella, una mesa pivotante anclada a la pared adapta su posición a las diferentes necesidades funcionales.

Even if the renovation of this small apartment relies on the standard technique for this type of project —locating the bed in a loft over the bathroom— its originality lies in the use that is made of the staircase leading to the upper level. By reason of its position in the one open space, it becomes a separator between the entryway and the kitchen/storage area; its design as a freestanding piece of furniture and its structure bring to mind a mountain that must be climbed to reach the sleeping area.

Obgleich das Umbauprojekt dieser kleinen Wohnung eines der üblichen Muster bei dieser Art von Eingriffen benutzt, bei der das Bett auf einem Zwischengeschoss über dem Bad platziert wird, liegt seine Eigenheit in der Art, wie die Zugangstreppe zur oberen Etage genutzt wird. Ihre Position indem einzigen Raum fungiert als Trennelement zwischen dem Eingang und dem Bereich Küche/ Stauraum. Seine Konzeption als Wohnraumn ohne Mobiliar und seine Gestaltung erinnern an einen „Berg", der erklommen werden muss, um in das Schlafzimmer zu gelangen.

Même si le projet de rénovation de ce loft reprend un modèle classique dans ce genre d'interventions où le lit se trouve sur une mezzanine, au-dessus de la salle de bains, sa singularité réside dans l'utilisation de l'escalier d'accès au niveau supérieur. Son emplacement dans la pièce unique joue le rôle de séparation entre l'entrée et l'espace cuisine et les rangements. Sa conception en tant que pièce sans mobilier et son design évoquent une « montagne » qui doit être escaladée pour accéder à la chambre.

Si bien el proyecto de reforma de este pequeño apartamento utiliza un patrón habitual en este tipo de intervenciones, que sitúa la cama en un altillo sobre la pieza del baño, su singularidad radica en la utilización que hace de la escalera de acceso al nivel superior. Su posición dentro del espacio único actúa como separador entre la entrada y la zona de cocina y almacenaje, y su concepción como pieza exenta del mobiliario y su diseño evocan una "montaña" que debe ser escalada para acceder al dormitorio.

292

LOFT ZURITA

Beriot, Bernardini Arquitectos

LOCATION **Madrid, Spain** AREA **28 m² / 301 sq ft** PHOTOS **© Yen Chen**

A small table, as an extension of one of the steps, has been integrated into the design of the ladder. The upper landing serves as the access point for a closet and acts as the seat for a folding table suspended over the entryway.

Als Verlängerung einer ihrer Stufen fügt sich ein kleiner Tisch in die Gestaltung der Treppe ein. Der obere Treppenabsatz dient als Zugang zu einem Wandschrank und als Auflage für eine herunterklappbare Holzplatte, die über dem Eingang hängt.

Une petite table intégrée à la conception de l'escalier vient en prolongement de l'une de ses marches. Le palier supérieur permet d'accéder à une armoire et sert d'assise pour un plateau rabattable suspendu au-dessus de l'entrée.

Una pequeña mesa se integra en el diseño de la escalera como prolongación de uno de sus peldaños. El descansillo superior sirve de acceso a un armario y como asiento para un tablero abatible suspendido sobre la entrada.

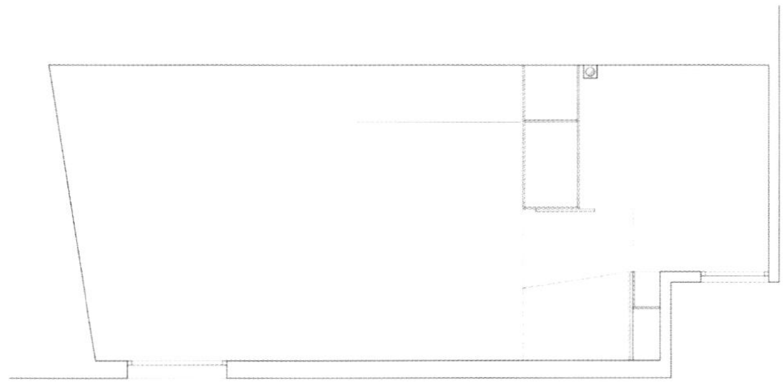

Mezzanine

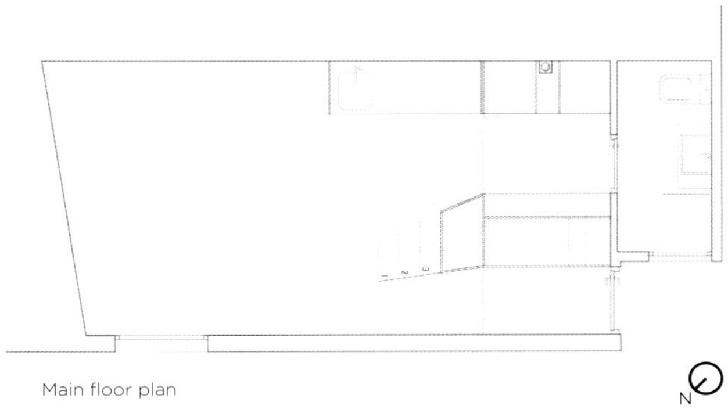

Main floor plan

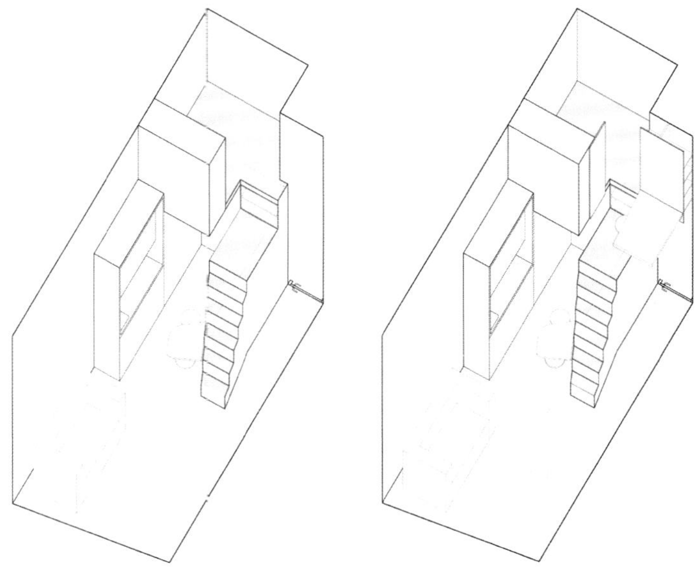

Axonometry

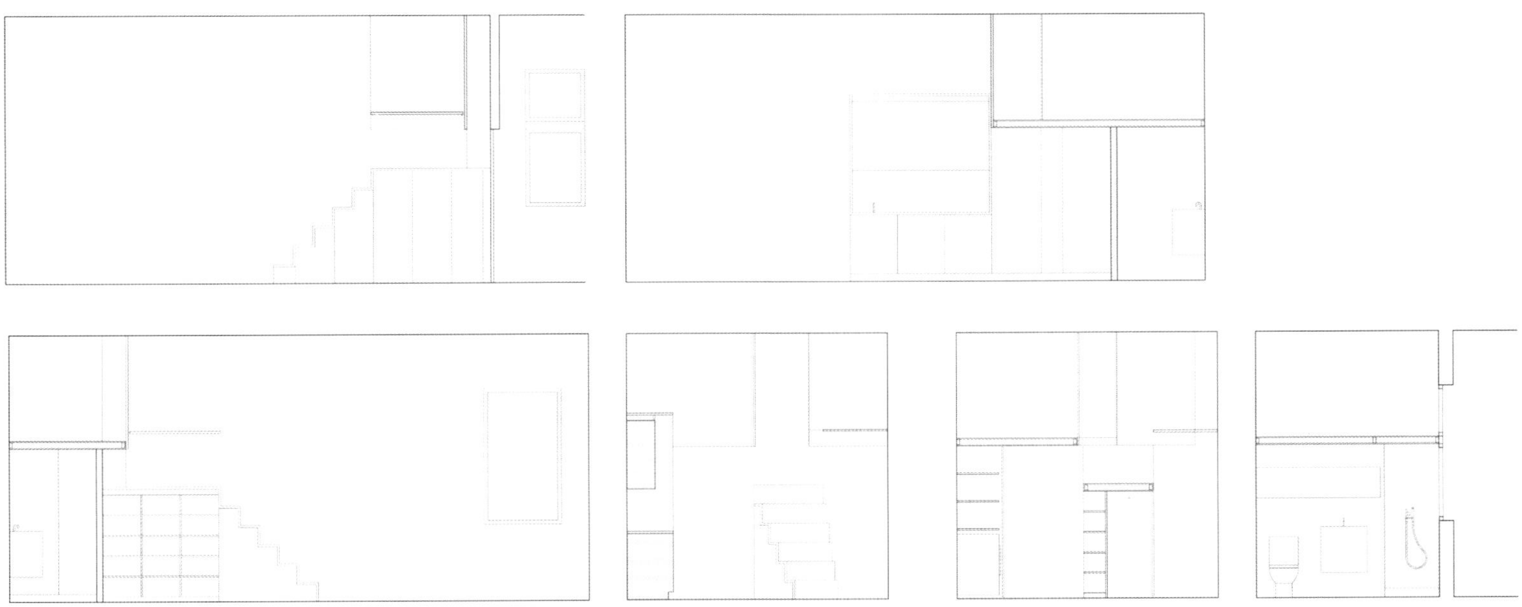

Sections

This renovation of the lower floor of an Edwardian home starts with the concept of intersecting two contrasting L-shaped elements. Designed as containers/furniture, one white and one black, these two elements incorporate closets, shelving, and kitchen appliances. Their intersection generates a singular point in the form of a glass opening between the living room and the master bedroom, which brings spatial continuity to this section of the house.

Der Umbau dieser Wohnung, die in der unteren Etage eines Gebäudes im edwardianischen Stil liegt, beruht auf der Idee der Überlagerung von zwei entgegengesetzten Elementen in der L-Form. Als jeweils ein weißes und ein schwarzes Containermöbelstück konzipiert, verbinden diese beiden Elemente Wandschränke, Regale und die Kücheneinrichtung. Seine Schnittstelle schafft dadurch einen einzigartigen Punkt in Form einer Glasöffnung, die zwischen Wohnzimmer und Hauptschlafzimmer liegt, welche diesem Bereich des Hauses eine räumliche Kontinuität verleiht.

Les travaux de cet appartement situé au rez-de-chaussée d'un édifice de style classique édouardien reposent sur l'idée de superposition de deux éléments opposés en forme de « L ». Conçus en forme de meubles containers, l'un blanc et l'autre noir, ces deux éléments rassemblent des armoires, des étagères et les éléments de cuisine. Leur intersection confère un point singulier en forme d'ouverture en verre, située entre le séjour et la chambre parentale qui confère une continuité spatiale à cet espace de vie.

La reforma de esta vivienda situada en el nivel inferior de un edificio de estilo eduardiano se basa en la idea de superposición de dos elementos opuestos en forma de "L". Concebidos a modo de muebles contenedores, uno blanco y otro negro, estos dos elementos aglutinan armarios, estanterías y el equipo de cocina, y su intersección genera un punto singular en forma de abertura de vidrio, situada entre la sala de estar y el dormitorio principal, que confiere continuidad espacial a esta zona de la vivienda.

296

NEVERN SQUARE APARTMENT

Daniele Petteno Architecture Workshop

LOCATION London, Great Britain AREA 69 m² / 743 sq ft PHOTOS © Daniele Petteno Architecture Workshop

The glass opening where the two L's intersect serves as one more window, allowing natural light to enter and doubling the visible possibilities from the two areas it connects.

Die Glasöffnung, die an der Schnittstelle des „L“ liegt, wirkt wie ein weiteres Fenster im Haus, sie lässt Tageslicht ein und verdoppelt die Augenlinien der beiden Bereiche, die sie verbindet.

L'ouverture en verre située à l'intersection des « L » joue le rôle de fenêtre supplémentaire dans la maison favorisant ainsi l'entrée de la lumière naturelle et doublant le champ de vision des deux espaces qu'elle relie.

La abertura de vidrio situada en el punto de intersección de las “L” actúa como una ventana más de la casa, contribuyendo a la entrada de luz natural y duplicando las visuales de los dos ámbitos que conecta.

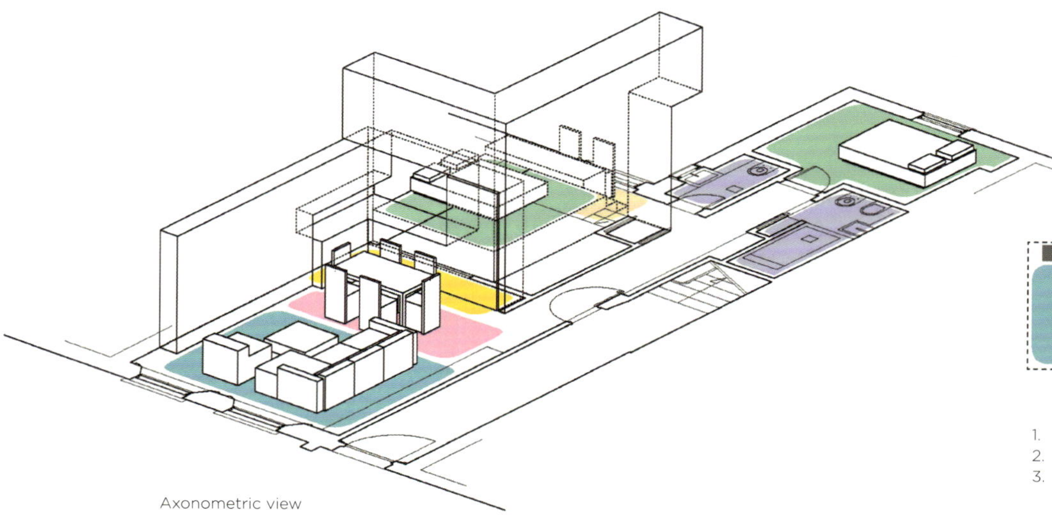

Axonometric view

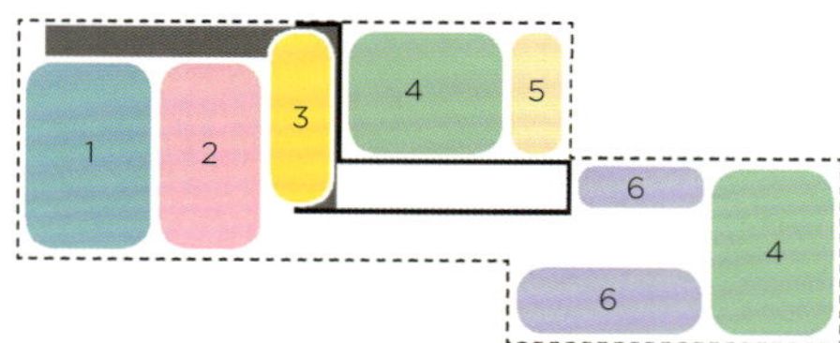

1. Living
2. Dining
3. Kitchen
4. Bedrooms
5. Study
6. Bathrooms

The two L-shaped elements define the layout of the rooms. The black one, 2.25 meters high, runs through the living-dining room, and ends in the kitchen area.

Beide Elemente in „L"-Form definieren die Aufteilung der Wohnräume im Haus. Das schwarze Element mit 2,25 Metern Höhe verläuft durch den Wohn-Essbereich und endet im Bereich der Küche.

Les deux éléments en forme de « L » définissent la disposition des espaces à l'intérieur de la maison. Celui en noir, de 2,25 mètres de hauteur, parcourt l'espace séjour-salle à manger pour terminer dans la cuisine.

Los dos elementos en forma de "L" definen la disposición de las estancias dentro de la vivienda. El de color negro, de 2,25 metros de altura, discurre por la zona del estar comedor y acaba en la zona de la cocina.

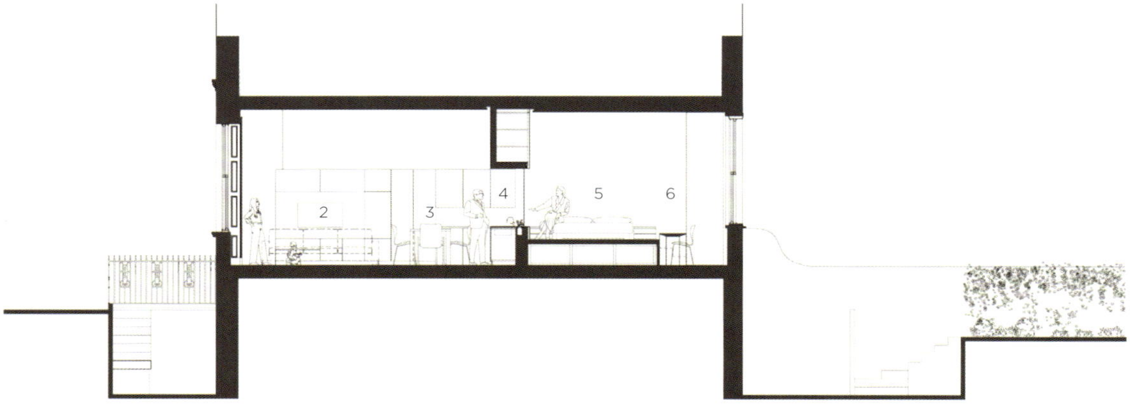

Section A - A

Section B - B

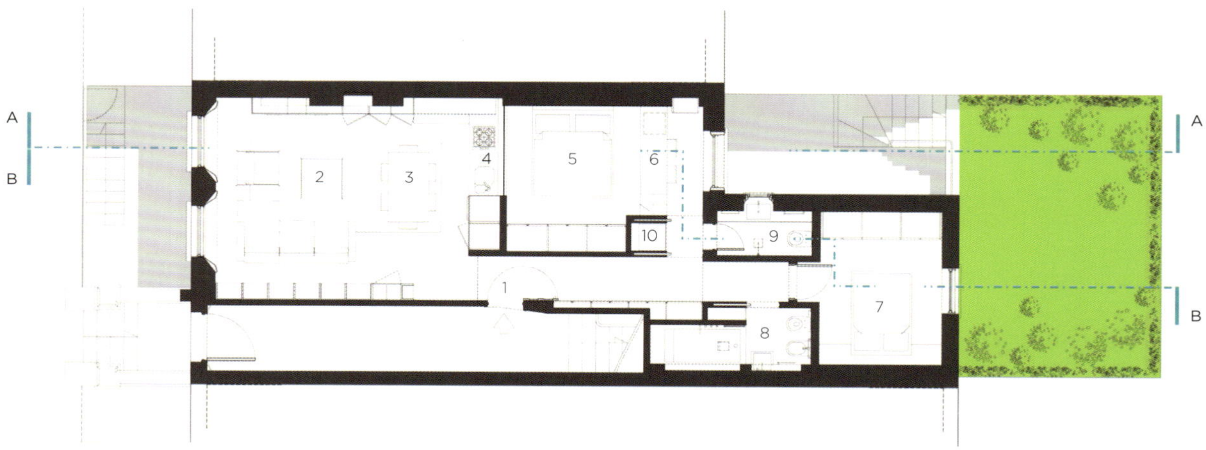

1. Entrance
2. Living
3. Dining
4. Kitchen
5. Master bedroom
6. Studio
7. Bedroom
8. Shared bathroom
9. Ensuite/Shared Wetroom
10. Utility

Ground floor plan

0 1 2 3 4 5m

N

Here, an apartment close to a university is remodeled to include three student bedrooms, a kitchen, two bathrooms, and an entryway that can be used as a common living space. The design of the bedrooms, conceived as cubes that are 2.5 meters on a side, creates flexible, functional spaces. Folding beds and desks are used, with generous storage capacity in the walls, thus allowing the rooms to be transformed into studies, bedrooms, or leisure spaces.

Umgestaltung einer Wohnung auf dem Unigelände. Die Zielsetzung lautete 3 Schlafzimmer für Studenten, Küche, zwei Bäder und einen Zugangsbereich, der sich als Gemeinschaftsraum verwenden lässt. Die Gestaltung der Schlafzimmer, als Würfel mit 2,50 Meter langen Schenkeln konzipiert, lässt flexible und funktionelle Räume entstehen. Durch den Einsatz von Klappbetten und Klappschreibtischen und die geräumigen Bereiche mit Stauraum, die in die vertikalen Wandflächen integriert sind, lassen sich die Zimmer in Studierzimmer, Schlafzimmer oder Orte der Freizeitgestaltung umwandeln.

Réaménagement d'un appartement à proximité d'une zone universitaire dont le programme comprend tois chambres pour étudiants, une cuisine, deux salles de bains et un espace d'accès qui peut service de séjour. La conception des chambres, réalisées en forme de cube de 2,50 mètres d'arête, confère des espaces modulables et fonctionnels. L'utilisation des lits et bureaux rabattables et les vastes rangements intégrés dans les murs permettent de transformer la pièce en bureau, chambre ou espace de loisir.

Remodelación de un apartamento cercano a una zona universitaria, cuyo programa incluye tres dormitorios para estudiantes, cocina, dos baños y una zona de acceso que puede utilizarse como sala común. El diseño de los dormitorios, concebidos a modo de cubos de 2,50 metros de arista, genera unos espacios flexibles y funcionales; el uso de camas y escritorios abatibles y las amplias zonas de almacenaje integradas en los paramentos verticales, permiten transformar las estancias en estudio, dormitorio o lugar de ocio.

304

XADREZ STUDENT'S APARTMENT

UMA Collective

LOCATION **Lisbon, Portugal** AREA **50 m² / 538 sq ft** PHOTOS **© Rui Cruz, UMA Collective**

The plan is to create a contemporary design using technically advanced materials such panels made of OSB (oriented strand board).

Der Eingriff zielt darauf ab, eine moderne Gestaltung zu schaffen, für die Material mit technisch fortschrittlicher Konzeption wie Grobspanplatten eingesetzt wird. Dieses Produkt wird aus Holz hergestellt, das aus ausgerichteten Spänen besteht.

L'intervention aspire à créer un design contemporain pour lequel on a utilisé des matériaux de conception technique avancée tels que les panneaux OSB, panneaux de copeaux encollés.

La intervención aspira a crear un diseño contemporáneo, para lo cual se utilizan materiales de concepción técnica avanzada como los paneles OSB, producto derivado de la madera compuesto de virutas orientadas y prensadas.

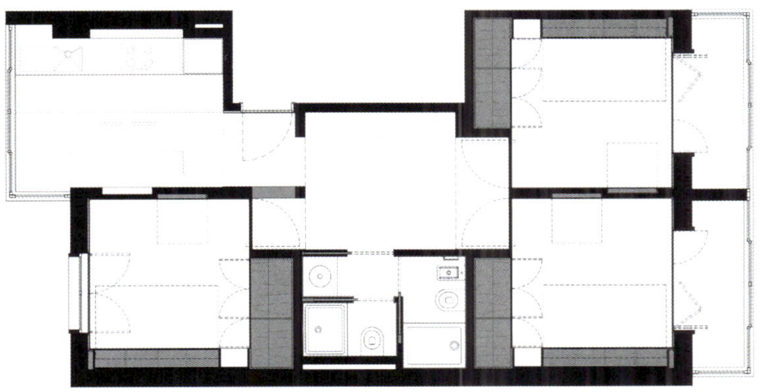

1. Kitchen
2. Entrance/Living area
3. Bedroom
4. Toilet

Floor plan

Two vertical faced walls, constructed of wooden panels, define the principal space in this small apartment. Their unique design allows them to bring together and conceal some of the household furniture, including a folding bed, and they contain the sliding doors that lead into the kitchen and bathroom. This frees up an open plan space that is very flexible in terms of layouts for different uses. A large picture window, flanked by two wooden walls, extends the interior space out toward the terrace.

Zwei sich gegenüberliegende vertikale Wandverkleidungen aus Holzpaneelen, definieren den Hauptbereich dieser kleinen Wohnung. Das besondere Design konzentriert und verbirgt Elemente der Wohnungseinrichtung, darunter ein Klappbett, und bindet die Schiebetüren zu Küche und Bad mit ein. Dadurch ergibt sich ein durchscheinender Raum, der für die verschiedenen Konfigurationen der Nutzung äußerst flexibel ist. Ein großes Fenster, flankiert von den beiden Holzwänden, dehnt den Innenraum Richtung Terrasse aus.

Deux parements verticaux face à face, construits avec des panneaux en bois, définissent l'espace de vie de ce petit appartement. Son design spécifique concentre et cache des éléments de mobilier de la maison, à savoir un lit escamotable, avec des portes coulissantes pour accéder à la cuisine et à la salle de bains. Ceci permet de libérer un espace ouvert, très modulable pour diverses configurations d'utilisation. Une grande baie vitrée, flanquée de deux murs en bois, prolonge l'espace intérieur vers la terrasse.

Dos paramentos verticales enfrentados, construidos con paneles de madera, definen el ámbito principal de este pequeño apartamento. Su especial diseño concentra y oculta elementos del mobiliario de la casa, incluyendo una cama abatible, e integra las puertas deslizantes de acceso a cocina y baño. De esta forma se libera un espacio diáfano, muy flexible frente a las diferentes configuraciones de uso. Un gran ventanal, flanqueado por las dos paredes de madera, extiende el espacio interior hacia la terraza.

308

BATIPIN FLAT

studioWok

LOCATION **Milano, Italy** AREA **28 m² / 301 sq ft** PHOTOS **© Federico Villa**

The kitchen and bathroom were designed as two monochrome blue spaces; this contrasts with the luminous white used in the living room, which enhances the grain of the wooden walls.

Küche und Bad werden als einfarbige Räume in Blau gestaltet als Gegensatz zu der hellen weißen Farbe, die im Wohnzimmer eingesetzt wird, welche die Textur der Wandflächen aus Holz betont.

La cuisine et la salle de bains sont conçues comme deux espaces monochromes de couleur bleue, en contraste avec le blanc lumineux du séjour, ce qui met en relief la texture des parements en bois.

La cocina y el baño se diseñan como dos espacios monocromos de color azul, en contraste con el luminoso color blanco utilizado en la sala de estar, que resalta la textura de los paramentos de madera.

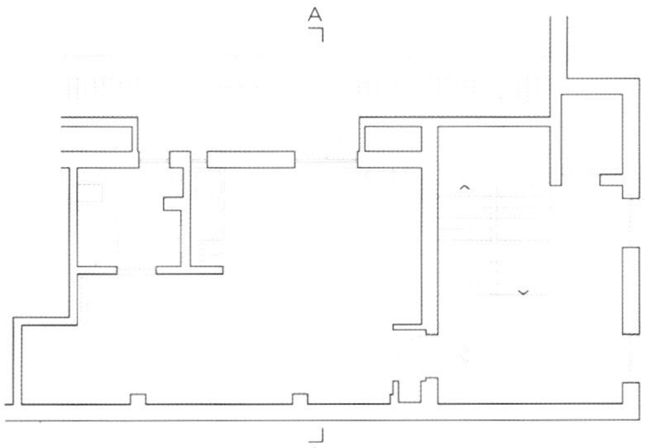

Existing floor plan

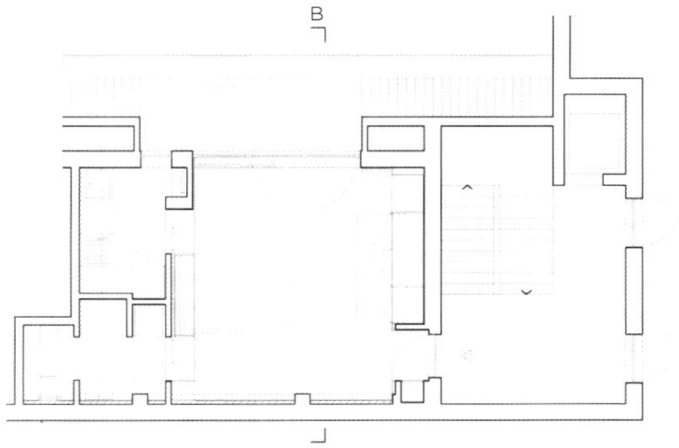

Project floor plan

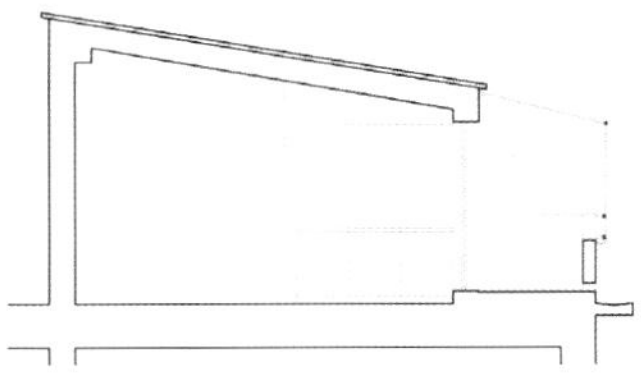

Section A-A

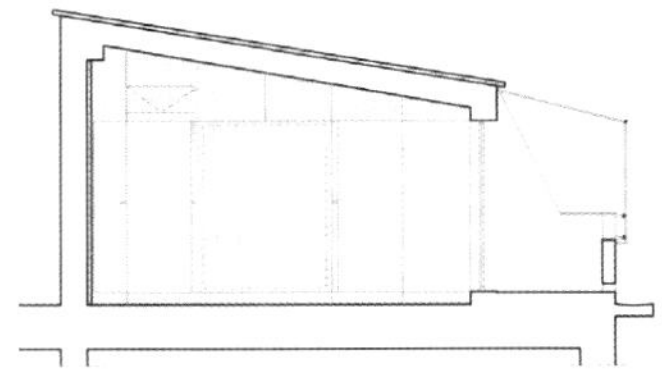

Section B-B

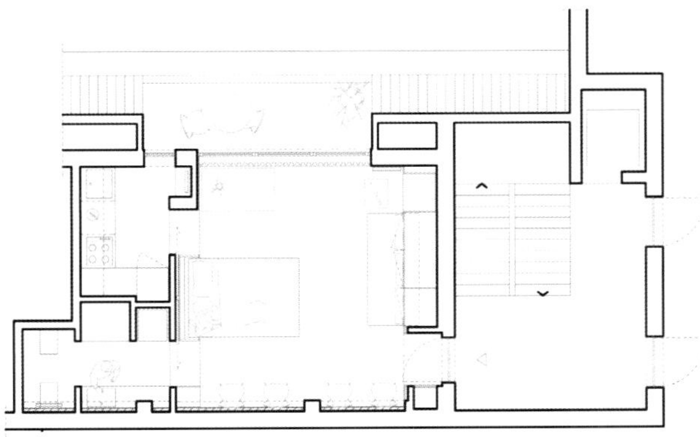

Wake up

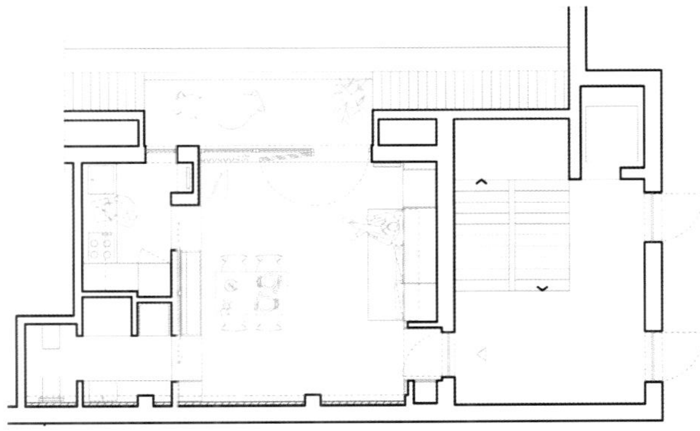

Lunch time

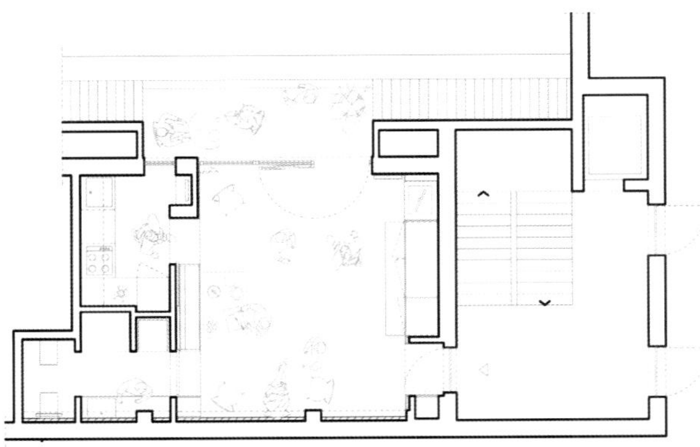

Let's party

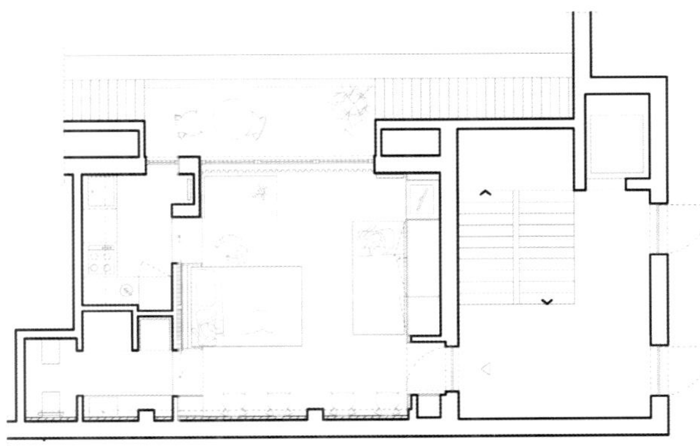

Sleeping time (with guest)

This older downtown apartment was remodeled around an airy, rectangular central space, created by grouping the functional pieces into an ell that was formed along two sides. Against one of the two free walls is a hinged screen that can fold like origami paper, and create many possible partitions, so that the dwelling becomes a flexible space suitable for numerous layouts.

Diese Renovierung einer alten Wohnung im Stadtzentrum strukturiert sich um einen durchscheinenden und rechteckigen zentralen Raum, erzeugt durch die Vereinigung des Funktionsprogramms in einem „L"-Entwurf, auf beiden Seiten entfaltet. Ein als Origami-Papier gegliederter Schirm, auf einer der beiden freien Wände des Viereckes integriert, erzeugt verschiedene Möglichkeiten der Einkapselung innerhalb der Wohnung, die zu einem flexiblen Raum wird, der für mehrere Konfigurationen offen ist.

Ces travaux d'un ancien appartement du centre de la ville sont structurés autour d'un espace central ouvert et rectangulaire, créé grâce au groupement du programme fonctionnel dans un schéma en forme de « L » développé sur deux de ses côtés. Un paravent articulé sous forme de papier d'origami, intégré à un des deux murs libres du rectangle, créé diverses possibilités de compartimentage au sein de l'appartement pour en faire un espace modulable et ouvert à plusieurs agencements.

Esta renovación de un antiguo piso del centro de la ciudad se estructura alrededor de un espacio central diáfano y rectangular, generado mediante la agrupación del programa funcional en un esquema en "L", desarrollado sobre dos de sus lados. Un biombo articulado a modo de papel de origami, integrado sobre una de las dos paredes libres del rectángulo, genera diversas posibilidades de compartimentación dentro de la casa, que deviene un espacio flexible y abierto a múltiples configuraciones domésticas.

314

BIOMBOMBASTIC

elii

LOCATION Madrid, Spain AREA 25 m² / 268 sq ft PHOTOS © Miguel de Guzmán, Rocío Romero

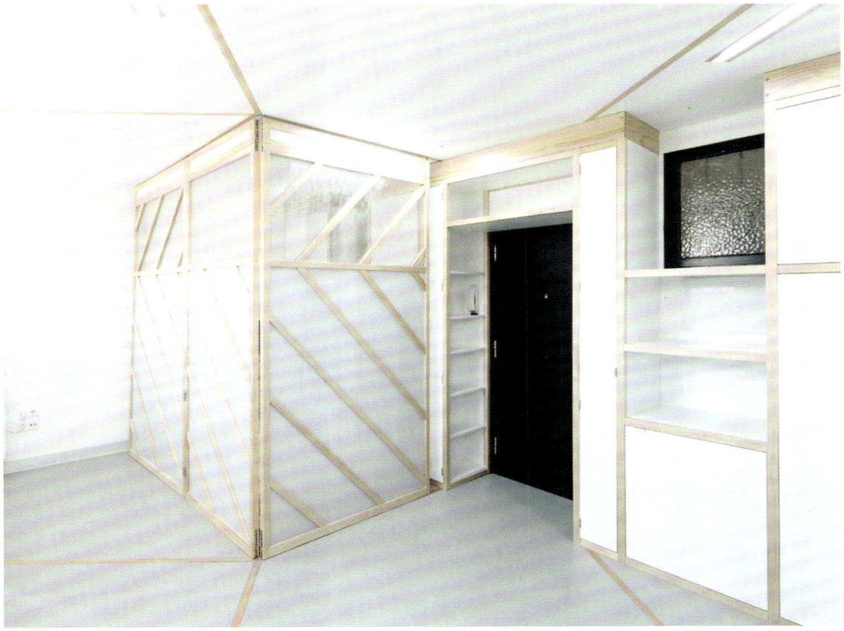
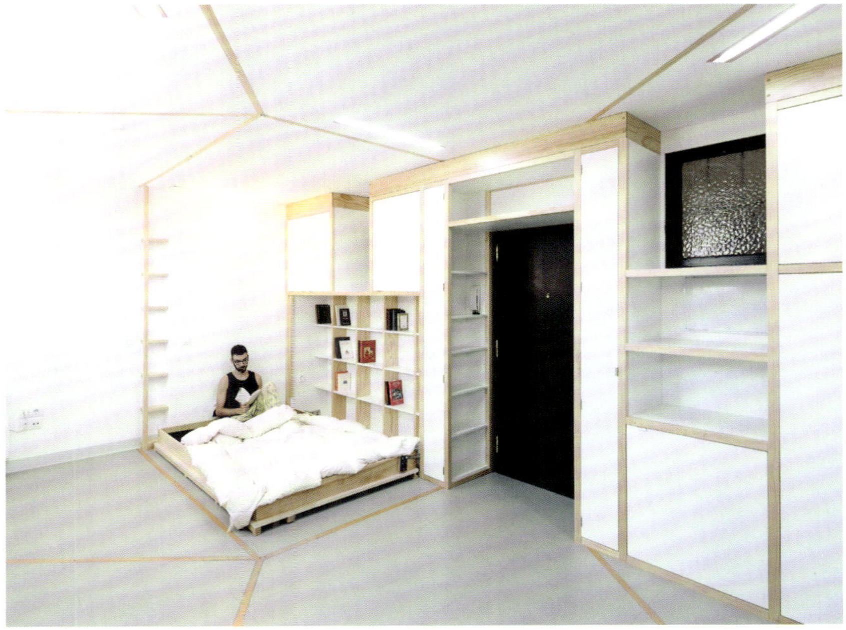

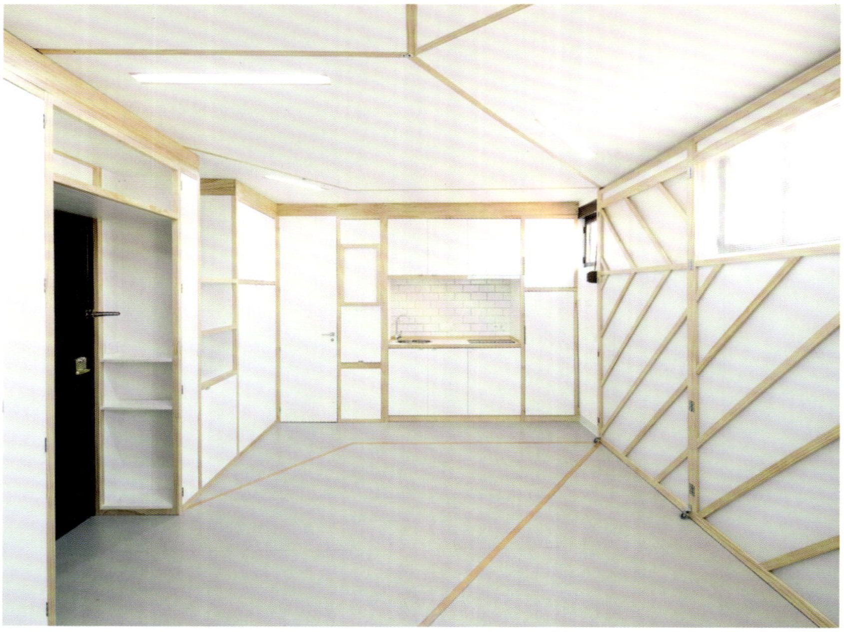
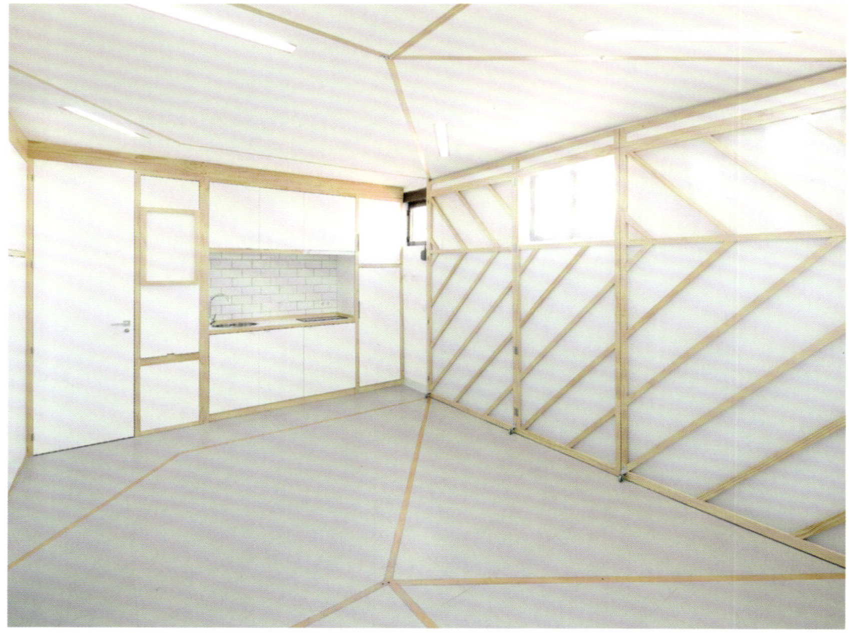

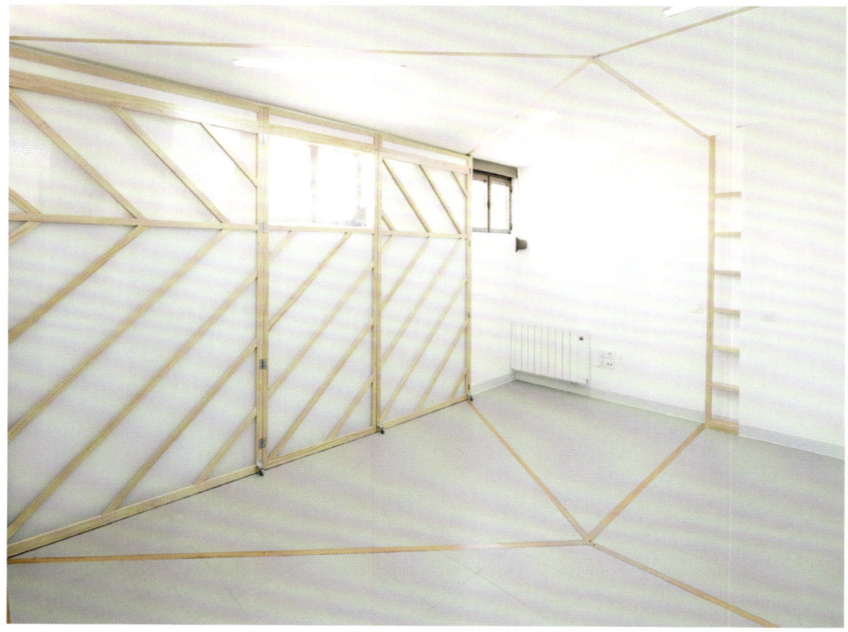

Wooden tracks on the floors, walls, and ceiling organize the space, showing where the screen could be placed when it is moved, and indicating the lighting for the different spaces that are formed.

Holzschienen, die in Boden, Wände und Decke eingelassen sind, ordnen den Raum und kennzeichnen Punkte zur Befestigung des Schirms beim Bewegen und die Beleuchtung der verschiedenen Bereiche, die dabei entstehen.

Des rails en bois fixés aux sols, murs et plafond, ordonnent l'espace et marquent les points de fixation du paravent en se déplaçant et l'éclairage des divers espaces qu'ils créent.

Unos carriles de madera situados en suelos, paredes y techo, ordenan el espacio y marcan los puntos de fijación del biombo al desplazarse y la iluminación de los diferentes ámbitos que se generan.

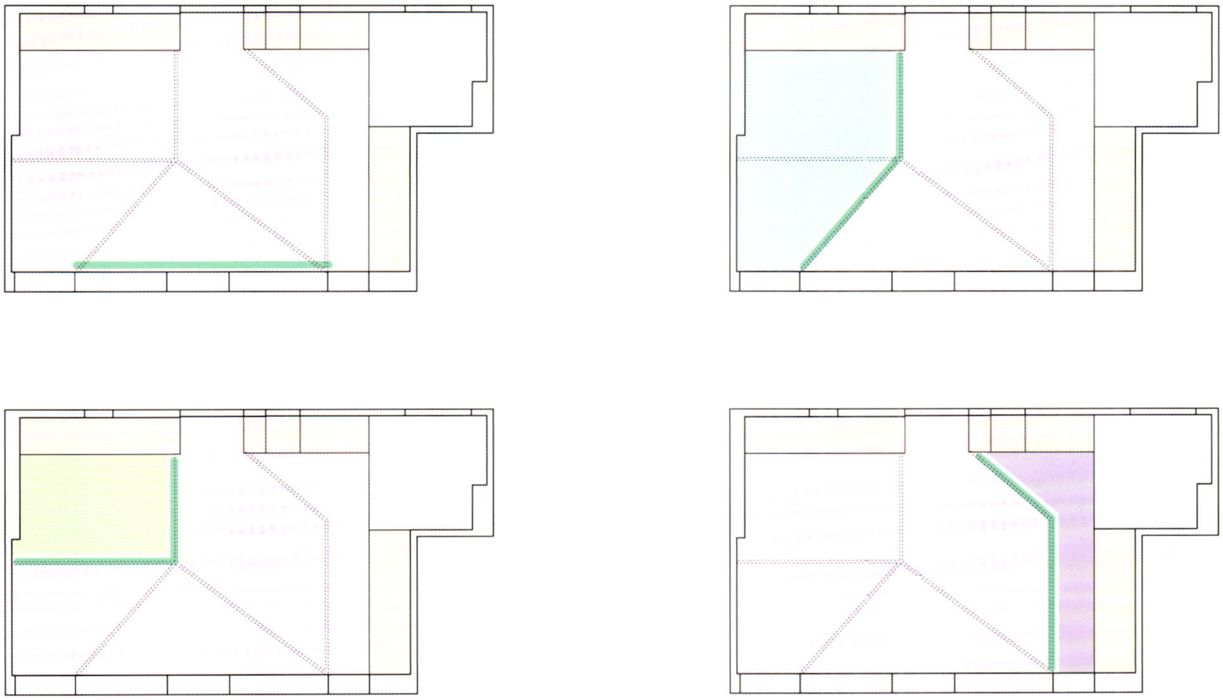

Layout options

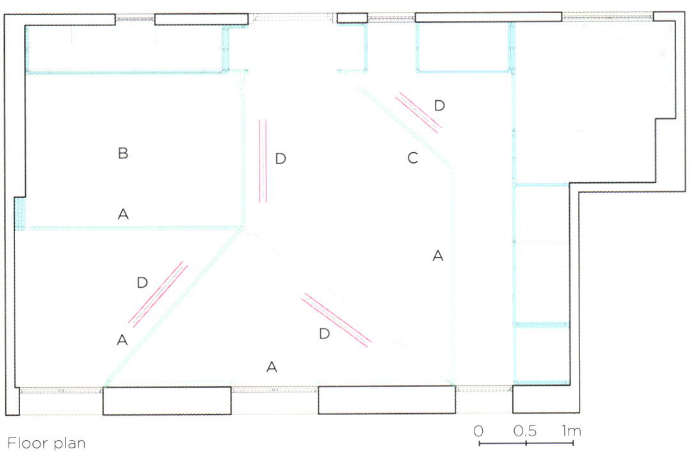

Floor plan

A. Sliding panel
B. Bed
C. Table
D. Light

Axonometric view

The plan here is to transform an existing home into two independent studios and have the option of connecting them to create one sole dwelling. The transformation has a functional central core that brings together kitchens, baths, storage and distribution spaces, thus freeing up the main space of each studio. The height of this central core, 60 centimeters above the original floor, provides a location for the new fixtures that were created by the project.

Das Projekt baut eine vorhandene Wohnung um und schafft dadurch zwei voneinander unabhängige Studios, die sich verbinden lassen, wodurch ein einziger Wohnraum entsteht. Der Eingriff entwirft einen zentralen Kern mit Funktionscharakter, der Küchen, Bäder, Stauraum und Flure verbindet und dadurch die Hauptwohnräume beider Studios davon befreit. Durch die Erhöhung dieses zentralen Kerns 60 cm über dem ursprünglichen Boden lassen sich die neuen Einrichtungen platzieren, die durch den Eingriff geschaffen werden.

Le projet transforme un bien immobilier existant en deux studios indépendants qui offrent la possibilité de communiquer entre eux et créer un seul logement. Les travaux prévoient un espace central fonctionnel qui centralise les cuisines, les salles de bains, les espaces de rangement et les espaces de répartition et qui libère les pièces principales de chacun des studios. La surélévation de cet espace de 60 centimètres par rapport au niveau du sol permet de nouvelles installations créées grâce à l'intervention.

El proyecto reforma una vivienda existente para crear dos estudios independientes que tienen la posibilidad de conectarse y de crear una única vivienda. La intervención plantea un núcleo central de carácter funcional que aglutina cocinas, baños, zonas de almacenamiento y espacios de distribución y que libera las estancias principales de cada uno de los estudios. La elevación de este núcleo central 60 centímetros sobre el suelo original permite ubicar las nuevas instalaciones generadas por la intervención.

318

INSIDER

elii

LOCATION **Zaragoza, Spain** AREA **76 m² / 821 sq ft** PHOTOS **© María Carmona**

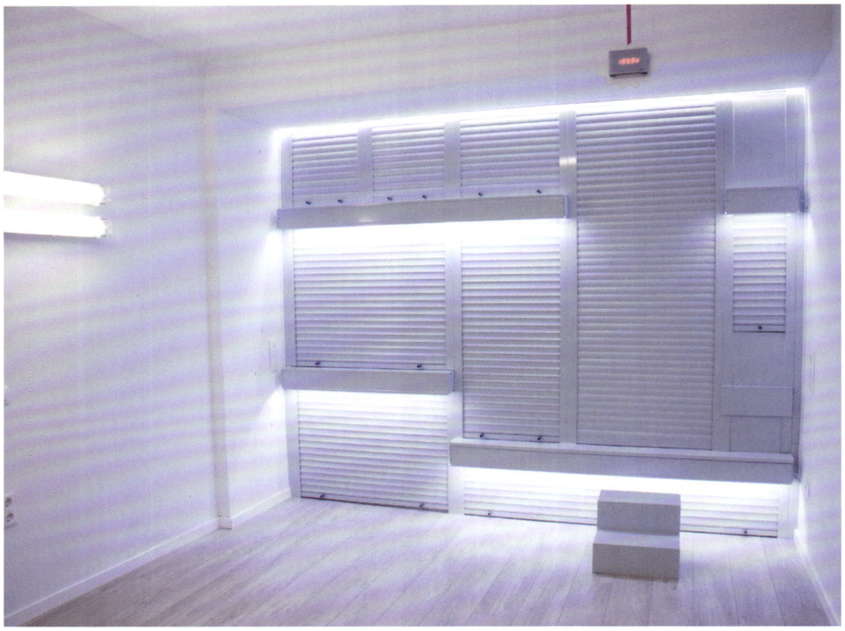

The relationship between the functional and living spaces is controlled by a set of blinds that can reveal or conceal different parts of the home, such as the kitchen, bed, or entryway.

Mithilfe einer Reihe von Jalousien, durch die sich die verschiedenen Elemente des Hauses, wie Küche, Bett oder Zugangsflur verbergen lassen, treten die Funktionsbereiche mit den Wohnbereichen in Verbindung.

Les espaces fonctionnels sont connectés au séjour par un jeu de persiennes qui permet de montrer ou cacher les divers éléments de l'appartement tels que la cuisine, le lit ou le couloir.

Las zonas funcionales se relacionan con las zonas de estar mediante un juego de persianas que permiten mostrar o esconder los diferentes elementos de la casa, como la cocina, la cama o el pasillo de acceso.

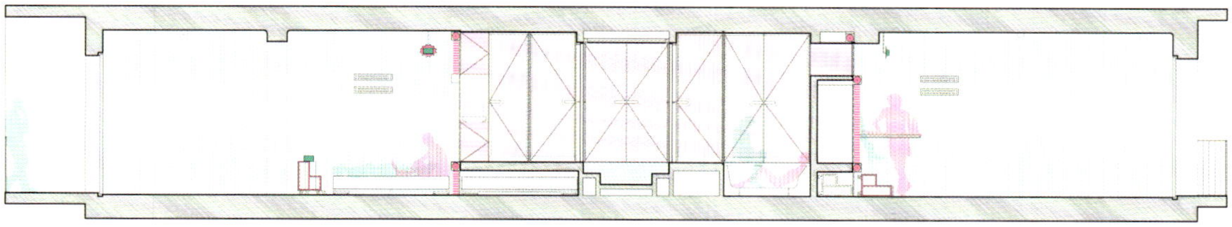

Section

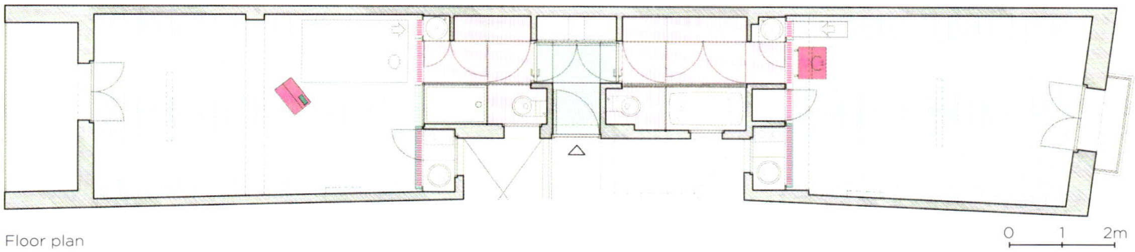

Floor plan

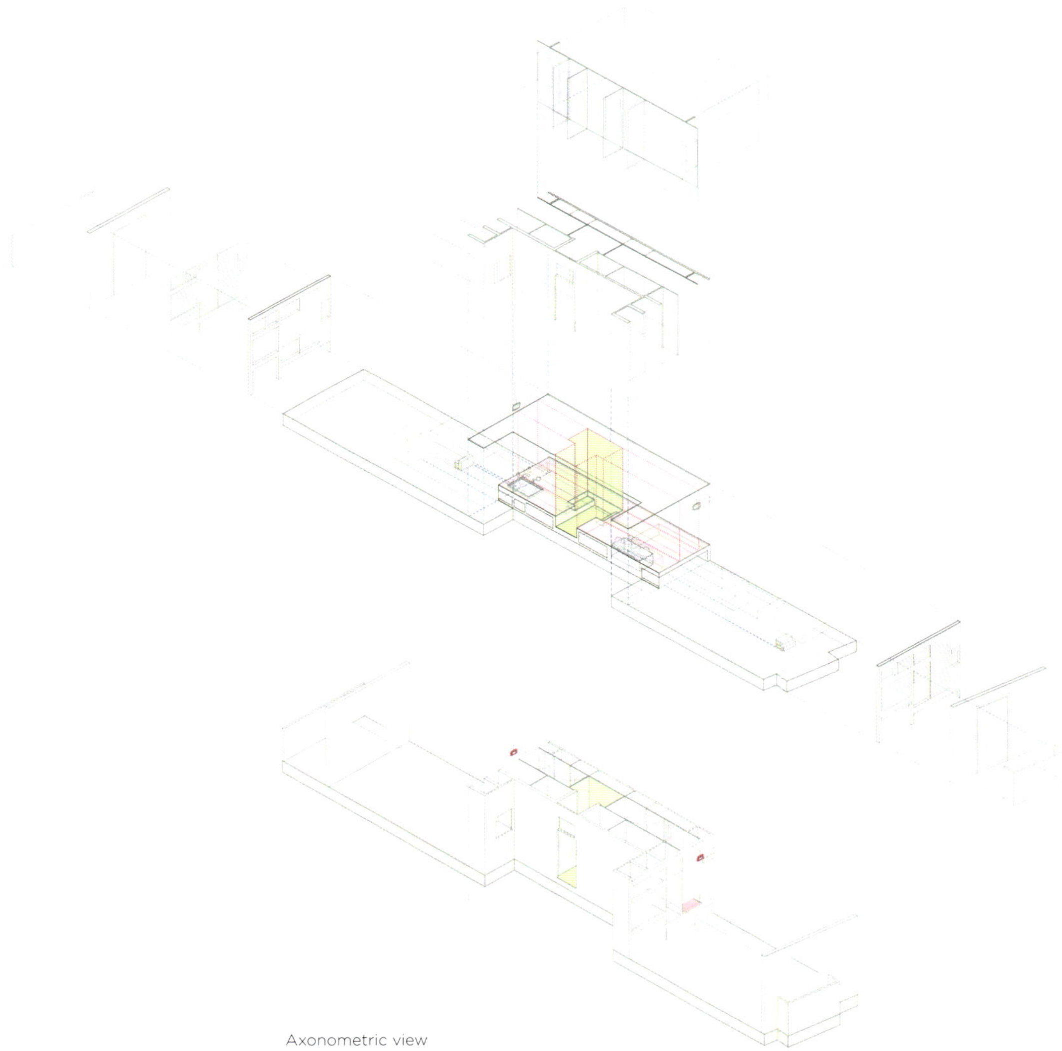

Axonometric view

TRAVELBOX OLOT

JUUST / juustdesign.com

PHOTOS © Stefan Prattes

A box measuring 209 x 124.5 x 38.5 centimeters and weighting 60 kilos, built of wood and housed in a thin aluminum casing, allows its users to carry with them on their lives' journeys the essential furniture for a home: bed, table, chair, and storage space. Its compact, rigid design protects it from the vicissitudes of long trips; then, once it has reached its destination, it unfolds to instantly create a new and comfortable living space.

Ein Kasten mit den Abmessungen 209 x 124,5 x 38,5 cm und 60 kg Gewicht, mit einem Holzrahmen und einem dünnen Gehäuse aus Aluminiumblech gebaut, ermöglicht dem Nutzer, die wesentlichen Bestandteile der Einrichtung einer Wohnstätte - Bett, Tisch, Stuhl und Stauraum - bei seiner Reise durch das Leben mitzunehmen. Dank seiner kompakten und stabilen Bauweise kann er die Höhen und Tiefen langer Reisen überstehen und nach der Ankunft an seinem Bestimmungsort ausgebreitet werden, um sofort einen neuen und bequemen Raum zum Leben zu schaffen.

Un caisson de 209 x 124,5 x 38,5 centimètres et 60 kilos construit avec une structure en bois et un fin châssis en tôle d'aluminium permet à ses utilisateurs d'emmener avec eux les éléments essentiels du mobilier d'un appartement : un lit, une table, une chaise et un espace de rangement, dans leur périple de vie. Sa conception compacte et rigide lui permet de supporter les aléas des longs voyages et, une fois arrivé à destination, se poser pour créer sur le moment un espace neuf et confortable pour y vivre.

Una caja de 209 x 124,5 x 38,5 centímetros y 60 kilos de peso, construida con una estructura de madera y una delgada carcasa de chapa de aluminio, permite a sus usuarios llevar consigo las piezas esenciales del mobiliario de una vivienda –cama, mesa, silla y espacio de almacenamiento– en su periplo vital. Su diseño compacto y rígido le permite soportar los avatares de los largos viajes y, una vez llegada a su destino, desplegarse para crear al instante un nuevo y confortable espacio para vivir.

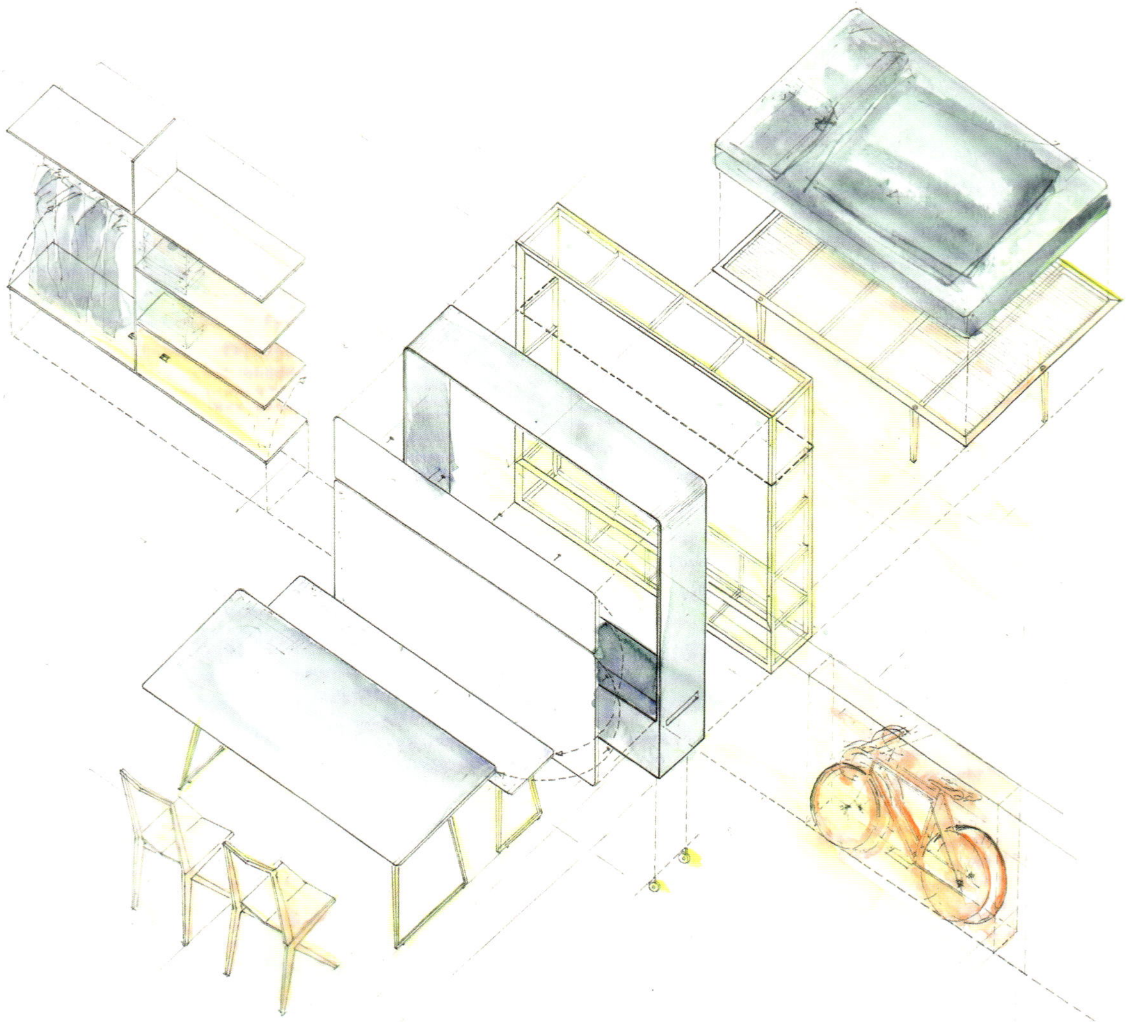

Expanded axonometric

The items that make up the Travelbox settle into their new environments, creating living spaces on their own or in combination with other furniture and decor.

Die Elemente der *Travelbox*besiedeln die Umgebungen, in denen sie sich ausbreitet, und schaffen alleine oder in der Verbindung mit anderen Einrichtungs- oder Dekorationselementen Wohnräume.

Les éléments de la *Travelbox* s'emparent des environnements où ils se déploient créant en soi des espaces habitables ou en combinaison avec d'autres éléments de mobilier ou de décoration.

Los elementos que componen la *Travelbox* colonizan los entornos en los que se despliegan, creando por sí solos espacios habitables o en combinación con otros elementos de mobiliario o decoración.

VOLUME: 1 m³ / 35.3 cu ft
WEIGHT: 60 kg / 132 lb
DIMENSIONS: 209 (l), 124,5 (h), 38,5 (w) cm / 82.3 (l), 49 (h), 15.1 (w) in

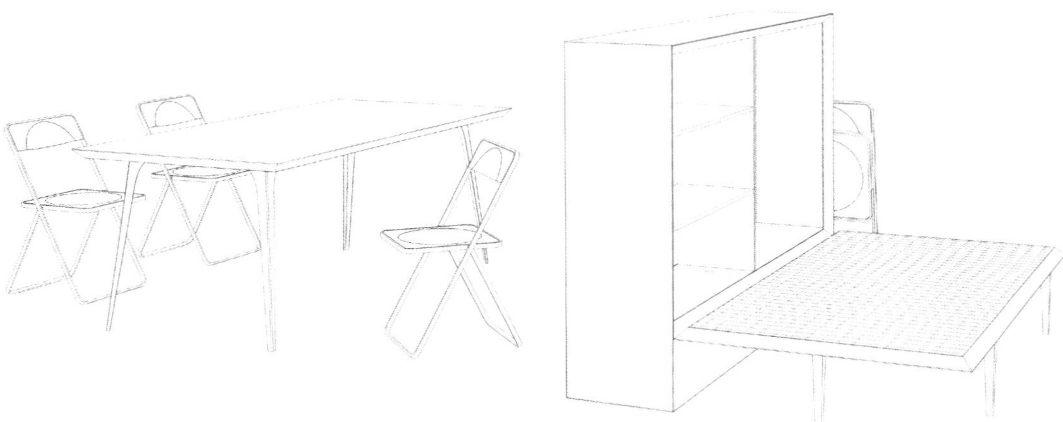

THE BIKE SHELF

KNIFE & SAW / **theknifeandsaw.com**

PHOTOS © Chris Brigham

This small wooden element, somewhere between a decorative item and a piece of furniture, offers an interesting combination of uses while solving the cumbersome problem of where in the house to store a bicycle. The bicycle hangs on this small wall-anchored shelf, which is large enough for books, keys, or even the bicycle helmet, and blends into the living space as one more component of the decor.

Dieses kleine Holzelement, das sich zwischen dekorativem Element und Möbelstück bewegt, bietet eine interessante Kombination von Nutzungsarten, wodurch sich ein manchmal verworrenes Problem, wie die Platzierung eines Fahrrades in einer Wohnung, lösen lässt. An einem kleinen, an der Wand befestigten Regal hängend, dessen Abmessungen es ermöglichen, Bücher, die Schlüssel oder den Sturzhelm des Radfahrers abzulegen, integriert sich das Fahrrad als ein weiterer Bestandteil der Innenausstattung in die Wohnstätte.

Ce petit élément en bois, situé à mi-chemin entre un élément de décoration et de mobilier, offre une intéressante combinaison d'utilisations qui permet de résoudre le problème parfois confus tel que le rangement de la bicyclette dans une maison. Accrochée à une petite étagère fixée au mur dont les dimensions permettent de placer quelques livres, des clés ou le casque du cycliste, la bicyclette est intégrée à la maison comme un élément supplémentaire de la décoration.

Este pequeño elemento de madera, situado a mitad de camino entre pieza ornamental y de mobiliario, ofrece una interesante combinación de usos que permite resolver un problema en ocasiones tan farragoso como es la ubicación de una bicicleta dentro de una casa. Colgada de una pequeña repisa anclada a la pared, cuyas dimensiones permiten colocar unos libros, las llaves o el propio casco del ciclista, la bicicleta se integra en la vivienda como un componente más de la decoración.

Walnut

DESCRIPTION: Solid Eastern Black Walnut. Danish Oil Finish
WEIGHT: 6,8 kg / 15.00 lb(s)
DIMENSIONS: 43,8 (w), 13,3 (h), 40,6 (d), 4,5 (Slot) cm
17.25 (w) / 5.25 (h) / 16"(d) / 1.75 (Slot) in

Walnut - Small

DESCRIPTION: Solid Eastern Black Walnut. Danish Oil Finish
WEIGHT: 5,4 kg / 12.00 lb(s)
DIMENSIONS: 36,8 (w), 14,6 (h), 35,6 (d), 5 (Slot) cm
14.5 (w) / 5.75 (h) / 14 (d) / 2 (Slot) in

Hickory

DESCRIPTION: Solid Rift Sawn Hickory. Hard-wax Oil
WEIGHT: 7,3 kg / 16.00 lb(s)
DIMENSIONS: 43,8 (w), 13,3 (h), 40,6 (d), 4,5 (Slot) cm
17.25 (w), 5.25 (h), 16 (d), 1.75 (Slot) in

Hickory - Small

DESCRIPTION: Solid Rift Sawn Hickory. Hard-wax Oil
WEIGHT: 6,3 kg / 14.00 lb(s)
DIMENSIONS: 36,8 (w), 14,6 (h), 35,6 (d), 5 (Slot) cm
14.5 (w) / 5.75 (h) / 14 (d) / 2 (Slot) in

Options

This item is handcrafted of walnut or ash; it comes in two sizes, which vary both the outer dimensions and those of the slot for the bicycle.

Dieses Teil wird von Hand aus Eschen- oder Walnussholz gefertigt, und sein Design bietet zwei mögliche Größen, welche in den äußeren Maßen und den Maßen des Verankerungsschlitzes des Fahrrads variieren.

Cette pièce a été réalisée manuellement, construite en noyer ou frêne, sa conception offre deux tailles possibles qui modifient les dimensions extérieures et celles de la rainure d'ancrage de la bicyclette.

La fabricación de esta pieza es manual, construida con madera de nogal o de fresno, y su diseño ofrece dos tamaños posibles, que varían las dimensiones exteriores y las de la ranura de anclaje de la bicicleta.

Passion & Fashion
The Clash
HAMBURGER EYES

Grid systems
Raster systeme

AMAZONS

Passion & Fashion
HAMBURGER EYES
DESIGN·SPONGE at HOME
Max Huber

DOMINO LOFT

Charles Irby, Peter Suen / icosadesign.com

PHOTOS © Brian Flaherty

A two-story multipurpose structure installed in this small apartment transforms it into a dynamic and more efficient space. Its factory-made components —concrete panels, wooden strips, and built-in furniture— were assembled inside the dwelling. The design provides several storage areas and a sleeping loft; there is also a space that can be used as either a dining room, a guest room, or a work space.

Die Platzierung eines Multifunktionsmöbelstücks mit zwei Ebenen verwandelt den Innenraum dieser kleinen Wohnung in einen dynamischen Raum mit mehr Funktionen. Aus Betonplatten, Holzlatten und integriertem Mobiliar bestehend, wurden seine Bestandteile in der Fabrik hergestellt und in der Wohnung zusammengebaut. Dank der Gestaltung kann der Bewohner in einem Zwischengeschoss über mehrere Bereiche für Stauräume und ein Schlafzimmer verfügen und - alternativ - über ein Esszimmer, ein Gästezimmer bzw. einen Arbeitsraum.

L'installation d'un meuble multifonctionnel de deux niveaux transforme l'intérieur d'un petit appartement dans un espace dynamique et aux prestations supérieures. Composée de blocs en béton, baguettes en bois et mobilier intégré, ses composants ont été fabriqués en atelier et assemblés dans la maison. Sa conception permet de disposer de plusieurs espaces de rangement et d'une chambre en mezzanine et, en alternance, d'une salle à manger, d'une chambre d'amis ou d'un espace de travail.

La implantación de un mueble multifuncional de dos niveles transforma el interior de un pequeño apartamento en un espacio dinámico y de mayores prestaciones. Formado por paneles de hormigón, listones de madera y mobiliario integrado, sus componentes fueron fabricados en taller y ensamblados en la casa. Su diseño permite disponer de varias zonas de almacenamiento y de un dormitorio situado en el altillo, y también, de forma alternativa, de un comedor, de un cuarto de visitas o de un espacio de trabajo.

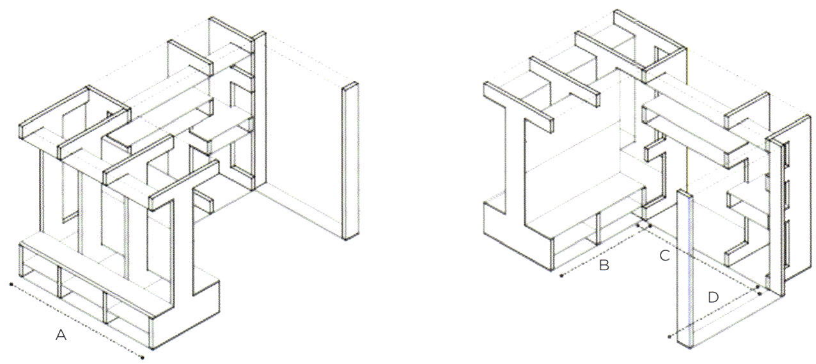

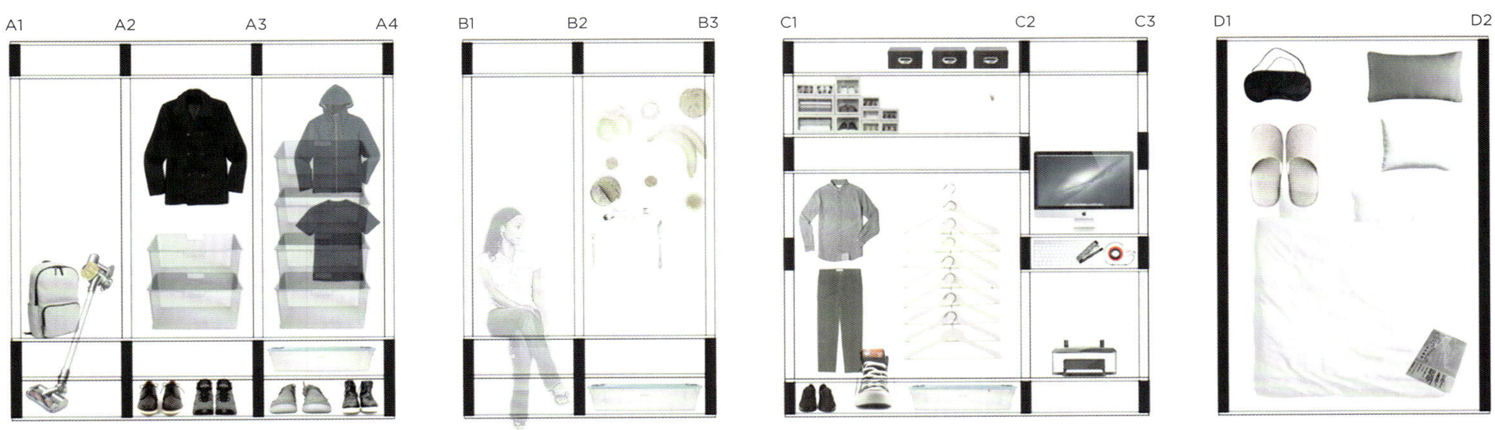

Functional diagrams

The design of the area under the loft features a continuous bench and furniture that can be unfolded as needed, like a dining table or a guest bed.

Die Gestaltung des Bereichs unter dem Zwischengeschoss umfasst eine Sitzbank und Elemente des Mobiliars, die sich je nach Bedarf aufklappen lassen, wie etwa ein Esstisch oder ein Gästebett.

La conception de la zone située en dessous de la mezzanine comprend une banquette et des éléments de mobilier qui peuvent être déployés selon les besoins comme une table à manger ou un lit d'appoint.

El diseño de la zona situada bajo el altillo incorpora un banco corrido y elementos de mobiliario que pueden desplegarse en función de las necesidades, como una mesa de comedor o una cama de invitados.